ROUTLEDGE LIBRARY EDITIONS:
PHONETICS AND PHONOLOGY

Volume 22

THE PHONOLOGY–MORPHOLOGY INTERFACE

THE PHONOLOGY–MORPHOLOGY INTERFACE
Cycles, Levels and Words

JOLANTA SZPYRA-KOZŁOWSKA

LONDON AND NEW YORK

First published in 1989 by Routledge

This edition first published in 2019
by Routledge
2 Park Square, Milton Park, Abingdon, Oxon OX14 4RN

and by Routledge
711 Third Avenue, New York, NY 10017

Routledge is an imprint of the Taylor & Francis Group, an informa business

© 1989 Jolanta Szpyra

All rights reserved. No part of this book may be reprinted or reproduced or utilised in any form or by any electronic, mechanical, or other means, now known or hereafter invented, including photocopying and recording, or in any information storage or retrieval system, without permission in writing from the publishers.

Trademark notice: Product or corporate names may be trademarks or registered trademarks, and are used only for identification and explanation without intent to infringe.

British Library Cataloguing in Publication Data
A catalogue record for this book is available from the British Library

ISBN: 978-1-138-60364-6 (Set)
ISBN: 978-0-429-43708-3 (Set) (ebk)
ISBN: 978-1-138-60436-0 (Volume 22) (hbk)
ISBN: 978-1-138-60437-7 (Volume 22) (pbk)
ISBN: 978-0-429-46851-3 (Volume 22) (ebk)

Publisher's Note
The publisher has gone to great lengths to ensure the quality of this reprint but points out that some imperfections in the original copies may be apparent.

Disclaimer
The publisher has made every effort to trace copyright holders and would welcome correspondence from those they have been unable to trace.

The Phonology–Morphology Interface
Cycles, levels and words

Jolanta Szpyra

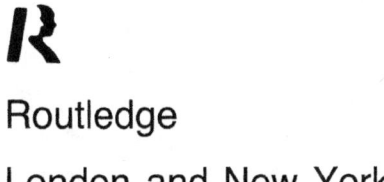

Routledge

London and New York

First published 1989
by Routledge
11 New Fetter Lane, London EC4P 4EE
29 West 35th Street, New York, NY 10001

© Jolanta Szpyra 1989

Typeset in 10/12pt Times, Linotron 202
by Columns of Reading
Printed in Great Britain
by T.J. Press (Padstow) Ltd, Cornwall

All rights reserved. No part of this book may be reprinted or reproduced or utilized in any form or by any electronic, mechanical, or other means, now known or hereafter invented, including photocopying and recording, or in any information storage or retrieval system, without permission in writing from the publishers.

Library of Congress Cataloging in Publication Data
applied for

0-415-00307-5

Contents

Introduction	vii
Abbreviations and symbols	xii

1 Separation versus integration – major approaches to the phonology–morphology interaction ... 1

2 Levels and cycles – some consequences of lexical and cyclic phonology ... 29
  Some consequences of adopting the lexical model for Polish ... 29
  Some consequences of adopting the lexical model for English ... 37
    Introduction ... 37
    Criteria used in establishing the class membership of English affixes ... 40
    Dual class suffixes: -ize, -ant/-ent, -ive, -able/-ible ... 46
    Other affixes ... 62
  Strict cyclicity ... 69
    Trisyllabic laxing in English ... 71
    Palatalization in Polish ... 77

3 The cycle revisited – the multiple application of phonological rules ... 84
  Complex verbs ... 85
    Primary verbs and their derivatives ... 85

	Secondary verbal stems and derived imperfective tensing	97
	Items based on DIs and verb suffix truncation	116
	Other cases	127

4 Phonetic inputs to WFRs – morphological evidence for the cycle ... 131
   Comparative degree formation ... 132
   Imperative formation ... 142
   Augmentative back-formation ... 158
   Other cases ... 167

5 Words – the morphological hierarchy versus the phonological hierarchy ... 178
   The phonology of English affixation ... 179
     The SPE analysis ... 181
     The phonological word, mapping and rebracketing ... 183
     Other prosodic categories ... 195
   The phonology of Polish prefixation ... 200
     Previous analyses ... 203
     Lower ... 209
     A prosodic solution ... 215
   Conclusion ... 225

Final remarks ... 230

Notes ... 244

References ... 259

Index of subjects ... 266

Index of rules ... 269

Introduction

The vigorous development of morphological and phonological theory within the broad framework of Generative Grammar poses a number of significant questions concerning the mutual relationship between phonology and morphology.

Do morphology and phonology constitute two separate components with morphological processes preceding phonological ones, or are phonological rules integrated with word formation rules?

What is the place of morphophonology? Is it a part of morphology, a part of phonology, or does it constitute a separate component?

What types of phonological information are needed in morphology? Are they present in underlying structures, or are they supplied by phonological rules?

What types of morphological information are needed in phonology? How are they encoded? To what extent can morphological structures influence the application of phonological rules?

Are morphological and phonological structures identical or are they different? Is there any need for some kind of an adjustment apparatus? What is its scope and form?

The present study is an attempt to answer some of these questions. On the basis of mainly Polish and English language material we endeavour to examine what we consider the most important aspects of the phonology–morphology interaction as well as trying to find the best model with which to describe these phenomena.

There are, it seems, two ways of approaching the interface of phonology and morphology. The first, which might be dubbed 'morphophonological', examines the issue from the morphological perspective and focuses on types of phonological information needed for the operation of word formation rules (WFRs). The other view, the 'phono-morphological', is mainly concerned with phonological aspects of the problem, i.e., it investigates in what ways phonological rules interact with morphology. Ours is basically the phonologist's approach. Therefore, in this book, with the exception of Chapter 4, we shall examine various phonological issues to a considerably greater extent than specifically morphological questions.

This is not the only limitation, unavoidable in a work of this sort. Thus, numerous problems which properly belong to the area of the interaction between phonology and morphology will be given only a brief consideration or even be bypassed altogether. It will, for instance, be assumed without any detailed discussion that phonological rules are morphophonological in character, in accordance with the traditional generative approach. This, in consequence, means that we shall not be concerned with those frameworks (such as, for example, natural generative phonology of Hooper 1976) in which the focus is on phonetically governed regularities. Various other models, although undoubtedly interesting, will not be treated at any length either. As a matter of fact, the discussion will centre mainly on the issues raised by lexical phonology and prosodic phonology, such as the integration of morphology and phonology in the lexicon, the validity of postulating derivational levels, the cyclicity of phonological rules, the nature of inputs to WFRs and the role of prosodic units in the application of phonological processes. Briefly, we shall deal with the phenomena which can be subsumed under the terms of cycles, levels and words.

The languages of exemplification are Polish and English. This means that in this book we rarely tread upon entirely virgin territory, for the phonologies of both languages have been thoroughly described within a variety of generative frameworks. Since the choice from among different viewpoints can only be made after a detailed scrutiny of each, much thought will be devoted to the discussion of the already existing analyses, their strong points as well as inadequacies. Only then will the necessary modifications be introduced. The restriction of our data base almost entirely to Polish and English necessitates testing the validity of various theoretical proposals which will be put forward here, against the ground of other languages. This remains a task for future research.

Chapter 1 is introductory in character and presents an overview of major generative approaches to the phonology–morphology interface, which fall into two types, termed 'separational' and 'integrational' respectively. The reader familiar with the SPE model and its further development will not find much new here, but someone less versed in various phonological and morphological frameworks will be provided with the necessary background.

In Chapter 2 we ask whether phonological rules should be combined with morphology in a single component, as suggested by lexical phonology, or whether phonology and morphology should be viewed as distinct and separate, as assumed in the traditional generative model. Particular attention is paid to the issue of derivational levels and the phonological consequences of their recognition. Finally, we consider whether phonological processes are strictly cyclic or non-cyclic.

The problem of rule cyclicity is taken up in Chapter 3, in which the inability of the existing frameworks to describe the derivation of complex verbs in Polish necessitates the introduction of the multiple application of phonological rules. This leads to a total reanalysis of the relationship between the morphological and the phonological components.

Chapter 4 provides more evidence for the organization of grammar proposed in Chapter 3. We deal with the issue of the nature of inputs to word formation rules, of which three possibilities are considered: phonological, intermediate and phonetic.

The relation between the morphological and the phonological hierarchies constitutes the major subject of Chapter 5. We return to the problems involved in describing the phonology of English affixation and Polish prefixation and demonstrate how the prosodic categories, such as the phonological word, can be successfully employed in solving them.

Introduction

In the Final Remarks we close our investigation, restating the most important findings of the previous chapters and presenting the model of the phonology–morphology interaction that has emerged in the course of our analysis. Additionally, the issue of morphological boundaries and their role in phonology is addressed in some detail.

A few technical comments are also in order. For the sake of clarity, we transcribe only those segments that are directly relevant to the discussion. In other instances conventional orthography is used. Below we list the symbols used in the transcription of Polish words, as well as the most important correspondences between letters and sounds.

[c, dz] – dental affricates, spelled *c* and *dz*, as in *cena* 'price', *dzwon* 'bell'

[č, dž] – postalveolar affricates, spelled *cz* and *dż*, as in *czas* 'time', *drożdże* 'yeast'

[š, ž] – postalveolar fricatives, spelled *sz* and *ż/rz*, as in *szynka* 'ham', *żaba* 'frog', *rzeka* 'river'

[ś, ź] – palatal fricatives, spelled as *ś* and *ź*, as in *śnieg* 'snow', *mroźny* 'icy', and *si, zi*, as in *siano* 'hay', *zima* 'winter'

[ć, dź] – palatal affricates, spelled as *ć* and *dź*, as in *ćma* 'moth', *dźwig* 'crane' and *ci, dzi*, as in *cicho* 'silently', *dzień* 'day'

[ń] – the palatal nasal, spelled as *ń*, as in *koń* 'horse', or *ni*, as in *nie* 'no'

[x] – the velar fricative, spelled as *h*, as in *hotel* 'hotel' or *ch*, as in *chyba* 'perhaps'

[w] – the bilabial glide, spelled *ł*, as in *koło* 'wheel'

[j] – the palatal glide, spelled *j*, as in *ja* 'I'

[v] – the voiced labio-velar fricative, spelled as *w*, as in *woda* 'water'

[p', b', m', f', v', t', d', s', z', k', g', x'] – palatalized consonants, spelled *pi, bi, mi, fi, wi, ti, di, si, zi, ki, gi, chi, hi*, as in, for example, *kino* 'cinema', *pies* 'dog', *wiatr* 'wind', *miasto* 'town', *tiul* 'tulle', *hiena* 'hyena'.

As clusters of obstruents must agree in voicing, letters are pronounced as voiced or voiceless, depending on the neighbouring segments, for example, *ławka* 'bench' – [wafka], *liczba* 'number' – [lidžba]. Word-finally all obstruents are devoiced, for example *sad* 'orchard' – [sat], *jeż* 'hedgehog' – [ješ].

[ɨ] – the high retracted unround vowel, spelled *y*, as in *ryba* 'fish'

[u] – the high back rounded vowel, spelled *u*, as in *lud* 'people' or *ó*, as in *lód* 'ice'

[ẽ,õ] – nasal vowels, spelled *ę* and *ą*, as in *kęs* 'morsel', *wąs* 'moustache.' The letters *ę* and *ą* are pronounced as nasal vowels only before fricatives. Before other consonants they are sequences of oral vowels followed by a nasal consonant homorganic with the following obstruent, for example *ząb* 'tooth' – [zomp], *ręka* 'hand' – [reŋka]. Before *ł* and *l*, *ę* and *ą* are pronounced as oral vowels, for example, *wziął* 'he took' – [vźoł], *wzięli* 'they took' – [vźeli].

The letter *i* stands for the high front vowel, for example, in *igła* 'needle', except for the cases when it follows consonants and precedes vowels, in which instances it marks the palatalization of the preceding consonant and is not pronounced, for example *ciocia* 'aunt' – [ćoća], *nie* 'no' – [ńe], *ziemia* 'earth' – [źem'a]. In the remaining cases there is one-to-one correspondence between letters and sounds, for example, *troska* 'worry' – [troska], *krokus* 'crocus' – [krokus].

The present study is a revised version of my doctoral dissertation. I should like to take this opportunity to thank some people who have contributed to its final shape. First and foremost, I wish to express my sense of deep personal and professional debt to my advisor Professor Edmund Gussmann, whose hearty encouragement as well as eager and extensive co-operation made this book possible. My warmest thanks are also extended to the referees of my thesis, Professors Jacek Fisiak and Walerian Świeczkowski, and to two reviewers for the publishers, for their comments and suggestions for improvement. I am also very grateful to Mr Jonathan Price, the linguistics editor for Routledge, for his valuable help. None of them, however, is to be blamed for any errors, which remain my sole responsibility.

Abbreviations and symbols

AOG	– affix ordering generalization
DI	– derived imperfective
NGP	– natural generative phonology
SPE	– *The Sound Pattern of English* by N. Chomsky and M. Halle (1968)
TSL	– trisyllabic laxing
VS	– verb suffix
VST	– verb suffix truncation
A, Ad, ad	– adjective
acc.	– accusative
augm.	– augmentative
comp.	– comparative
dat.	– dative
dim.	– diminutive
exp.	– expressive
fem.	– feminine
gen.	– genitive
imper.	– imperative
instr.	– instrumental
loc.	– locative
masc.	– masculine
N, n	– noun
nom.	– nominative
pl.	– plural
Pref.	– prefix
sg.	– singular
V, v	– verb
v̌	– lax vowel

Abbreviations and symbols

∇	– tense vowel
ω	– the phonological word
ω'	– the phonological compound
φ	– the phonological phrase
σ	– the syllable
F	– the foot
μ	– the morpheme

Chapter one

Separation versus integration – major approaches to the phonology–morphology interaction

Although several books and papers espousing the model of generative phonology appeared in the late 1950s and the early 1960s (most notably Halle 1959), the publication of Chomsky and Halle's *The Sound Pattern of English* (henceforth SPE) marked 1968 as 'the year in which generative phonology was substantiated and legitimized' (Anderson 1985:328). This event can be claimed to have determined the development of phonological theory and practice for many years afterwards. It is rightly said that the majority of phonological works that have appeared since 1968 have been either a positive or a negative reaction to SPE, which in itself demonstrates the outstanding significance of this study. We shall therefore start our sketchy presentation of the most influential approaches to the phonology–morphology interaction with a brief summary of the relevant claims and assumptions put forward in *The Sound Pattern of English*.

One of the major features of the SPE analysis and of generative phonology in general is its morphophonemic character. This means that no distinction is made between the alternations conditioned purely phonologically and those which are, to some extent, morphologized; a set of ordered phonological rules derive all the allomorphs from a single underlying form set up for every morpheme. In other words, SPE rejects the need for a separate morphophonemic component (in the structural sense) as well as the taxonomic phonemic level. As a result, in the SPE type of approach many instances can be found of what structural linguists would regard as the 'mixing of levels', i.e., cases in which phonological rules must refer to non-phonetic information.

There are several types of non-phonetic information relevant to the application of phonological processes. They fall into two groups: extragrammatical and grammatical (Kenstowicz and Kisseberth 1977). The former comprise such factors as the tempo and the style of speech, and will not be discussed here. The latter involve syntactic, morphological and lexical features. Of these morphological information in phonology will be our primary concern.

As is well known, in the early days of Generative Grammar morphology did not exist as a separate component. A part of it was assigned to syntax and a part to phonology. Thus, in SPE phonological rules operate on syntactic rather than on morphological structures. Nothing is said about the system of rules that generate words. Therefore, the question of the phonology–morphology interaction does not, in fact, arise. Rather the issue at stake is that of mapping syntactic structures onto phonological ones. The syntax-phonology mapping is effected by means of three different devices: labelled bracketing, morphological boundaries and readjustment rules. We shall now discuss them briefly one by one.

According to SPE, the syntactic component assigns to each sentence a surface structure which consists of a string of formatives with labelled bracketing. Brackets refer to such categories as 'sentence', 'noun phrase', 'noun', 'verb', 'adjective'. Labelled bracketing of syntactic structure has several functions. One of them is to delimit the domain of application of phonological rules by restricting them to certain lexical and grammatical categories. An example of a phonological process that refers to such distinctions is stress in English, which operates in a different fashion depending on the lexical category of words. The word *torment*, for instance, is stressed on its first syllable if it is a noun (*'torment*), and on its second syllable if it is a verb (*tor'ment*).

Another significant function of labelled bracketing is to determine the mode in which phonological rules apply. SPE classifies them into two types: transformational phonological rules and non-transformational or word-level rules. The presence of bracketing is essential to the operation of the former; 'transformational phonological rules first apply to the maximal strings that contain no brackets, and after all relevant rules have applied the innermost brackets are erased, the rules then reapply to maximal strings containing no brackets, and again innermost brackets are erased after this application; and so on, until the maximal domain of phonological processes is reached' (SPE:15).

In English transformational rules relate basically to such phenomena as stress and vowel reduction. Consider the placement of stress in the compound

$$\overset{1}{\text{black}}\overset{3}{\text{board}} \overset{2}{\text{eraser}}$$

where the numbers refer to the degree of stress. The structure of this compound can be presented in the following way (SPE:21)

$$[_N [_N [_A \text{ black}]_A [_N \text{ board}] {}_N]_N [_N \text{ eraser}]_N]_N$$

On the first cycle the adjective *black* and the noun *board* receive stress

$$[_A \overset{1}{\text{black}}]_A \quad [_N \overset{1}{\text{board}}]_N$$

The same happens with the noun *eraser*

$$[_N \overset{1}{\text{eraser}}]_N$$

Now the innermost brackets between *black* and *board* are erased and the compound stress rule applies

$$[_N \overset{1}{\text{black}} \overset{2}{\text{board}}]_N$$

Then the next pair of brackets is erased and the compound stress rule reapplies

$$[_N \overset{1}{\text{black}} \overset{3}{\text{board}} \overset{2}{\text{eraser}}]_N$$

Word-level rules are not cyclic, i.e., they apply only once and are not dependent on bracketing in the way cyclic rules are. An example is the rule of palatalization exemplified in

gra[d]e – gra[ǰ]ual
depar[t] – depar[č]ure

Here the alveolar obstruents are turned into the corresponding palato-alveolars with the subsequent deletion of the conditioning palatal glide. In SPE transformational phonological rules and word-level rules are interspersed although their mutual ordering raises some doubts (Fischer-Jørgensen 1975:249).

The second device employed in SPE is the use of morphological boundaries. They are of several kinds:

1. The internal word boundary, expressed by #, which is inserted at the beginning and end of every string dominated by a major lexical category (such as noun, verb or adjective). For example, the word *differ* can be presented as

$$[_V \# \text{ differ } \#]_V$$

2. The full word boundary, ##, which is assigned in agreement with the convention specified under 1. The word *differing* has thus the following structure

$$[_V\# [_V \# \text{ differ } \#]_V \text{ ing } \#]_V$$

It should be added that the full word boundary plays an important role in defining the notion 'word', which can now be described as a unit bound with ## _____ ##, with no internal occurrences of ##.

3. The morpheme boundary, symbolized by +, which separates two formatives (morphemes), for example *tele+graph*. These three boundaries are syntactically motivated.

4. The prefix boundary, marked by means of =, which separates the prefixes from the stems in words such as *per=mit, com=bat, con=de=scend*. This juncture has no syntactic justification and is postulated for the sake of phonological rules only. It is introduced by the readjustment apparatus.

Morphological boundaries are very important for the operation of phonological rules. They have either an inhibiting function, which means that a phonological process is blocked when a certain boundary intervenes, and a conditioning function when the application of a phonological rule is contingent on the presence of some boundary. Boundaries differ in terms of their strength (Kenstowicz and Kisseberth 1977).

The morpheme boundary is the weakest of all and cannot block any phonological rule. This means that a rule which, for example, applies in the context

___ V

can also operate in three other environments:

___ + V   ___ V +   ___ + V +

An example of an SPE rule which operates regardless of the presence or absence of + is velar softening, which turns velar plosives /k, g/ into /s/ and /ǰ/ respectively. It is claimed to affect the phonological voiceless plosives in *recite* and *electricity* in the context of the following non-low front vowel

/re=kīt/   /elektrik+iti/

although in the first case the conditioning vowel is in the same morpheme as the plosive while in the other example the two segments are separated by +. In some cases, however, the morpheme boundary can condition a phonological process. For instance, spirantization, which converts alveolar plosives into the corresponding spirants, takes place, among other things, in the context of the palatal glide preceded by the morpheme boundary (SPE:229):

___ + y

This ensures the application of spirantization in

democra[s]y   from   /demokræt+y/

and, at the same time, disallows it in

novel[t]y   from   /novel+ty/

in which there is no morpheme boundary between /t/ and /y/ (in both cases the phonological glide undergoes later vocalization to [i]).

The prefix boundary can, in turn, both condition and block a phonological rule. For example, it is necessary in order to trigger the rule of s-voicing in prefixed forms (when the voiceless spirant is preceded and followed by a vowel, of which the second one must be stressed), for example

    re=[z]ume vs as=[s]ume
    de=[z]ign vs as=[s]ign

This is expressed by means of an appropriate condition placed in the rule itself (SPE:228):

$$V = \underline{} \acute{V}$$

On the other hand, the presence of = in the words such as *per=mit* prevents the shift of stress to the first syllable, since the process in question is not allowed to cross the prefix boundary.

The word boundary, whether word internal or full, is the strongest of all and its presence prevents a phonological rule from applying unless this boundary is explicitly mentioned in the structural description of the rule. Thus, velar softening never applies across word boundaries, for example

    bi[g] egg   *bi[ǰ] egg

which means that the boundary in question delimits the domain of application of word-level processes. An example of a process that is triggered by the word boundary is sonorant syllabification, which inserts the vowel schwa in the following context (SPE:85),

$$C \underline{} [+\text{sonorant}] \#$$

e.g., in *hinder* from /hindr/, *cylinder* from /silindr/, *remember* from /remeNbr/.

Nevertheless, the presence of the word boundary in certain contexts becomes problematic. Consider the word *hindrance*, for example

$[_N \# [_V \# \text{hindr} \#]_V \text{ance} \#]_N$

Since # is present after the sonorant, the schwa vowel should be inserted. This, however, yields the incorrect form

*hind[ə]rance

To avoid such undesirable consequences, SPE proposes to replace certain occurrences of # by +. This is effected by readjustment rules, which in this particular case modify the initial structure in the following manner:

$[_N \# [_V \# \text{hindr} \#]_V \text{ance} \#]_N \rightarrow$
$[_N \# [_V \# \text{hindr} +]_V \text{ance} \#]_N$

The change of this sort must be restricted to certain affixes only since other formatives behave as if they were associated with the word boundary. Take the word *hindering* as an example. The attachment of the suffix *-ing* has the same phonological effect as the word-final position: the schwa is inserted

hind[ə]ring

Consequently, the word boundary before *-ing* must be retained for the sake of some phonological rules. This is additionally supported by the fact that appending *-ing* does not cause any shift of stress, i.e., the stress rule operates as if the suffix in question were not present at all. We shall deal more extensively with the issue of boundaries in other chapters of this book.

Thus, SPE distinguishes two classes of affixes in English, which differ in terms of their phonological properties. The first group, the word boundary affixes, block the application of those word-level rules in which # has no conditioning function. Such affixes do not affect the placement of stress in a word, for example

'délicate – 'délicately   'démonstrate – 'démonstrating

and are often referred to as 'stress-neutral' (for example, *-ness*, *-less*, *-ing*, *-ly*, *un-*, etc.). The second type, the morpheme boundary affixes, lie in the domain of almost all phonological rules and, first of all, the stress rule, for example

'lucid – lu'cidity   'atom – a'tomic

Such affixes are known as 'stress-determining' (for example, *-ic*, *-ion*, *-ate*, *in-*, etc.). What is important is the fact that both groups of affixes in SPE are identical at the syntactic level, i.e., prephonologically. The differentiation is introduced by readjustment rules, which we shall briefly present here.

Chomsky and Halle note that surface structure is two things at once: it is both the output of the syntactic component and the input to the phonological component. Although these coincide to a significant degree, there are also certain discrepancies. These discrepancies are removed by means of readjustment rules, which relate syntax to phonology and modify surface structure in a number of ways. First of all, they divide surface structures into phonological phrases. This is necessary since although sometimes the whole sentence is a single phonological phrase, in other cases it might consist of several such units. Phonological phrases constitute the maximal domain for the application of phonological rules. Secondly, readjustment rules may change the syntactic categorization of a constituent (for example from 'noun phrase' to 'noun'), replace some occurrences of # by + or = and assign to abstract grammatical formatives strings that have phonetic content, for example

past → /d/

Finally, readjustment rules effect some changes which take place in certain idiosyncratic morphological contexts, for example, (SPE:238)

$$t \rightarrow [+\text{voice}] / = \begin{Bmatrix} \text{mi} \underline{\quad} + \text{ive} \\ \text{ver} \underline{\quad} + \text{iVn} \end{Bmatrix}$$

(*inversion, permissive*).[1]

Apart from syntactic/morphological information, phonological rules must sometimes refer to the features of words or morphemes which are specified in the lexicon. For instance, some processes appear to be sensitive to such lexical features as [foreign], [romance] etc. The best-known example of this sort is velar softening, which operates exclusively within items marked as [+latinate], but is blocked in native English words, for example

criti[k]al – criti[s]ism   vs   bla[k] – bla[k]ish
ri[g]our – ri[j]id   do[g] – do[g]y

Moreover, other categories such as 'present tense', 'masculine', 'animate', etc. may also be referred to by phonological rules. An example of this sort can be found in Polish. The process known as second velar palatalization converts velar consonants into affricates and fricatives in the following grammatical contexts: dative and locative singular of feminine nouns, nominative plural of masculine personal nouns, nominative plural of masculine personal adjectives, and deadjectival adverbs, for example

mu[x]a 'fly' – *mu[š]e* 'id. dat. sg.'
ryba[k] 'fisherman' – *ryba[c]y* 'id. nom. pl.'
na[g]a 'naked, fem.' – *na[dz]y* 'id. nom. pl.'

Finally, an issue that deserves at least a brief mention is the treatment of exceptions in SPE. Since Chomsky and Halle's analysis of English has attempted to cover almost all morphophonological alternations, it comes as no surprise that numerous exceptions to general rules must be noted. Basically two ways of dealing with exceptions are employed in SPE. One method consists in marking idiosyncratic items with exception features in the lexicon. Another way is to postulate underlying forms which allow for regularizing exceptions (for instance by setting up phonological geminates, adding phonetically nonexistent segments, etc.). For example, to account for the penultimate stress in the words such as *vanilla*, *umbrella* and *gorilla* Chomsky and Halle suggest that these items should contain a cluster of two laterals at the phonological level (SPE:83).

However much approbation the SPE framework received, the year of its publication was also the time from which, as Anderson (1985:328) notes, the reaction against the theory must be dated. In fact, none of the claims and assumptions which have just been summarized has survived in an unmodified form. In the following pages we intend to trace the most significant developments of the relevant concepts.

First, the SPE idea of the transformational cycle has been heavily criticized. Some linguists (for example Ross 1972) attempted to demonstrate that English stress rules can be formulated in such a way that no phonological cycle is required at the word level. The Goyvaerts and Pullum (1974) volume illustrates well this critical tendency (especially the papers by Langendoen and Lee) of the years following the appearance of SPE. It has been claimed that the concept of the transformational cycle is of little usefulness in the description of languages in which stress plays no important role. Consequently, numerous generative descriptions of the phonologies of various languages have been produced in which no recourse to the cycle was made. The idea of cyclic phonological rules can be said to have started falling into decline. Labelled bracketing lost its function of determining the mode of application of phonological rules and retained its role of indicating grammatical categories to which phonological rules could refer.

With Chomsky's (1970) 'lexicalist hypothesis' and the subsequent works on word structure (Halle 1973, Siegel 1974, Aronoff 1976, Booij 1977, Allen 1978 – to mention just a few contributions from the 1970s) it has become clear from the SPE assumption that there is nothing between syntax and phonology could no longer be maintained. Early generative attempts at reducing morphology to other domains have proved largely unsuccessful and it has gradually become evident that word structures are governed by different properties than syntactic structures. In brief, an autonomous morphological component has been postulated. A crucial issue has now been to establish the degree of its independence or, to put it differently, its interaction with the remaining components. The problem of the morphology–syntax overlap has become most prominent and resulted in a number of still unresolved debates concerning, for instance, the nature of morphological operations (the 'transformationalist' versus the 'lexicalist' approach), their scope (does inflection belong to morphology or to syntax?), the nature of derivational units (word-based versus root-based morphology), etc. (for an introduction to these issues see Scalise 1986).

Another issue, initially considered of less relevance, has been the relationship between morphology and phonology. Now, as word structures and not only syntax structures have become important in phonological analysis, more significance has begun to be attached to the morphological justification of phonological descriptions.

One of the first aspects of the SPE framework that came under criticism was Chomsky and Halle's theory of boundaries. It has been pointed out (for example, by Aronoff 1980) that the boundaries in SPE resemble the structural 'juncture phonemes', that is, they are treated as sequential units on a par with underlying segments. For example, such 'distinctive features' as [segment], [formative boundary] and [word boundary] serve to describe them, which is objectionable since properties of this sort have no phonetic contents and are phonetically arbitrary. Second, and more important, boundaries have been criticized for their morphological arbitrariness. Recall that all affixes in SPE appear with the word boundary at the syntactic level and are later modified by means of readjustment rules for the sake of phonological processes. In other words, they are phonologically, but not morphologically motivated. A typical example of a morphologically suspicious juncture is the prefix boundary, which acts as a diacritic for the mere purpose of triggering or blocking some phonological rules.

It has been generally felt that the use of boundaries must somehow be constrained. As Kenstowicz and Kisseberth (1977:105) observe, 'the concept of boundary is rather vacuous unless some restrictions on positing boundaries in a string of morphemes and referring to boundaries in phonological rules can be established'. In other words, boundaries must be justified by the morphological structure of a given language. Otherwise they become mere tricks, likely to increase in number, that the phonologist uses to make his analysis work. If phonology is the sole reason for postulating boundaries, this might lead to total arbitrariness. In brief, SPE has been accused, and rightly so, of an inadequate approach to English morphology. Consequently, it has been assumed that an adequate morphological analysis is a necessary prerequisite to an adequate phonological description. In view of numerous morphological controversies and the lack of comprehensive morphological analyses of various languages, however, this requirement has remained largely theoretical and actual phonological practice had little or almost no recourse to morphology.

Needless to say, the concept of readjustment rules has also undergone considerable revisions since now it is not the syntactic structure, but rather morphological structure that serves as input to the phonological component. This means that there is no longer a need for the SPE rules such as

$$[_V [_V \text{mend}]_V \text{past}]_V \rightarrow [_V [_V \text{mend}]_V \text{d}]_V$$
$$[_V [_V \text{sit}]_V \text{past}]_V \rightarrow [_V \text{sæt}]_V$$

since the past tense ending of *mended* has earlier been introduced by morphological rules, and suppletive forms such as *sat* can simply be listed in the lexicon. Furthermore, there seems to be no need to replace certain occurrences of # by + as affixes are represented in the lexicon with either of the boundaries, which is their lexical property.

Nevertheless, morphological structures must be frequently modified in a number of ways before they can be subject to phonological processing. The most detailed, and at the same time the most influential treatment of readjustment has been proposed by Aronoff (1976). Aronoff's theory of (re)adjustment is considerably more constrained than the SPE approach; according to him adjustment rules are those which are restricted to specific morphemes and which take place only in the environment of other specific morphemes. Aronoff isolates two types of such rules, i.e., allomorphy and truncation.

An allomorphy rule (Aronoff 1976:88), 'adjusts the shape of a designated morpheme or class of morphemes in the immediate environment of another designated morpheme or morpheme class'. Clearly, the SPE readjustment rule which concerns the voicing of the alveolar plosive in *mit-* before *-ive* and in *vert-* before *-ion* can be treated as an allomorphy rule. Allomorphy might refer either to the base or to the suffix. An example of the first kind is verbs in *-fy* and *-ply* which nominalize in *-ication*, for example

amplify – amplification   imply – implication

SPE (p. 201) suggests the following rule

$$k \rightarrow \phi \:/\: + C_1 \bar{\imath} \underline{} \#\#$$

which, in Aronoff's framework, is a typical example of stem allomorphy. Allomorphy within the suffix is illustrated with the variants *-ion/-tion/-ation*. Aronoff assumes (1976:100–5) that *-ation* is the basic (unrestricted) variant, which is modified in the following way

$$\textit{-ation} \rightarrow \begin{Bmatrix} +\text{ion} \\ +\text{tion} \end{Bmatrix} / \: X \begin{Bmatrix} +\text{cor} \\ -\text{cor} \end{Bmatrix}$$

where X α cor is one of a set of specified latinate roots.

A truncation rule (Aronoff 1976:88) 'deletes a designated stem-final morpheme before a designated suffix'. An example of truncation is the nominalization of verbs in *-ate* by means of *-ee*; when the nominalizing suffix is appended, *-ate* is truncated, for example

nomin+ate → nomin+ee not *nomin+at+ee
evacu+ate → evacu+ee not *evacu+at+ee

It should be noted here that while Aronoff's allomorphy rules are generally accepted, the same cannot be said about truncation rules. The latter are absolutely necessary in Aronoff's model, in which words are formed from other words. In morphological frameworks that are root-based, truncation can be dispensed with. We shall return to this issue in Chapter 3, where the need for truncation rules in Polish will be argued for.

A different and not so widely accepted view of readjustment is put forward by Lieber (1980, 1982). She argues that the structure of the lexicon should be considerably enriched so as to allow the listing of allomorphs formerly derived by means of allomorphy rules. The listed allomorphs are related by the so-called morpholexical rules, which are non-directional redundancy statements. Thus, according to Lieber, the lexical entries for the verbs *nominate* and *amplify* will contain two items each:

$$\begin{Bmatrix} \text{nominate} \\ \text{nomin\_} \end{Bmatrix} \quad \begin{Bmatrix} \text{amplify} \\ \text{amplific\_} \end{Bmatrix}$$

which can all be subject to further morphological processes. Consequently, in Lieber's framework the need for a separate adjustment apparatus disappears altogether; the lexicon contains a list of those allomorphs that cannot be derived by any regular processes and which, without any further modifications, undergo the operation of both morphological and phonological rules. Lieber's proposal will be discussed in Chapter 3 in connection with the derivation of verbs and deverbal words in Polish. Let us only note in passing that Aronoff's theory seems to be advocated by more linguists (for example Booij 1977, Scalise 1986). Lieber's approach, however, has been adopted by, for example, Marantz (1982) and Spencer (1985).

Let us summarize now the major features of the 'standard' or 'traditional' (bearing in mind that the 'tradition' is only two decades old) generative approach to the phonology–morphology interaction that has emerged from all these developments. The rules of the morphological component apply first and produce word structures. These, after being modified by the (re)adjustment rules, constitute the input to the phonological component.[2] This way of organizing a grammar can explain the fact that phonological rules have access to morphological information in the form of labelled bracketing and morphological boundaries as they operate on fully specified morphological structures. On the other hand, the separation of the two components means that morphological processes can refer to phonology only in a very limited sense, i.e., they can only employ the information present in the underlying structure of words. We shall refer to this approach as to the 'traditional generative' or the 'separational' model.

Within this general approach to the interaction between phonology and morphology several phonological models have been suggested, all basically modifications of the SPE framework. Many linguists have reacted strongly against what they felt was the excessive abstractness of the SPE type of phonology. The debate which has come to be known as 'the abstractness controversy' centred around the question of – to use the title of Kiparsky's (1968) paper – 'how abstract is phonology?'. It has been generally thought that the descriptions carried out within the standard generative framework achieve a considerable degree of regularity at a disproportionately high cost, i.e., by creating psychologically totally unrealistic analyses. Consequently, almost every point of the SPE model has come under criticism. Objections have been raised, for instance, against abstract phonological representations which comprise phonetically non-occurring segments, retaining no distinction between morphologically and phonetically conditioned rules, an attempt at regularizing obvious exceptions, etc.

An extreme position has been taken by natural generative phonology (NGP), in which the structuralist division of phonological rules into morphologically and phonetically conditioned has been revived. NGP constrains the power of the phonological component considerably by allowing phonological rules merely to relate surface forms. Morphophonological alternations are of secondary importance with the alternants being listed in the lexicon and related by means of morphophonemic rules and 'via-rules'. A significant claim made by NGP is that in true phonological processes grammatical boundaries play no role. Hooper (1976:14) argues that, 'the phonological boundaries are the syllable boundary and the pause boundary'. In this way attention has been brought to the syllable, to which SPE gave no formal recognition. NGP has been subject to heavy criticism and, as Anderson (1985:342) observes, by the mid-1980s the great majority of phonologists regarded NGP as 'unsatisfactory as a basis for understanding the sound structures in natural languages'.

Another, much more influential trend of generative phonology, also aimed at restricting the abstractness of phonological analyses, is associated with Kiparsky's (1971, 1973) works. Kiparsky (1971) notes that SPE has introduced a very powerful and totally unconstrained mechanism of absolute neutralization, i.e., postulating a phonological contrast which is never manifested on the surface. Analyses involving absolute neutralization should, according to Kiparsky, be disallowed or made very costly. In other words, in those cases in which there are no alternations, the underlying representation of a morpheme should not be very distinct from its surface shape. This can formally be expressed by means of the so-called Alternation Condition of the following form:

Obligatory neutralization rules cannot apply to all occurrences of a morpheme.

On further study of neutralization rules, Kiparsky (1973) has observed that they appear to apply under special circumstances: either when the morpheme boundary is present in the string subject to the rule, or when the conditions for the application of a given rule are created by an earlier process (the situation known as 'feeding relation'). To put it differently, neutralization rules seem to apply in what Kiparsky refers to as 'derived environment'.

Kiparsky's Finnish example can be used to demonstrate the application of a phonological rule in derived environment. Finnish has the following two rules:

$t \rightarrow s / \underline{\quad} i$

and

$e \rightarrow i / \underline{\quad} \#$

The rule of spirantization appears to operate in two contexts only: either when the conditioning high front vowel is separated from the plosive by the morpheme boundary, or when /i/ is not underlying, but derived from /e/ via the 'e → i' rule. No 't → s' change takes place when the sequence /ti/ is found at the phonological level, for example

	/halut+i/ 'wanted'	/vete/ 'water'	/tili/ 'account'
e → i	–	veti	–
t → s	[halus+i]	[vesi]	–

Another example of a rule which applies in derived environment is trisyllabic laxing (TSL) in English. It neutralizes the distinction between tense (or long) and lax (or short) vowels in the antepenultimate syllable,[3] for example

sāne – sănity   līne – lĭnear
brīef – brĕvity   derīve – derĭvative

Kiparsky (1973:71) brings attention to the fact that TSL fails to apply in morphologically simple words such as nīghtingale   Ōberon   stēvedore

which is exactly the situation predicted by the derived-environment application of neutralization rules; in these cases there is no feeding relation involving TSL, or the conditioning morpheme boundary. The latter, however, is present in

săn+ity   lĭn+ear
brĕv+ity   derĭv+ative

so the rule in question is free to apply. Nevertheless, it should be added that although Kiparsky's principle can account for the peculiar behaviour of such rules as spirantization in Finnish and TSL in English, as it stands it is a stipulation on the application of neutralization processes which does not follow from any general properties of a grammar.

Further elaboration of the alternation condition as well as the attempt at incorporating it into a comprehensive phonological analysis has been made by Kean (1974), Mascaró (1976) and Halle (1979). These authors have suggested that the processes which apply in derived environments constitute a special class of cyclic rules. Consequently, the claim is that

Cyclic rules apply to derived forms.

This statement has come to be known as the strict cyclicity principle and has subsequently been employed as a basis for models of cyclic phonology (for a discussion of the development of the relevant concepts see Kiparsky 1982a).

Generally speaking, cyclic phonology assumes that phonological rules fall into two types: cyclic and postcyclic. The former apply in accordance with strict cyclicity and are, therefore, barred from applying morpheme-internally. Moreover, cyclic rules are allowed to operate several times in the derivation of morphologically complex items. Postcyclic rules of SPE resemble word-level rules of SPE in that they apply only once and are not sensitive to the constituent structure of words. This lack of sensitivity to the morphological properties of derivatives is accounted for by a convention known as bracket erasure, which removes morphological brackets after the application of cyclic rules. An example of a postcyclic rule which disregards morpheme boundaries and operates inside morphemes is vowel shift in English, for example

house /hūs/ → [haus]   keep /kēp/ → [ki:p]

In cyclic phonology the two types of rules form separate blocks and cannot be intermingled: the block of cyclic rules invariably precedes the block of postcyclic rules.

A sample derivation within the cyclic model will clarify the theoretical principles.

	nightingale /nītVngǣl/	sane /sǣn/	sanity /sǣn+iti/
Cycle 1 TSL	/nītVngǣl/ –	/sǣn/ –	/sǣn/ –
Cycle 2 TSL	/nītVngǣl/ –	/sǣn/ –	/sǣn+iti/ ǣ
Postcyclic Diphthongization Vowel shift Other rules	/nītVngǣl/ iy æy ay ey ŋ [naitiŋgeil]	/sǣn/ æy ey [sein]	/sæniti/ – – [sæniti]

No rules apply on Cycle 1 since here the derived environment condition is not fulfilled.[4] On Cycle 2 TSL applies in *sanity* in which two morphemes are combined. Nothing happens in monomorphemic items *sane* and *nightingale*. At the postcyclic stage vowel shift affects tense vowels.

Let us recall at this point that the idea that phonological rules apply in a cyclic fashion is not an invention of cyclic phonology and has been present already in SPE. However, the understanding of cyclicity in these two frameworks is significantly different. In the SPE model it is not absolutely necessary for every language to have cyclic rules. Cyclic phonology assumes that the division of phonological rules into cyclic and postcyclic is universal. Second, cyclic rules of cyclic phonology must observe the principle of strict cyclicity, whereas there is no such restriction on transformational phonological rules. Finally, within the standard generative model word-level rules and cyclic processes can be interspersed in one derivation – an impossibility in cyclic phonology, in which cyclic and postcyclic rules form two independent blocks.

As regards the phonology–morphology interface, cyclic phonology assumes that WFRs precede phonological rules, i.e., the framework in question can be treated as a version of a separational model. Nevertheless, the connection of phonology and morphology is much stronger here than in the traditional approach in that cyclic rules of cyclic phonology must apply in the order dictated by the operation of WFRs. In other words, in the latter model the role of morphological bracketing becomes very important since it determines phonological cycles.

It should be added that since in cyclic phonology, as in SPE, morphology precedes phonology, morphological and phonological structures do not always have to be identical. If the two components require a different bracketing of a given item, this can be done by means of adjustment rules, which modify the output of morphological rules before it can serve as the input to phonological processes. An example of this sort is provided by Russian (Pesetsky 1979), in which prefixes must be processed on the last cycle although they are attached to their bases by WFRs much earlier. A similar problem involves Polish prefixes as well and will be subject to discussion in Chapter 5. Moreover, some consequences of adopting the strict cyclicity principle in English and Polish will be examined in the following chapter.

Before we present the more recent development of cyclic phonology in the shape of lexical phonology, we should like to devote some thought to a different line of research which has become prominent in phonology of late. We mean here a variety of approaches which can generally be termed prosodic phonology.

Many linguists have noted that the SPE model offers no satisfactory ways of describing such prosodic phenomena as tone and stress. The fault in Chomsky and Halle's framework is, first of all, an oversimplified conception of phonological representations, which traditionally consist of a linear string of segments and boundaries. Phonological segments are claimed to have no internal structure (although they are regarded as bundles of unordered distinctive features). Moreover, the failure to recognize such prosodic categories as syllables and feet in the standard generative model is also regarded as unjustified since they allow us to describe stress and tone patterns in a more adequate way than segments and morphemes do. The need to take into account the internal structure of segments in the analysis of tones has led to the rise of autosegmental phonology (particularly as elaborated by Goldsmith 1976, 1979), according to which phonological representations can be viewed as consisting of several tiers that are linked to each other by association lines. The assumption of the hierarchical organization of phonological units constitutes the basis for metrical phonology (represented, for example, by Liberman and Prince 1977, Hayes 1980, Halle and Vergnaud 1980, Selkirk 1984). It soon became obvious that these theories, originally devised to describe tones (autosegmental) and stress (metrical), have much broader applications (see, for instance, van der Hulst and Smith 1982). Particularly interesting is McCarthy's (1979) attempt to employ the autosegmental framework to the description of nonconcatenative morphology of Semitic languages.

Furthermore, prosodic phonology appears to be applicable in the analysis of many phenomena of segmental phonology as well. Kahn (1976), for example, has been one of the first generative phonologists to demonstrate that many generalizations about English phonology that were regarded as morpheme-dependent are, in fact, syllable-based. Other prosodic units also can be shown to function in the application of phonological rules. Thus, according to many linguists (for example Liberman and Prince 1977, Selkirk 1982, 1984, Booij 1983, 1985a and 1985b, Nespor 1985, Nespor and Vogel 1986), apart from morphological units such as the morpheme, the morphological word, the compound and the phrase, it is necessary to recognize in phonology such units as the syllable, the foot, the phonological word, the phonological phrase, the intonational phrase and the phonological utterance.

In brief, according to prosodic phonology, phonological representations can be conceived of as multi-tiered, multi-dimensional objects simultaneously organized into both the morpho-syntactic and the prosodic hierachies. As Halle and Clements (1983:15) observe, this approach makes it possible to solve a long-standing problem involving the fact that on the one hand words consist of a sequence of morphemes, and on the other hand, of a sequence of syllables. Such organization of phonological structure can be presented at the word-level in the following way (based on van der Hulst and Smith 1985a:8)

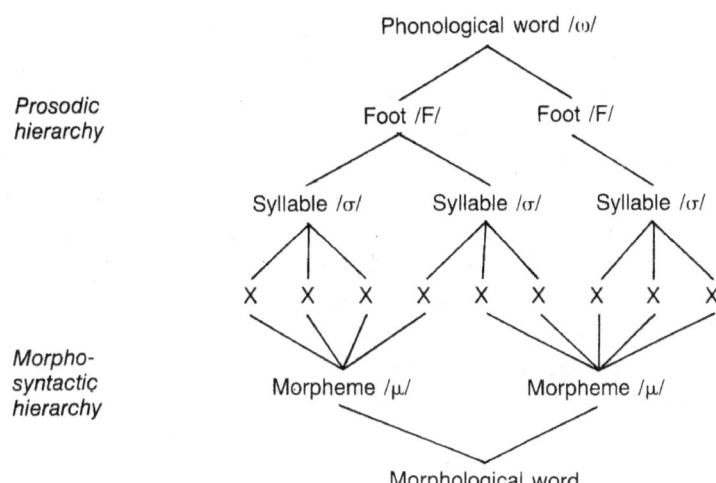

It must be made clear that the number and types of prosodic categories needed in the description of various languages are subject to an open debate, which is far from being settled. As a matter of fact, apart from the syllable, whose role in phonology is generally recognized, the status of the remaining units has been called into question and attempts have been made to dispense with some categories altogether (for example, Selkirk 1984). We discuss the role of some prosodic units, especially of the phonological word, in English and Polish in Chapter 5.

An interesting issue is why prosodic units have not been recognized in earlier generative descriptions of the SPE type. The major reason was, it seems, that they did not appear necessary. Simply, it was assumed that all the relevant phonological facts could be adequately accounted for by reference to sequences of segments and to the morphological hierarchy. As a matter of fact, in many cases the problem did not arise at all since frequently morphological and phonological structures coincide to a significant degree and there is no discrepancy between them.

example, it is usually the case that syllable boundaries fall at morphological word boundaries. Consequently, phonological rules which apply in this context, i.e., word-finally, can often be formulated in such a way as to refer either to the syllable or to the word boundary.

Nevertheless, the two types of units are not always identical. The most trivial and obvious example is the lack of identity between syllables and morphemes. For instance, the hypothetical word whose structure has been earlier presented consists of two morphemes, but three syllables. Consequently, phonological rules that make reference to the edges of morphemes and syllables will make different predictions. This follows from the fact that the division of a word into morphemes is independent from its division into syllables (and feet).

Considerably less trivial is the relationship between morphological and phonological words. It appears that frequently there is no one-to-one correspondence between these units, a fact which has already been observed in SPE. Chomsky and Halle (SPE:388) suggest that the sentence

The book was in an unlikely place.

actually consists of three phonological words

1. # the # book #
2. # was # in # an # un # likely #
3. # place #,

which follows from the convention of boundary assignment discussed earlier. Words understood in this fashion need not be syntactic constituents (for example, *was in an unlikely*).

We shall now pass to the presentation of some morphological models which make significant claims concerning the phonology–morphology interaction.

Bloomfield (1933) observed that in English normal roots combine with normal affixes and learned roots with learned affixes, where 'normal' means native and 'learned' non-native respectively. The same observation has been made by Siegel (1974), who has noted that the existence of two phonological classes of affixes, i.e., 'stress-neutral' and 'stress-determining', is supported by morphological facts, or, to be more exact, by their distribution. Thus, stress-neutral affixes (called also Class II affixes) appear only outside the nonneutral ones (called also Class I affixes), and nonneutral affixes never occur outside the neutral ones. For example, the word

histor + ical$_I$ # ness$_{II}$

is possible as the # boundary affix is attached here outside the + boundary affix, whereas

*kind # ness$_{II}$ + ical$_I$

cannot be an English word since the ordering of affixes is violated.

This observation, later termed the affix ordering generalization (AOG), has given rise to models of level-ordered morphology (for example Allen 1978). According to them, morphology is organized into a series of levels, with affixes of one level attached before those of the next level, and so on. Level-ordering is thus meant to account for the 'stacking up' properties of affixes.

Moreover, if we assume that stress rules in English apply after Class I (stress-determining) affixation, but before Class II (stress-neutral) affixation, i.e.,
1. Class I affixation (for example, +*ion*, +*ity*, +*ate*, *in*+)
2. Stress rules
3. Class II affixation (for example #y, #ly, #ness, un#)
then the accentual properties of affixes can be accounted for in a straightforward manner; Class I affixes lie in the domain of stress rules while Class II affixes are stress-neutral since stress applies before they are appended.

This way of organizing grammar has an additional significant advantage. As has been pointed out by several linguists (for example, Siegel 1974), some word formation rules appear to be sensitive to the placement of stress within the derivational base. The most celebrated example is the *-al* (noun-forming) suffixation. The suffix *-al* attaches to verbs which are stressed on the last syllable and end in a single consonant, for example

re'fuse – re'fusal   re'move – re'moval
sub'due – sub'dual   ar'rive – ar'rival

If this condition is not fulfilled, -al cannot be attached, for example

re'cover – *recoveral   con'sider – *consideral

The conclusion is simple: verbs must be stressed before they are subject to -al suffixation. This appears to have another property in common with other cases of the same sort discovered by Siegel (1974), namely that only Class II affixes may display sensitivity to stress placement, and never Class I affixes. These facts support the assumption that stress rules are ordered after Class I, but before Class II affixation. As noted by Strauss (1979), level-ordered morphology scores also in another point, which has escaped Siegel's (1974) or Allen's (1978) attention; it renders boundary distinctions in morphology superfluous. Simply, proper results can be obtained by ordering Class I affixation before Class II affixation.

The campaign 'against boundary distinctions in morphology' – to employ the title of Strauss's (1979) paper – was accompanied by a similar trend in phonology. First Siegel (1974) has demonstrated convincingly that the prefix boundary postulated by SPE is unnecessary even within the standard model. If one type of boundary can be dispensed with, the question arises whether the same can be done with the remaining junctures. It has turned out that a further reduction in the number of morphological boundaries might be achieved if WFRs are allowed to be interspersed with phonological rules.

The latter assumption has been adopted by models of lexical phonology, which was originally proposed by Pesetsky (1979) and later developed by Kiparsky (1982a, 1983, 1984, 1985), Mohanan (1982), Strauss (1982), Rubach (1984a), Booij and Rubach (1984, 1987), Halle and Mohanan (1985), Pulleyblank (1986) and others. Since the number of contributions to lexical phonology is constantly growing, it is impossible to present different varieties of this approach (for an introduction to lexical phonology see Archangeli 1984, Kaisse and Shaw 1985). What all these proposals have in common is the claim that the lexicon consists of several ordered levels, called also strata (whose actual number for English varies from two to five). Phonological rules, i.e., a subset of them known as lexical phonological rules, are assigned to these levels (sometimes a rule can be assigned to more levels than one, as in Halle and Mohanan 1985), which act as the domain of rule application. This means that morphological rules and phonological rules are no longer separated but intermingled. As Strauss (1982:157–8) has put it, in lexical phonology, 'the process of word-formation is intrinsically interspersed with the application of cyclic phonological rules. They apply immediately after that affix is attached which, on attachment, contributes to satisfying the structural description of the rule. Word-formation rules and cyclic phonological rules alternate with each other in the process of word formation.'

This approach entails the claim that lexical phonological rules can, and, in fact, are expected to interact with WFRs, which is expressed in the mode of application of such rules. As the quoted passage shows, lexical phonological rules are claimed to be cyclic, i.e., mirroring the operation of morphological processes. They apply in agreement with the strict cyclicity principle (for the idea of cyclicity being the property of lexical levels rather than individual rules, see Halle and Mohanan 1985). The remaining phonological rules called postcyclic or postlexical operate outside the lexicon and apply in a non-cyclic fashion.[5] Postlexical rules cannot interact with WFRs, nor can morphological processes have any influence on them. This is ensured by a convention which erases morphological bracketing prior to the application of postcyclic rules.

In brief, in the model under discussion phonological rules fall into two classes: lexical, which operate in the lexicon and are interspersed with WFRs, and postlexical, which apply outside the lexicon and do not interact with WFRs. Thus, lexical phonology is a model that attempts to account for both the morphological properties of affixes (through level-ordering) and the phonological ones (through the assignment of rules to different modules). As it is mainly characterized by the integration of (some) phonological rules with WFRs in the lexicon, we shall refer to it as the 'integrational' approach.

The operation of the lexical model can be clarified with a simple example taken from Kiparsky (1982a:139). Two English negative prefixes *in-* and *non-* differ in a number of properties. The phonological difference is that the final nasal of *in-* assimilates to the following consonant, whereas in *non-* it does not, for example

in+legible → il+legible
non+legible → non+legible   /*nollegible/

Morphologically, *non-* can be attached to a word with *in-*, while *in-* cannot be added to a *non-* word, for example

non+il+legible vs *in+non+legible

These phenomena are explained by claiming that *in-* is appended at level 1 and *non-* at level 2. Nasal assimilation, which is assigned to level 1, can affect *in-*, but not *non-*. Furthermore, level 1 forms can undergo level 2 affixation, but not vice versa. Hence, *non-* can freely attach to *in-* items, but *in-* cannot be prefixed to *non-* words. In this way both the phonological and morphological properties of *in-* and *non-* are elegantly explained. The facts pertaining to *in-* and *non-* might be graphically presented in a simplified form (without the degemination of the prefix consonant) as follows:

	[legible]
Level 1	
WFR: *in-* prefixation	[in [legible]$_A$]$_A$
Phonological rules:	
Stress	[in [légible]$_A$]$_A$
Nasal assimilation	[il [légible]$_A$]$_A$
Level 2	[illègible]$_A$
WFR: *non-* prefixation	[non [illégible]$_A$]$_A$
Phonological rules	—
	[nonillégible]$_A$

As Kiparsky (1982b:1) states, 'the significance of level-ordered morphology is that it relates the "positional" properties of affixes to their phonological properties'. A more detailed discussion of lexical phonology and its predictions for English and Polish can be found in Chapter 2.

To conclude, in the broadly understood generative framework there are basically two major approaches to the phonology–morphology interaction, which can be termed separational and integrational. According to the former, represented for example by the standard generative model (its more abstract and less abstract varieties, prosodically oriented or not, cyclic and non-cyclic), morphology and phonology constitute two separate components with phonological rules operating on the output of morphological rules (modified by the readjustment apparatus). Here the possibility of the interaction of the two components is limited to phonological rules making use of morphological information mostly in the form of syntactic brackets and morphological boundaries. WFRs can have access to the segmental structure of lexical items as well as to their idiosyncratic phonological properties which are stored in the lexicon. However, morphological rules are not supposed to refer to the information that becomes available due to the application of phonological rules.

The second proposal, represented by lexical phonology, is entirely different; here morphological processes and lexical phonological rules are not separate and found in two distinct components, but are all placed in the lexicon and alternate in the formation of lexical items. In lexical phonology every lexical phonological rule directly interacts with WFRs of the level(s) to which it is assigned. This means that WFRs now have access not only to underlying structures, but also to the strings which arise in the course of phonological derivation, or, more exactly, they can refer to the information supplied by lexical phonological rules. The latter make use of morpho-syntactic bracketing, and the need for several boundary symbols disappears altogether.

These two models of the phonology–morphology interaction can be presented in a largely simplified way as shown on p. 28.

It is clear that the major issue within the area of the phonology–morphology interaction, which to a large extent determines the remaining aspects, is deciding which approach: separational or integrational, is more adequate. This problem will be addressed in the next chapter.

Separation versus integration

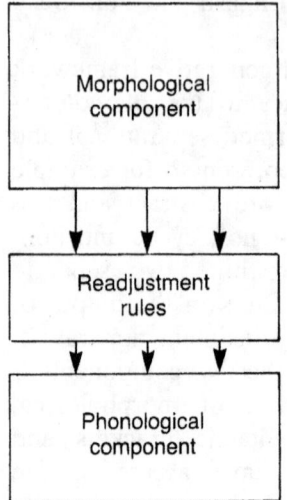

A simplified separational model

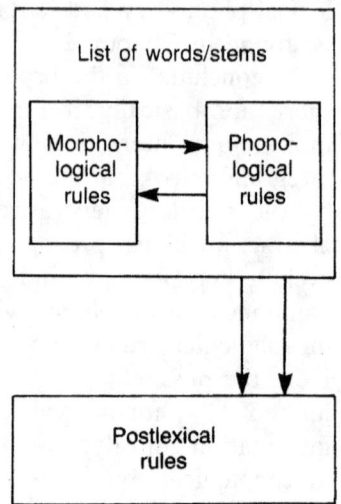

A simplified integrational model

Chapter two

Levels and cycles – some consequences of lexical and cyclic phonology

In this chapter we shall examine the validity of combining phonological rules with WFRs in the lexicon as suggested by lexical phonology. Some of the consequences that the integrational approach leads to when applied to the description of Polish and English will be considered with a special emphasis on the theory of derivational levels and their phonological justification. Another issue which will be of concern in this chapter is the problem of the cyclic application of phonological rules which follows from adopting the principle of strict cyclicity. To put it differently, we shall try to weigh up the advantages as well as the shortcomings of regarding some phonological processes as strictly cyclic.

2.1 Some consequences of adopting the lexical model for Polish

As mentioned in Chapter 1, one of the major assumptions of lexical phonology is that the lexicon consists of a series of levels, which comprise some morphological rules as well as phonological processes. To our knowledge, no description of Polish has ever argued for the need to distinguish several derivational strata in it. The existing lexical analysis of Polish (Rubach 1984a) also admits that there is no justification for any such division of the lexicon and concludes that levels are not universal but language-specific. Curiously enough, the lack of morphological strata in Polish has been taken for granted rather than proved in concrete analyses. It is therefore worthwhile examining whether indeed no lexical levels can be isolated for Polish.

Generally speaking, the reason for postulating a separate

morphological level is the existence of a class of derivatives whose morphological and phonological properties set them off from the remaining items of the language. English Class I and Class II forms, briefly presented in the preceding chapter, are an example of such a case. The starting point is thus to examine whether a given language contains a class of formatives whose behaviour systematically makes them different from other units. It appears that Polish does possess such a special type of affixes.

A well-known fact of Polish is that prefixes differ from suffixes in that the majority of phonological rules do not apply across the prefix boundary. For instance, anterior palatalization, which changes hard consonants such as [t, d, s, z] into their palatal equivalents [ć, dź, ś, ź] in the context of the following front vowel or the palatal glide, for example

ko[t] cat – *ko[ć]e* id. loc. sg.
bu[d]a shack – *bu[dź]e* id. loc. sg.
ro[s]a dew – *ro[ś]e* id. loc. sg.
oa[z]a oasis – *oa[ź]e* id. loc. sg.

is blocked on prefixation, for example

po[d']=jechać drive up *ro[z']=iskrzyć* sparkle
[z']=jeść eat   *[z']=ignorować* ignore

In the latter examples only a slight phonetic modification, known as surface palatalization, can be observed. Other phonological rules which fail to apply when prefixes are involved are vowel deletion, vowel retraction and DI tensing, all discussed in detail in Chapter 5.

These facts indicate that it is justifiable to assume that prefixes are attached at a separate derivational level and that suffixation, but not prefixation, constitutes the domain of the majority of phonological rules such as anterior palatalization. In other words, two lexical strata, prefixation and suffixation, are needed in order to account for the phonology of Polish affixation. What has to be decided is the mutual ordering of prefixation and suffixation, i.e., the 'stacking up' properties of the two classes of affixes.

In many cases suffixes appear to be attached prior to prefixes. For example, the superlative degree prefix *naj-* can only be appended to comparative degree adjectives, which are formed by means of the suffix *-sz(y)* (*-i* and *-y* are the inflectional endings of nominative singular forms of masculine adjectives), for example

biał+y white – *biel+sz+y* whiter – *naj+biel+sz+y* whitest
głup+i silly – *głup+sz+y* sillier – *naj+głup+sz+y* silliest
now+y new – *now+sz+y* newer – *naj+now+sz+y* newest

Here the *-sz(y)* suffixation must precede the *naj-* prefixation since the prefix *naj-* can never be attached to absolute degree (unsuffixed) forms, for example

*naj+biał+y   *naj+głup+i   *naj+now+y

Another example in which prefixes are attached outside suffixes involves the prefix *prze-* ([pše]), which serves to intensify adjectives, for example

mił+y nice – *prze+mił+y* extremely nice
bogat+y rich – *prze+bogat+y* extremely rich

In Polish adjectives can frequently be formed from nouns with the suffix *-n(y)*, for example

ozdob+a ornament – *ozdob+n+y* ornamental
rozkosz delight – *rozkosz+n+y* delightful

Such adjectives may be subject to *prze-* prefixation:

ozdob+n+y ornamental – *prze+ozdob+n+y* over-ornamental
rozkosz+n+y delightful – *prze+rozkosz+n+y* extremely delightful

Clearly, nouns must be turned into adjectives before they can be intensified simply because *prze-* does not attach to nouns,

*prze+ozdob+a   *prze+rozkosz

It follows that in such instances prefixes are attached after suffixes.

Nevertheless, quite frequently prefixation can also be shown to precede suffixation. Many verbs, for instance, must be prefixed before they are subject to nominalization, for example

chow+a+ć hide → *prze+chow+a+ć* store →
prze+chow+alni+a store room
my+ć wash → *z+myw+a+ć* wash up →
z+myw+ark+a dish-washer
mierz+y+ć measure → *przy+mierz+y+ć* try on →
przy+mierz+alni+a fitting room

That this is indeed the case can be seen from the fact that prefixes such as *prze-*, *z-*, and *przy-* do not, as a rule, attach to nouns, but to verbs. Consequently, unprefixed nouns such as

**chow+alni+a* **myw+ark+a* **mierz+alni+a*

do not exist. Furthermore, the meaning of deverbal nouns is directly derivable from the meaning of prefixed verbs, for example

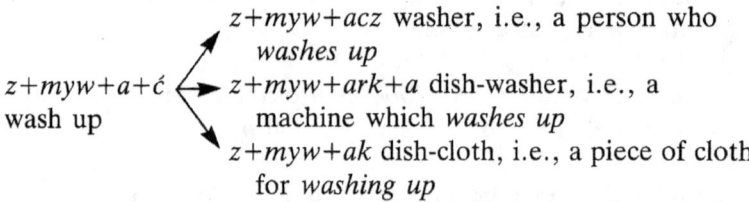

which, in view of the general unpredictability of the meaning of prefixed forms can only be explained if prefixes are first attached to verbs and then the prefixed verbs are nominalized.

In short, morphologically, suffixation appears both to precede and follow prefixation. The noun *zamrażarka* freezer, for instance, is derived in the following fashion: first the noun *mróz* frost is verbalized by the suffix *-i(ć)* – *mroz+i+ć* freeze, then the verb is made perfective by the attachment of the prefix *za-* – *za+mroz+i+ć*. The process of secondary imperfectivization changes *za+mroz+i+ć* into *za+mraż+a+ć* and, finally, the nominalizing suffix *-ark(a)* is appended. Schematically,

suffixation: *mróz* → *mroz+i+ć*
prefixation: *mroz+i+ć* → *za+mroz+i+ć*
suffixation: *za+mroz+i+ć* → *za+mraż+a+ć* →
za+mraż+ark+a

These facts indicate that at least three derivational levels are needed in Polish: level 1 – suffixation, level 2 – prefixation and level 3 – suffixation. This suggestion can be graphically presented as follows:

level 1 – suffixation	(*-ny, -szy*)
Phonological rules	1. ......
of level 1	2. ......
	n. ......
level 2 – prefixation	(*prze-, naj-, z-*)
Phonological rules	1. ......
of level 2	2. ......
	n. ......
level 3 – suffixation	(*-arka, -acz-, -ak*)
Phonological rules	1. ......
of level 3	2. ......
	n. ......
Postcyclic rules	1. ......
	2. ......
	n. ......

It seems, however, that this model is unworkable. First of all, it finds no support in phonological facts; phonological rules of Polish need to distinguish between prefixes and suffixes, but not between two types of suffixes. In other words, phonological properties of level 1 and level 3 suffixes are very much the same. Take the rule of anterior palatalization. It is frequently induced by level 1 suffixes such as *-sz(y)* and *-n(y)*,[1] for example

bia[w]+y white – *bie[l]+sz+y* whiter
gło[s] voice – *gło[ś]+n+y* loud

The process in question fails, however, to affect prefixed items, tentatively assigned to level 2, for example

be[z']=imienny nameless   not **be[ź]imienny*
[z']=jawić się appear   not **[ź]jawić się*

Palatalization is again applicable at level 3, with such suffixes as *-arka*, for example

myd[w]+o soap – *myd[l]+arka* soaping machine
ceg[w]+a brick – *ceg[l]+arka* brick press

Thus, anterior palatalization must be assigned to level 1 and to level 3, but not to level 2. This means that isolating two levels of suffixation is not justified from the phonological point of view as their phonological properties are identical. Moreover, assigning anterior palatalization to both level 1 and level 3 violates a principle, formulated by Halle and Mohanan (1985), according to which the domain of a rule cannot be a set of discontinuous strata.

Furthermore, this model is not confirmed by the morphological facts either. Isolating two separate levels of suffixation is implausible not only phonologically, but also morphologically, since frequently the same suffixes must be appended both at level 1 and at level 3. For example, the suffix *-owy*, which forms adjectives from nouns, attaches both to prefixed and unprefixed words, for example

płeć sex → *płci+ow+y* id.adj. → *bez+płci+ow+y* sexless
dźwięk sound → *dźwięk+ow+y* id.adj. →
  nad+dźwięk+ow+y supersonic

versus

bieg+a+ć run → *o+bieg+a+ć* revolve → *o+bieg* rotation →
  o+bieg+ow+y rotary
słuch+a+ć listen → *pod+słuch+a+ć* listen in → *pod+słuch*
  tapping, noun → *pod+słuch+ow+y* tapping, adj.

In the first case *-owy* must be attached prior to prefixation, i.e., at level 1, while in the second case *-owy* is appended after prefixation, i.e., at level 3. This shows that level 1 and level 3 suffixations are not only phonologically but also morphologically identical. Consequently, this distinction would be very difficult to maintain; rather all suffixes should be viewed as belonging to one and the same stratum. Since suffixation takes place both before and after prefixation, it follows that all these processes must also take place at one lexical level. In consequence, no derivational strata can be postulated for Polish.

This also means that lexical levels cannot be resorted to in order to account for the phonological properties of prefixes, and the model under consideration is forced to employ some other devices to cope with the issue (a discussion of this problem is provided in Chapter 5). In other words, despite the fact that prefixes are phonologically systematically different from suffixes, the most obvious lexical solution, i.e., that of setting up distinct derivational levels is unavailable to handle this situation. This seems to us an important flaw of lexical phonology.

Let us pinpoint the major source of difficulty. Lexical strata can be isolated if a given class of items is characterized by both morphological *and* phonological properties that set it off from all the remaining words. It is not enough if only one group of factors, i.e., either morphological or phonological, differentiates two kinds of derivatives; within one lexical level phonology and morphology must always go hand in hand. This requirement, however, is not met in all the cases (for example, with Polish prefixes), which means that the level approach has limited applicability.

At this point one may legitimately ask whether lexical phonology, with the division of the lexicon into ordered levels as one of its major assumptions, is a viable model for Polish, in which no such strata can be distinguished. In order to answer this question, the most significant advantages of integrating phonological rules with morphology should be recalled. On the morphology side the following aspects of lexical phonology are claimed to be its strongest points.

1. Lexical phonology accounts for the 'stacking up' properties of affixes and relates them to their phonological properties.
2. It explains the fact that WFRs can have access to the information provided by phonological rules.

From the phonological point of view, the lexical model has the following major advantages:[2]

3. It accounts for the phonological properties of affixes by assigning them and phonological rules to different derivational levels. In this way the mechanism of rule conditioning and rule blocking can be described without the necessity of employing distinct boundary symbols.

4. The cyclicity of lexical phonological rules does not have to be stipulated, but follows from the organization of the lexicon: cyclic rules apply as a result of the successive attachment of affixes to the derivational base.[3]

The first point is clearly applicable only to languages with several lexical levels, since lexical phonology does not predict the ordering of affixes within one level. As to the second point, the lexical description of Polish (Rubach 1984a) provides no evidence as to WFRs which are dependent in their application on the information supplied by phonological rules (see, however, Chapter 4). Thus, on the morphology side, little seems to be gained by its integration with phonology.

Let us consider now the second group of lexical assets. Point 3 refers to derivational levels and is therefore inapplicable to languages such as Polish, which lack level distinction. Point 4 concerns the cyclicity of lexical rules and is the only one that is of interest to Polish phonology. As a matter of fact, the cyclic and the lexical analyses of Polish (Rubach 1981 and 1984a) differ very little from each other and the former is incorporated into the latter with only minor modifications.[4] This decision, however, is not dictated by the fact that lexical phonology solves more problems and describes Polish in a more adequate manner than cyclic phonology, but on the basis of the greater theoretical coherence of the lexical framework (mainly the fact, mentioned in point 4, that the cyclicity of phonological rules does not have to be stipulated). Consequently, the accuracy of the lexical analysis crucially depends on the correctness of the cyclic framework. At this point it should be stressed that it is the validity of the cyclic description of Polish that raises doubts in the first place (Szpyra 1985, Gussmann 1985c, and see also section 2.3.2 of the present chapter).

To conclude, Polish provides no compelling evidence for the integration of morphology and phonology suggested by the lexical model. It remains just one of the numerous descriptive possibilities whose superiority over other analyses has yet to be demonstrated.[5] We should also like to add that the existing generative descriptions of Polish morphology (for example, Laskowski 1977, 1981, Malicka-Kleparska 1985, Szymanek 1985), in which a crucial distinction is made between the rules of derivation and the rules of affixation, exclude the possibility of level-ordering and, consequently, interspersing phonological rules with WFRs.

2.2 Some consequences of adopting the lexical model for English

2.2.1 Introduction

In this section we shall consider some aspects of the application of the lexical framework to the analysis of English. This is not meant to be a detailed review of lexical phonology, within which a number of divergent and often competing proposals have been put forward; rather we shall concentrate on the shared assumptions that refer to the integration of phonological and morphological rules in the lexicon. In consequence, several significant aspects of the model such as Kiparsky's (1982a) theory of underspecification and structure-preservation, Halle and Mohanan's (1985) concept of cyclic and non-cyclic strata, etc., as not directly relevant to the integration issue, will not be discussed here.

In contradistinction to Polish, the evidence amassed in support of the conflation of phonology and morphology in English is truly impressive. This is not surprising in view of the fact that it was English that served as a basis for models of level-ordered morphology (Siegel 1974, Allen 1978).

Thus, the existence of several derivational levels and phonological rules associated with them is fairly well documented and evidenced by numerous neat analyses. Recall here Kiparsky's (1982a) treatment of the negative prefixes *in-* and *non-* (presented in Chapter 1), whose 'stacking up' and phonological properties are both accounted for by assigning *in-* and *non-* to two derivational levels and by restricting nasal assimilation to one of them. More examples of this sort can be found in the lexical literature.

Furthermore, English is frequently mentioned as a language in which some WFRs use the information that results from the application of phonological rules. Siegel (1974) discusses three such examples: the *-al* (nominalizing), *-ful* and *(e)teria* suffixations, all of which involve stress conditions on their bases.

In what follows, however, we shall demonstrate that all these advantages are nullified by numerous cases in which the lexical framework makes wrong predictions.

We shall start with a list of major morphological objections to lexical phonology (for more detailed criticism see Sproat 1985).

1. First of all, as noted by some linguists (for example, Aronoff and Sridhar 1983), the affix ordering generalization, on which lexical phonology is based, can be formulated merely as a tendency since there are open classes of items that contradict it, for example

$$[[[\text{patent}] \text{able}_{II}] \text{ity}_I] \quad [[[\text{govern}] \text{ment}_{II}] \text{al}_I]$$
$$[[[\text{standard}] \text{ize}_{II}] \text{ation}_I]$$

In these examples Class I suffixes are appended to Class II suffixes, which is contradictory to AOG. For instance, the suffix *-ize* in *standardize* is stress-neutral (Class II) and yet stress-changing (Class I) suffix *-ation* attaches outside it – *standardization*.

2. There are cases in which morphological and phonological structures of words are different rather than identical, for example

morphological structure	*phonological structure*
$[[\text{re}_{II} [\text{organize}]] \text{ation}_I]$	$[\text{re}_{II} [[\text{organize}] \text{ation}_I]]$
$[[\text{extra}_{II} [\text{metrical}]] \text{ity}_I]$	$[\text{extra}_{II} [[\text{metrical}] \text{ity}_I]]$
$[[\text{un}_{II} [\text{grammatical}]] \text{ity}_I]$	$[\text{un}_{II} [[\text{grammatical}] \text{ity}_I]]$

The morphological structure of *ungrammaticality*, for instance, requires the adjunction of *un-* to *grammatical* since the prefix attaches to adjectives and not to nouns. Consequently, the nominalizing suffix *-ity* is placed outside the adjective *ungrammatical*. From the phonological point of view, however, the prefix *un-* must be regarded as external to the noun *grammaticality* since it fails to undergo nasal assimilation. Hence the two types of bracketing.

3. Frequently there are also discrepancies between the morphological and the semantic structure of words, for example

morphological structure	*semantic structure*
[un [[happy] er]]	[[un [happy]] er]
[[transformational]	[[[transformational]
[[grammar] ian]]	[grammar]] ian]

For instance, the word *unhappier* is formed by the attachment of the comparative degree suffix *-er* to the adjective *happy* since only bisyllabic items can be graded in this fashion. Thus, morphologically, the prefix *un-* is bracketed outside *happier*. This is in disagreement with the meaning of the whole word, which is not 'not happier', as predicted by morphological bracketing, but 'more unhappy'. The latter reading requires that semantically *un-* be attached to *happy* and then the negative adjective can be subject to grading.

The types of structures presented under 2 and 3 came to be known as 'bracketing paradoxes'. An attempt at reconciling them with the lexical model has been made by Kiparsky (1983) and Pesetsky (1985) (for the critical assessment of these proposals see Sproat 1984, 1985).

4. Lexical phonology lacks control over the number of derivational levels (Aronoff and Sridhar 1983), which leads to their proliferation (for instance, the following proposals have been put forward with respect to English: Siegel 1974 – two levels, Allen 1978 – three levels, Kiparsky 1982a – three levels, Kiparsky 1983 – three levels, Mohanan 1982 – four levels, Halle and Mohanan 1985 – five levels).

5. Those lexical models which posit the level of compounding as distinct from the level of affixation (for example, Halle and Mohanan 1985, Mohanan 1982), require the introduction of an additional device of the loop (which allows the output of a later level to become the input to an earlier level) in those cases in which compounding precedes affixation, for example

    [[air] [condition]] → [re [[air] [condition]]]
    compounding →   affixation

The loop constitutes a considerable weakening of the level-ordering hypothesis (Halle 1986).

6. Lexical phonology, at its current stage of development, represents an oversimplified approach to morphology and

fails to address, let alone solve, various morphological issues such as (Gussmann 1986):
- the ordering of affixes within one derivational level, for example the fact that we can have both *-less-ness* (*care-less-ness*) and *-ness-less* (*tender-ness-less*), but only *-ic-ity* (*atom-ic-ity*) and not *-ity-ic* (*atom-ity-ic).
- the selection of competing affixes, for example why the adjective formed from the noun *period* is *period+ic*, and not *period-al* or *period-y*.
- the problem why sometimes two derivations are possible with suffixes from different strata (for example *periodic$_I$-ness$_{II}$*) and *period-ic$_I$-ity$_I$*), while in other cases this is not possible (for example, *im$_I$-polite* versus **un$_{II}$-polite*).

We shall now proceed to demonstrate some phonological consequences of adopting the lexical framework in English. The issue of primary importance is how many lexical strata have to be isolated to account for the phonological properties of this language. The different number of levels posited by various linguists (see point 4) seems to indicate that the evidence for several such distinctions is scarce if not altogether non-existent (Kaisse and Shaw 1985). We shall, therefore, assume that the only well-documented phonological distinction is the one between the SPE stress-neutral and stress-determining affixes, which were subsequently referred to as Class I and Class II affixes by Siegel (1974), level 1 and level 2 affixes by Allen (1978), root and word affixes by Selkirk (1982) and primary and secondary affixes by Kiparsky (1982a). The following discussion centres around the properties of these two types of affix.

2.2.2 Criteria used in establishing the class membership of English affixes

According to lexical phonology, the two types of English affixes are appended at separate derivational levels and are systematically distinguished by a set of morphological, phonological and semantic properties, which are cumulatively listed below.

Levels and cycles

Class I Affixes	Class II Affixes
Morphological properties:	
1. Class I affixes can attach to non-word bases, for example *sub-mit, dict-ate, re-duce*.	1. Class II affixes attach to words only (Siegel 1974), for example *re-print, kind-ness, treat-ment*.
2. Class I affixes attach only outside Class I affixes and never outside Class II affixes, for example **beauti-ful$_{II}$-ity$_{I}$, atom-ic$_{I}$-ity$_{I}$*.	2. Class II affixes can never be followed by Class I affixes – the affix ordering generalization (Siegel 1974), for example **wretch-ed$_{II}$-ity$_{I}$*.
3. Class I affixes can trigger allomorphy and truncation, for example *nomin-ate → nomin-ee$_{I}$ simpl-ify → simpl-ific-ation$_{I}$*.	3. Class II affixes never trigger allomorphy or trunction (Aronoff 1976) *nomin-ate → nomin-at-ed$_{II}$ simpl-ify → simpl-ify-ing$_{II}$*.

Phonological properties: Generally speaking, the application versus non-application of phonological rules is contingent on the nature of the appended affix.

Class I Affixes	Class II Affixes
1. Class I affixes are stress-determining, for example, *'curious – curi'os-ity$_{I}$*.	1. Class II affixes are stress-neutral (SPE), for example *'demonstrate – 'demonstrat-ing$_{II}$*.
2. *g* does not drop after the velar nasal before Class I suffixes, for example *diptho[ŋg]-al$_{I}$*.	2. *g* drops after the velar nasal before Class II suffixes (SPE), for example *diphtho[ŋ]-s$_{II}$*.
3. Sonorants are not syllabified before Class I affixes, for example, *remem[br]-ance$_{I}$*.	3. Sonorants are syllabified before Class II affixes (SPE), for example *remem[bər]-ing$_{II}$*.
4. Class I suffix *-y* induces spirantization, for example *democra[t] – democra[s]-y$_{I}$*.	4. Class II suffix *-y* blocks spirantization, for example *tren[d] – tren[d]-y$_{II}$*.
5. Class I affixes evince degemination, for example *in$_{I}$-numerable → i[n]umerable*.	5. Class II affixes block degemination (SPE), for example *un$_{II}$-natural → u[nn]atural*.
6. Class I affixes trigger nasal assimilation, for example *in$_{I}$-possible → i[mp]ossible*.	6. Class II affixes block nasal assimilation (SPE), for example *un$_{II}$-popular → u[np]opular*.
7. Class I affixes trigger trisyllabic laxing, for example *provōke – provŏc-ative$_{I}$*.	7. Class II affixes block trisyllabic laxing (Kiparsky 1982a), for example *mīght – mīght-i$_{II}$-ly$_{II}$*.

(continued overleaf)

Levels and cycles

(continued)

Class I Affixes	Class II Affixes
8. Consonant clusters (plosive + nasal, nasal + plosive, nasal + nasal) are preserved before Class I affixes, for example $bo[mb]\text{-}ard_I$, $da[mn]\text{-}ation_I$.	8. Consonant clusters are simplified before Class II affixes (Halle and Mohanan 1985), for example $bo[m]\text{-}er_{II}$, $da[m]\text{-}ing_{II}$.
9. Class I affixes also trigger other word-level rules which do not refer to the word boundary.	9. Class II affixes block other word-level rules which do not refer to the word boundary (SPE).
Semantic properties:	
1. Class I derivatives tend to have non-compositional semantics, for example in re_I-*duce*, re_I-*sume*, *re-* has no constant meaning.	1. Class II derivatives tend to have compositional semantics (Siegel 1974), for example in re_{II}-*wash*, re_{II}-*make*, *re-* means 'to do something again'.

Class I suffixes comprise, for example, *-y* (noun-forming), *-ate*, *-ion*, *-ity*, *-(i)fy*, *-al* (adjective-forming), *-ous*, *-ory*, *-ic*, *-ary*, *-use*, *-itude*, *-ial* (Siegel 1974), *-th*, *-ette*, *-ian*, *-a*, *-ese*, *-esque* (Selkirk 1982), *-an*, *-ious*, *-is* (Strauss 1982), while Class II *-y* (adjective-forming), *-ness*, *-less*, *-ly*, *-ish*, *-like*, *-some*, *-ful*, *-al* (noun-forming), *-ed*, *-ing* (Siegel 1974), *-hood*, *-age*, *-ling*, *-let*, *-dom*, *-worthy* (Selkirk 1982), *-ship*, *-er* (Strauss 1982). Class I prefixes include *in-*, *con-*, *per-*, *ab-*, *sub-*, *dis-*, *trans-*, *inter-*, *para-*, *de-* (Siegel 1974), Class II *anti-*, *pro-* (Siegel 1974), *non-*, *step-*, *ex-* (Selkirk 1982). Moreover, as several linguists (for example Siegel 1974, Aronoff 1976, Selkirk 1982) have noted, while the majority of English affixes can be assigned either to Class I or to Class II, some seem to display the properties of both classes. Consequently, they may be termed 'dual class' affixes. They comprise, according to Selkirk (1982), such suffixes as *-ize*, *-ment*, *-able*, *-ism*, *-ist*, *-ive*, *-y* (noun-forming) and prefixes such as *hyper-*, *circum-*, *neo-*, *auto-* and *mono-*.

Before we proceed to discuss some phonological problems concerning the two types of English affixes, we should like to comment briefly on the criteria employed in establishing their class membership. First of all, it must be noted that not all the factors which have been enumerated are unanimously accepted by the linguists working within the lexical framework. As a matter of fact, it is frequently impossible to say what criteria have been used in individual instances as the proper justification of such decisions is not always provided.[6] More specific comments also seem in order.

One of the hallmarks of level-ordered morphology as well as lexical phonology is that they reject Aronoff's (1976) word-based hypothesis, according to which all regular word formation processes are word-based, and assume that non-words can also serve as the input to WFRs. Consequently, the nature of the derivational base (word versus non-word) can be used to distinguish Class I and Class II derivatives. It should be mentioned that Strauss (1982) opposes this view, pointing out that since WFRs are optional, there is no reason why non-words should undergo any affixation at level 1. Non-words can, in his opinion, be subject directly to Class II affixation, evidenced in the following examples:

hap-less$_{II}$ feck-less$_{II}$
grue-some$_{II}$ ful-some$_{II}$

It is striking, however, that the number of forms with Class II affixes attached to non-words is very low, hence they do not constitute serious counterevidence to the criterion under discussion, which is recognized by the majority of lexical linguists.

Nevertheless, the assumption that WFRs operate on items which are not words raises several problems. First of all, there seems to be no principled way of determining which strings are morphologically simple and which are complex. The usual procedure is to resort to the phonetic identity of recurring sequences of segments. For example,

native and local

can be treated as morphologically divisible since *nat* and *loc* recur in

nat-ion and loc-ate

and *-ive* as well as *-al* are regular suffixes of English (for example in *creat+ive, environment+al*). On analogy, other items, such as

    possible and decent

can also be regarded as morphologically complex (*-ible* and *-ent* are suffixes in *divis+ible, persist+ent*), even if *poss* and *dec* do not seem to recur in any other words. Alternatively, *possible* and *decent* might be treated as simple items. Since, to our knowledge, no definite principles of morphological segmentation have been formulated within lexical phonology, it is not clear what decisions would be made in individual instances (such as the interpretation of the adjectives *possible* and *decent*).

Consider now a different set of examples. The forms such as

    participant   navigable
    hesitant   cultivable

can be approached in two ways. On the one hand, it can be claimed that the suffixes *-ant* and *-able* are attached to non-word bases

    particip-   navig-
    hesit-   cultiv-

Alternatively, the adjectives above may be regarded as derived from the verbs

    participate   navigate
    hesitate   cultivate

with the subsequent truncation of the suffix *-ate* (along the lines suggested by Aronoff's 1976 model). The latter approach has a significant advantage of accounting for the deverbal meaning of the adjectives in question, for example

    participant – someone who *participates*
    cultivable – something that can be *cultivated*

It is not always obvious which approach individual lexicalists subscribe to.

It has already been mentioned that lexical phonology accepts the affix ordering generalization. Again Strauss (1982) has to be singled out since his position is that the AOG holds true, but only for suffixes and prefixes separately. In other words, he claims that the left and right adjunction are independent of each other. In this way Strauss manages to avoid 'bracketing paradoxes' which involve both prefixes and suffixes, but still has to cope with the cases of Class I suffixes attached outside Class II suffixes (the '-*ability*' type). Nevertheless, for the majority of lexicalists the AOG is one of the major diagnostics of class membership.

As far as the phonological criteria for distinguishing Class I and Class II affixes are concerned, there is no complete agreement as to the diagnostic status of individual rules either. For example, if a phonological process is regarded as postcyclic, then it cannot serve to distinguish the two classes of affixes. Similarly, if a rule is assigned to level 2, but is not conditioned by the morphological features of that level, it can also affect the structures created at earlier levels. Such is, for instance, the approach of Halle and Mohanan (1985) to spirantization and palatalization, which they treat as level 2 rules applicable also to level 1 items.

A few remarks are also necessary with regard to the analysis of dual class affixes specifically. In this case the decision concerning their class membership cannot be made on any *a priori* grounds, but every word with a dual class affix has to be individually examined. In the overwhelming majority of cases, however, it is impossible to decide the status of an affix since no significant phonological or morphological phenomena might be involved in a given affixation.

Aronoff (1976) argues, for example, that two -*able* suffixes must be isolated as they differ in a number of features. None of these factors can help us to establish the status of -*able* in

blamable	checkable	burnable
drinkable	kissable	swimmable

in which no phonological rules of importance are applicable.

Similarly, the fact that -*ize* can be both stress-neutral and stress-determining is of no use in the case of many short (i.e., mono- and disyllabic) bases since their stress pattern cannot be affected by the addition of -ize anyway, for example

'logic – 'logicize   'fluid – 'fluidize
'formal – 'formalize   'human – 'humanize

The lack of generally accepted criteria for establishing the class membership of English affixes frequently results in contradictory assignments. Therefore, in our subsequent discussion we shall employ as many and as uncontroversial factors as possible. Moreover, only conclusive and already attested examples will be used, even though sometimes these are forms infrequent in colloquial use. The variety of English is basically received pronunciation although in almost all cases the presented facts hold true of other types of English as well.[7]

2.2.3 *Dual class suffixes:* -ize, -ant/-ent, -ive, -able/-ible

We shall start examining the contention of lexical phonology that it can account for the properties of English affixes with the analysis of dual class suffixes. If I understand the lexical framework correctly, a given affix can be said to possess 'dual membership' if, when attached to one item, it displays morphological and phonological features of Class I and if, when appended to a different form, it behaves as a member of Class II. In other words, duality is both phonological and morphological since in a model whose major assumption is that (Kiparsky 1982b:33), 'phonological rules operate in tandem with morphology in the lexicon', there cannot be cases of systematic disparity between the morphological, phonological and semantic structure of words.[8]

Below we examine the morphological and phonological properties of some selected dual class suffixes. We start with the verbalizing suffix *-ize*.

-ize

The suffix *-ize* displays considerable productivity. It attaches to nominal bases, for example

Levels and cycles

alcohol – alcoholize   carbon – carbonize
victim – victimize   robot – robotize

It also attaches to adjectives, for example

familiar – familiarize   velar – velarize
erotic – eroticize   legal – legalize

Phonological properties The behaviour of *-ize* with regard to phonological rules clearly reveals its dual nature: the required phonological processes are triggered in some cases, whereas in others they are blocked.

Stress It appears that *-ize* sometimes is stress-neutral, sometimes stress-determining and in some cases it admits fluctuations, for example

(a) Nominal bases
   stress-neutral   *stress-determining*
   'skeleton – 'skeletonize   'dialogue – di'alogize
   'alphabet – 'alphabetize   'synonym – sy'nonymize
   'vitamin – 'vitaminize   'gelatin – ge'latinize
   'nicotin – 'nicotinize   'nitrogen – ni'trogenize
   'vagabond – 'vagabondize   'diamond – di'amondize
   'hospital – 'hospitalize   ca'nal – 'canalize
   'alcohol – 'alcoholize   'misanthrope – mi'santhropize

   fluctuating forms

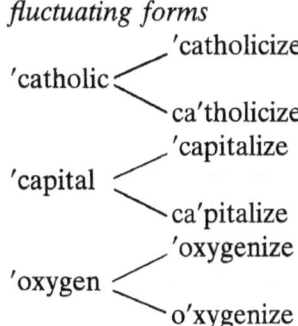

(b) Adjectival bases
   stress-neutral   *stress-determining*
   'rational – 'rationalize   'Arabic – a'rabicize

(b) Adjectival bases
'decimal – 'decimalize   di'vine – 'divinize
'masculine – 'masculinize   i'mmune – 'immunize
'anglican – 'anglicanize   dia'bolic – di'abolize
'prodigal – 'prodigalize   meta'bolic – me'tabolize

fluctuating forms

'volatile ⟨ 'volatilize / vo'latilize

It should be added that there seem to be more forms with stress-neutral *-ize*.

Sonorant syllabification The number of conclusive examples is fairly low, but sufficient to demonstrate that, again, the suffix *-ize* has two different effects on the final sonorants of words to which it is attached, for example

syllabification	*no syllabification*
so[bər]ize (so[br]iety)	thea[tr]ize (thea[tə])
win[tər]ize (win[tr]y)	idola[tr]ize (idola[tə])

Cluster simplification We have been able to find only one example

sole[mn]ize (sole[m]n)

where the consonant cluster is preserved before *-ize*, which points to its Class I nature. Other forms such as

reco[gn]ize   co[gn]ize

are also pronounced with two consonants although no alternations can be observed in this case.

Trisyllabic laxing Trisyllabic laxing does not seem to affect tense vowels in the words to which *-ize* is added, for example

vāpourize	nāturize	mājorize	dēmonize
vōwelize	ītemize	schēmatize	mīcronize
nāsalize	pēnalize	vēlarize	lēgalize
pōlarize	fīnalize	vītalize	sōlarize

This feature of the items above suggests that *-ize* should be regarded here as belonging to Class II.⁹

On the other hand, the vowel in the penultimate syllable is frequently shortened on the attachment of *-ize*, for example

satīre – satĭrize   divīne – divĭnize
mobīle (BE) – mobĭlize   fertīle (BE) – fertĭlize
sterīle (BE) – sterĭlize volatīle (BE) – volatĭlize

which, however, is not true of such items as

stȳle – stȳlize   echō – echōize
herō – herōize   zerō – zerōize

These facts support the dual class nature of *-ize*.

G-deletion   There are only two verbs in *-ize* which are derived from the velar nasal bases

monophtho[ŋg]ize / monophtho[ŋ]ize
diphtho[ŋg]ize   / diphtho[ŋ]ize

Here two pronunciations are possible: with and without the velar plosive. Although drawing any definite conclusions on the basis of two examples is not justified, it is evident that the suffix *-ize* displays no uniform phonological behaviour.

Generally speaking, *-ize* appears to have phonological properties of both Class I and Class II. The rules of stress and trisyllabic laxing demonstrate that more forms appear to possess the characteristics of Class II.

Morphological properties   Several morphological arguments can be brought forward to show that *-ize*, in spite of its phonological properties, is uniformly Class I.
1. All verbs in *-ize* are, without exception, subject to nominalization by means of stress-changing Class I suffix *-ation*, for example

alcoholization   carbonization   nasalization
legàlization   velarization   palatalization
divinization   immunization   hospitalization

This is one of the most serious examples of the violation of the affix ordering generalization, particularly significant because of the absolute exceptionlessness of the process (Aronoff and Sridhar 1983).

2. *-ize* always attaches outside Class I, but never outside Class II suffixes, for example

> centr-al$_I$-ize   *grate-ful$_{II}$-ize
> republic-an$_I$-ize   *worth-less$_{II}$-ize
> poet-ic$_I$-ize   *Jew-ish$_{II}$-ize
> perfect-ion$_I$-ize   *mad-ness$_{II}$-ize

3. *-ize* can attach to non-word stems, for example

> catech-ize (catech-ism)   bapt-ize (bapt-ism)
> minim-ize (minim-al)   mechan-ize (mechan-ic)
> egot-ize (egot-ism)   recogn-ize (recogn-ition)

4. When *-ize* is attached to nouns in *-y*, the *-y* gets truncated, for example

> category – categorize   allegory – allegorize
> melancholy – melancholize   symmetry – symmetrize

Moreover, nouns terminating in *-is* lose this ending on verbalization by means of *-ize*, for example[10]

> hypothesis – hypothesize   parenthesis – parenthesize
> emphasis – emphasize   synthesis – synthesize

Let us take stock of the situation. It has been established that from the morphological point of view the suffix *-ize* is uniformly Class I. Its behaviour with respect to phonological rules, however, indicates that it belongs to two different classes. In other words, phonological differences have no morphological correlates. Thus, *-ize* is 'dual' only in terms of its phonology, not in terms of its morphology. Consequently, it cannot be assigned either to level 1 or to level 2; if *-ize* is appended at level 1, its phonological properties cannot be fully accounted for; if it is attached at level 2, its morphological features will be inexplicable. Appending *-ize* at both levels is impossible because of its uniformly Class I morphology. All in all, the lexical framework appears incapable of handling all the properties of *-ize*.

Below we present another suffix which poses similar problems for the lexical description.

-ant/-ent[11]

The suffix *-ant/-ent* is usually attached to verbs and forms deverbal nouns and adjectives. Quite frequently one word functions both as a noun and as an adjective.

nouns
attend – attendant
adhere – adherent
inhabit – inhabitant

adjectives
resemble – resemblant
indulge – indulgent
diverge – divergent

nouns and adjectives
exhale – exhalant
repel – repellent
absorb – absorbent

Phonological properties Like *-ize*, the suffix *-ant/-ent* appears to have a dual nature in terms of its phonology.
Stress The suffix *-ant/-ent* can be both stress-determining and stress-neutral.

stress-determining
'signify – sig'nificant
pre'fer – 'preferent
pro'test – 'protestant
per'tain – 'pertinent
'execute – ex'ecutant

stress-neutral
perse'vere – perse'verant
de'fy – de'fiant
re'ly – re'liant
in'hale – in'halant
re'pel – re'pellent

fluctuating forms

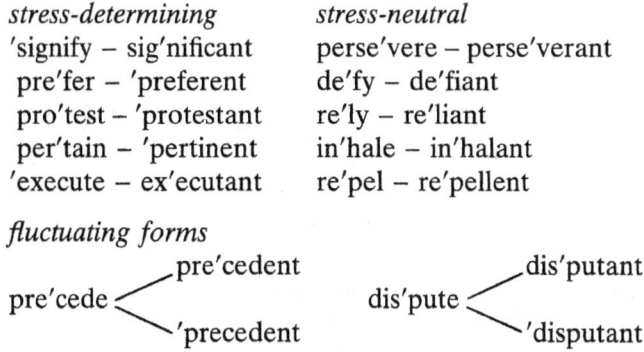

The items with stress-neutral *-ant/-ent* constitute the majority (Fudge 1984).

Laxing It is a well-known fact of English that laxing is triggered by some suffixes (for example, by *-ic*, *-ish* and *-id*, according to SPE:241). We have already demonstrated the phenomenon with the suffix *-ize*. It appears that *-ant/-ent* has such an effect on stem vowels of the verbs to which it is attached, for example

    presīde – presĭdent   resīde – resĭdent
    confīde – confĭdent   provīde – provĭdent
    prevāil – prevălent   coincīde – coincĭdent

In other cases, however, no laxing takes place on the attachment of *-ant/-ent*, for example

    cohēre – cohērent   defȳ – defīant
    complȳ – complīant   relȳ – relīant
    inhāle – inhālant   exhāle – exhālant

which points to the dual character of the suffix in question. It should also be noted that laxing affects only those forms in which the shift of stress has taken place.

Cluster simplification It appears that usually the prenasal consonant is not deleted before *-ant/-ent*, for example

    malig[n] – mali[gn]ant   repug[n] – repu[gn]ant
    benig[n] – beni[gn]ant   oppug[n] – oppu[gn]ant

which points to Class I character of *-ant* in these examples.

Morphological properties Morphological arguments demonstrate that *-ant/-ent* should be treated as a member of Class I.

1. Nouns in *-ant/-ent* are often subject to adjectivization by means of stress-changing and also spirantization and palatalization inducing Class I suffix *-ial*, for example

    'precedent – prece'dential   'president – presi'dential
    ex'istent – exi'stential   ex'ponent – expo'nential
    re'ferent – refe'rential   'reverent – reve'rential

This refers to stress-neutral and stress-determining forms alike.
2. Adjectives in *-ant/-ent* usually take the negative Class I prefix *in-*, for example

incoherent	independent	insufficient
irradiant	irrelevant	insignificant
irreverent	improvident	inconvenient

and only rarely Class II *un-*, for example, *undefiant, unrepentant*. Again, the attachment of *in-* is true of both stress-neutral /inco'herent/ and stress-determining /ir'reverent/ *-ant/-ent*.
3. The suffix in question truncates the verb suffix *-ate*, for example

stimul-ate → stimul-ant	domin-ate → domin-ant
devi-ate → devi-ant	hesit-ate → hesit-ant
particip-ate → particip-ant	emigr-ate → emigr-ant

4. The suffix *-ent*, when attached to *pose* stems, induces the allomorphic s→n change, for example

propose → proponent	oppose → opponent
expose → exponent	depose → deponent

5. *-ant/-ent* attaches only to underived verbs and never to Class II derivatives, for example

attend → attendant	to house → *housant
irritate → irritant	to sharpen → *sharpenant
absorb → absorbent	to de-louse → *de-lousant

The suffix *-ant/-ent* confronts us with exactly the same situation as *-ize*: morphologically it belongs to Class I, but phonologically to both classes. In other words, phonological and morphological structures are different rather than identical. It is important to add that the same seems to be true about other suffixes such as *-ance/-ence* and *-ancy/-ency*, whose behaviour parallels exactly that of *-ant/-ent*.

Now we turn to the discussion of a slightly different group of dual class suffixes.

-ive

The suffix *-ive* is usually attached to verbs from which it forms adjectives, for example[12]

affect – affective   attract – attractive
possess – possessive   corrode – corrosive
omit – omissive   comprehend – comprehensive

Occasionally *-ive* is appended to nominal bases, for example

adjunct – adjunctive   gerund – gerundive
instinct – instinctive

Phonological properties When *-ive* is attached to verbs, it usually leaves the stress on the verbal base. In the case of verbs in *-ate*, however, in some forms we observe the shift in stress-placement, whereas in others we do not. Some items have two possible pronunciations.

stress-neutral -ive
'generate – 'generative
'cumulate – 'cumulative
'stimulate – 'stimulative
'legislate – 'legislative
in'vestigate – in'vestigative
co'mmemorate – co'mmemorative

stress-determining -ive
'demonstrate – de'monstrative
'contemplate – con'templative
'indicate – in'dicative
'correlate – cor'relative
'derogate – de'rogative
nar'rate – 'narrative

fluctuating forms

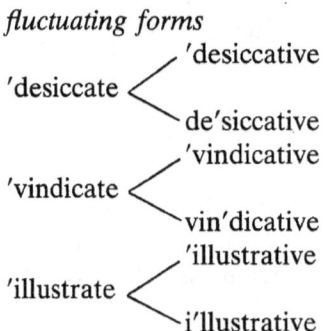

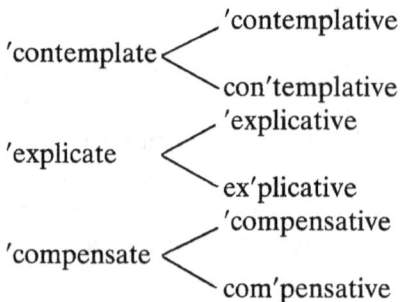

Clearly, from the phonological point of view, two classes of *-ive* should be distinguished.

Morphological properties It appears that *-ive* in some derivatives displays the morphological properties of Class I, in others of Class II, which points to its dual status.
Properties of Class I:
1. Although the *-ive* adjectives normally nominalize by means of the Class II suffix *-ness*, for example,

collective – collectiveness   attractive – attractiveness
productive – productiveness   suggestive – suggestiveness

occasionally Class I nominalizations with the suffix *-ity* are attested, for example

corrosive – corrosivity   regressive – regressivity
emissive – emissivity   diffusive – diffusivity
exclusive – exclusivity   productive – productivity

2. Almost all *-ive* adjectives are subject to Class I negative *in*-prefixation, for example

indecisive   inadhesive   incommunicative
irrelative   inoffensive   indiscriminative
inoperative   irresponsive   irradiative

3. The attachment of *-ive* often induces various types of allomorphy within the stem, for example

permi[t] – permi[s]ive   cohe[r]e – cohe[s]ive
explo[d]e – explo[s]ive   produ[s]e – produ[kt]ive
destr[oi] – destru[kt]ive   corro[d]e – corro[s]ive

4. *-ive* can be claimed to attach to non-word stems, for example

nat-ive /nat-ion/   fict-ive /fict-ion/
volit-ive /volit-ion/   cognit-ive /cognit-ion/
attent-ive /attent-ion/   lenit-ive /lenit-ion/

Properties of Class II:
1. Marchand (1969:317) observes that -ive can be attached to whole phrases, which is particularly true of American English, for example

afterthoughtive	stick-to-itiveness
hang-to-itiveness	wide-awake-ativeness
go-ahead-ativeness	stay-at-home-ativeness

although some of these examples may not be in frequent use.[13]

It is clear that -ive is a dual class affix with respect both to phonological and morphological properties. The most significant issue is whether phonological differences are correlated with morphological differentiation. It appears that in many cases no such correlation can be found. For instance, Class I negative prefix in- can be appended to adjectives with stress-neutral -ive, for example

inco'mmunicative	indis'criminative
in'operative	in'cogitative

Allomorphy, which is a feature of Class I affixation, can also take place when -ive is stress-neutral, for example

per'mi[t] – per'mi[s]ive	'multipl[ai] – 'multipl[ik]ative
e'va[d]e – e'va[s]ive	'modif[ai] – 'modif[ik]ative

Thus, the suffix -ive is different from -ize and -ant/-ent. In the cases discussed previously, morphologically uniform suffixes displayed phonologically divergent behaviour, which could not be explained by the morphological structure of the analysed items. Here morphological evidence shows that -ive is a truly dual class affix. This duality has been confirmed by phonological facts: in some forms -ive is stress-neutral, in others stress-determining. Nevertheless, it appears that even if we do need to distinguish two kinds of phonological -ive suffixes, there is no one-to-one correspondence with morphological classes. Thus, one suffix within the same item may have morphological properties of one class, but phonological features of another. Let us recall once again that such cases prove problematic for the lexical framework. Below we demonstrate that this is not an isolated example.

-able/-ible[14]

The suffix in question has been extensively discussed by Aronoff (1976), who claims that in English there are two distinct *-able* suffixes differing in a number of phonological, morphological, semantic and syntactic properties. The suffix *-able* is used mainly for forming deverbal adjectives, for example

remove – removable   forgive – forgivable
love – lovable   advise – advisable
adapt – adaptable   recover – recoverable

Phonological properties   The suffix *-able* is dual class in terms of its phonology: in some cases it induces phonological processes, in others it blocks them.
Stress   The stress pattern of *-able* adjectives is not uniform: sometimes the suffix is stress-neutral, sometimes stress-determining, and sometimes fluctuating forms occur, for example[15]

stress-determining   *stress-neutral*
re′pute – ′reputable   for′give – for′givable
′remedy – re′mediable   ′govern – ′governable
la′ment – ′lamentable   di′vide – di′visible

fluctuating forms
′reconcile – ′reconcilable / recon′cilable
′recognize – ′recognizable / recog′nizable
′criticize – ′criticizable / criti′cizable
re′voke – re′vocable / ′revocable
a′pply – a′pplicable / ′applicable
′transfer – ′transferable / trans′ferable
re′spire – re′spirable / ′respirable

In the majority of cases, however, the stress of the verbal base is unmodified by the attachment of *-able*.[16]
Sonorant syllabification   The attachment of *-able* has two different effects on stem-final sonorants: in some forms they are syllabified, in others they are not, for example

syllabification
remem[bər]able (remem[br]ance)
fil[tər]able (fil[tr]ate)
han[dl]eable (han[dl]er)

no syllabification
arbi[tr]able (arbi[tə]r)
fil[tr]able (fil[tə]r)
minis[tr]able (minis[tə]r)
seques[tr]able (seques[tə]r)
regis[tr]able (regis[tə]r)

Cluster simplification The dual status of *-able* is also confirmed by cluster simplification, for example

simplification　*no simplification*
assig[n]able　　　　　impre[gn]able
consig[n]able　impu[gn]able
desig[n]able　expu[gn]able
sig[n]able　da[mn]able
bo[m]bable　conde[mn]able

G-deletion The voiced velar stop seems to be dropped before *-able* after the velar nasal, which points to the Class II nature of *-able* in the forms below, for example

ha[ŋ]able　ri[ŋ]able
swi[ŋ]able　cli[ŋ]able
si[ŋ]able　prolo[ŋ]able

Morphological properties: Several morphological facts show the need for distinguishing two *-able* suffixes: one Class I, another Class II.

1. As Aronoff (1976:123) demonstrates, in some cases *-able* triggers stem allomorphy whereas in others it does not, even if the same verb serves as a derivational base, for example

defend – defen[s]ible – defen[d]able
divide – divi[z]ible – divi[d]able
perceive – perce[pt]ible – percei[v]able

2. Aronoff also observes that *-able* appended to verbs in *-ate* sometimes truncates the verb suffix and sometimes does not, for example

toler-ate – toler-able　　　vs　deb-ate – deb-at-able

negoti-ate – negoti-able   rel-ate – rel-at-able
communic-ate – communic-able   cre-ate – cre-at-able

This sometimes leads to doublets, for example

cultiv-ate – cultiv-able / cultiv-at-able
educ-ate – educ-able / educ-at-able
irrig-ate – irrig-able / irrig-at-able

3. Although -*able* usually attaches to verbs, sometimes it is found appended to non-word stems (Aronoff 1976:125), for example

poss-ible   refrang-ible
vulner-able   horr-ible

On the other hand, -*able* may sometimes be attached not only to words or stems, but also to whole phrases (Marchand 1969:230), for example

get-at-able   un-get-at-able
come-at-able   un-come-at-able
         go-up-able

-*able* appears also in such phrases as

livable in   livable with
unspeakable to   unget-on-able with

4. According to Aronoff, the necessity of distinguishing two kinds of -*able* can be seen in the fact that some adjectives under consideration form negatives by means of Class I prefix *in-*, whereas others do so by means of Class II *un-* (the former contain Class I -*able*, the latter Class II -*able*), for example

im-possible   vs   un-regulatable
in-divisible   un-dividable
ir-revocable   un-revokable

5. It should additionally be noted that, apart from the differences between Class I -*able* and Class II -*able* mentioned

under 1–4, all -*able* adjectives are characterized by a common 'stacking up' property; they are subject to Class I stress-changing nominalization with the suffix -*ity*. This type of suffixation takes place regardless of whether the adjective contains the stress-determining or stress-neutral -*able*, for example

-*ity with stress-changing -able*	-*ity with stress-neutral -able*
'comparable – compara'bility	re'movable – remova'bility
'applicable – applica'bility	en'joyable – enjoya'bility
'reputable – reputa'bility	'governable – governa'bility

Here the right-hand examples are another instance of the violation of the AOG since Class I -*ity* is found outside Class II -*able*. Such cases are inexplicable within the lexical framework, which is particularly important in view of the fact that the process in question is absolutely without exception and all -*able* adjectives can form -*ability* nouns.

The situation we encounter with -*able* words seems perfectly clear and unambiguous: there are two morphological -*able* suffixes and two phonological -*able* suffixes. What remains to be proved is that these two classes are the same, i.e., that morphological Class I coincides with phonological Class I, and that morphological Class II means exactly the same as phonological Class II. Unfortunately, it is exactly at this point that the elaborately built parallel breaks down completely.

Thus, apart from those instances in which phonology and morphology go hand in hand, i.e., where, for example, allomorphy and/or truncation are accompanied by the stress shift, for example

a'pply – 'applicable   'explicate – ex'plicable

or the lack of allomorphy co-occurs with the preservation of the stress-pattern, for example

a'pply – a'ppliable   'signify – 'signifiable

there are many cases in which phonological properties of -*able* adjectives appear to contradict their morphological features. For instance, a large group of words with Class II -*able* is subject to

Class I negative prefixation with *in-*, for example[17]

incontrollable	inadvisable	incomputable
inconceivable	inapproachable	indescribable
inappeasable	inaccessible	inconsolable
incommutable	incompliable	incondensable

What is more, nasal assimilation assimilates the nasal consonant of the prefix *in-* to the following consonant regardless of whether *-able* is stress-neutral or stress-determining, for example

i'rrefutable – irre'futable   irrecon'cilable – i'rreconcilable
i'rrevocable – irre'vokable   i'rreparable – irre'pairable

No consistency can be detected with regard to the stress pattern of *-able* adjectives and allomorphy. Thus, allomorphy affects also stress-neutral *-able* adjectives, for example

a'pply – a'pplicable   'multiply – 'multiplicable

The same is true of *-ate* truncation, which does not have to be accompanied by the change in stress placement, for example

'explicate – 'explicable   'extricate – 'extricable

Clearly, phonological properties of *-able* adjectives cannot always be explained in terms of their morphological structure since, as was the case with *-ive* words, morphological and phonological levels in English are often distinct rather than identical.

Let us now summarize the major observations concerning dual class suffixes.[18] We have demonstrated that they do not form a homogeneous group; the suffixes *-ize* and *-ant/-ent* (as well as *-ance/-ence*, *-ancy/-ency*) consistently display morphological properties of Class I and phonological features of both classes, while the suffixes *-ive* and *-able/-ible* (but also, it seems, *-ist* and *-ism*) appear to be members of both classes in terms of their morphology and phonology, although in many instances there is no one-to-one correspondence between these two groups of factors. Consequently, all such cases constitute significant counter examples to the lexical model, in which the assumption of level-ordering excludes systematic discrepancy between the morphological and phonological structure of words.

One objection to our conclusion concerning the inadequacy of the lexical framework might be that dual class affixes are marginal in English and can therefore have certain peculiarities and idiosyncracies. This seems to be the prevalent attitude of lexicalists, who, on the whole, devote little more than scattered remarks to them. Nevertheless, dual class affixes cannot be treated as trivial exceptions since in all cases we are dealing with synchronically productive formations whose number runs into hundreds. Moreover, the instances of the disparity between the morphological and phonological structure of lexical items in English are much more numerous than has been assumed in current morphophonological literature. What is more, they are not restricted to dual class affixes. In what follows we discuss some examples of this sort.

2.2.4 Other affixes

Fudge (1984:105 and 133) lists 23 suffixes, which he calls 'mixed', whose effect on stress placement is twofold: in some words they are stress-neutral, in others stress-determining. His list includes all dual class affixes, but also many of those formatives whose morphological status is unambiguous, i.e. which belong uniquely to Class I or to Class II. Below we provide some examples.

The suffix *-ary* is morphologically Class I (Siegel 1974). When attached to nouns terminating in *-ment*, however, it is stress-neutral with bisyllabic bases, for example

'pigment – 'pigmentary   'fragment – 'fragmentary
'segment – 'segmentary   'moment – 'momentary

but stress-changing with longer items, for example

'parliament – parlia'mentary   'rudiment – rudi'mentary
'complement – comple'mentary   'element – ele'mentary
'supplement – supple'mentary   'instrument – instru'mentary

Phonological duality can also be observed in the case of the noun-forming suffix -y, which belongs to Class I (Siegel 1974). In some instances it induces the shift of stress, whereas in others it has no such effect, for example

stress-determining -y *stress-neutral -y*
'aristocrat – ari'stocracy 'heterodox – 'heterodoxy
'diplomat – di'plomacy le'gitimate – le'gitimacy
'synonym – sy'nonymy 'monarch – 'monarchy
'telescope – te'lescopy 'polymorph – 'polymorphy
'hypocrite – hy'pocrisy 'accurate – 'accuracy

Examples can also be given of Class II suffixes, which, although generally stress-neutral, in some (isolated) forms appear to have influence upon the placement of stress, for example

-age
'parent – 'parentage vs 'concubine – con'cubinage
per'cent – per'centage e'quip – 'equipage

-or
'govern – 'governor 'execute – e'xecutor
'prosecute – 'prosecutor o'rate – 'orator

In all the presented cases, morphologically uniform suffixes have phonological features of both classes. Notice that the dual membership solution would not work here as it presumes morphological correlates of phonological differentiation absent in the items under discussion. We conclude that assigning English affixes to two derivational levels cannot account for all their accentual properties. The same is true of other phonological processes as well.

Consider, for instance, the rule of trisyllabic laxing, which, according to Kiparsky (1982a), applies only within Class I affixation. The suffix *-ify* belongs to Class I as seen in its stress-changing effect

'syllable – sy'llabify   'solid – so'lidify

Curiously enough, when *-ify* is appended, in some cases laxing takes place, while in other words it is blocked, for example

Levels and cycles

laxing	no laxing
mētre – mĕtrify	spēech – spēechify
tȳpe – tўpify	tōwn – tōwnify
cōde – cŏdify	stēel – stēelify
divīne – divĭnify	rāre – rārefy
vīle – vĭlify	prēach – prēachify
clēar – clărify	chȳle – chȳlify
sāne – sănify	nītre – nītrify

Obviously, the forms on the right might simply be regarded as exceptions to trisyllabic laxing, but this approach would not be able to explain the fact that there are as many exceptions as the items that actually undergo the rule. An alternative is to assume that phonologically there are two types of *-ify* and that this differentiation is not reflected in the morphological structure.

Several examples of a similar sort are discussed by Kastovsky (1987 and forthcoming). Degemination, for instance, operates within Class I derivatives and is blocked with Class II affixes. The process can be illustrated with the two negative prefixes *in-* and *un-*; the consonant of *in-* undergoes degemination and the nasal of *un-* is preserved, for example

in-navigable → i[n]avigable   vs un-natural → u[nn]atural
in-numerable → i[n]umerable   un-navigable → u[nn]avigable

The adverbial suffix *-ly*, which belongs to Class II since it is stress-neutral, for example

'beautiful – 'beautifully   'wonderful – 'wonderfully

is expected to block degemination. Study the following examples

normal-ly → norma[l]y   casual-ly → casua[l]y
simpl-ly → simp[l]y   singl-ly → sing[l]y
real-ly → rea[l]y   ful-ly → fu[l]y

All these words are pronounced with a single lateral, which means that the rule of degemination has applied in spite of the presence of a Class II suffix. In other words, *-ly* in these examples morphologically belongs to Class II, but displays the properties of a phonologically Class I affix.

Another interesting case is the process of sonorant syllabification, which syllabifies sonorants in the context of Class II suffixes (and the word boundary). There exist numerous words, however, in which Class II suffixes such as *-ing*, *-er* and *-y* (adjectival) fail to induce the rule under consideration, for example

ang[l]e – ang[l]er, ang[l]ing   ang[ə]r – an[gr]y
wigg[l]e – wigg[l]er, wigg[l]ing   hung[ə]r – hun[gr]y
nibb[l]e – nibb[l]er, nibb[l]ing   bubb[l]e – bubb[l]y

This is clearly another example of the disparity between the morphological and phonological structure of English words.

Further corroboration of our criticism is provided by some compounds. As frequently noted (for example, by Allen 1980), vowel reduction applies in certain compounds as if they were simple words, for example

mainl[ə]nd   vs   waste-l[æ]nd
chairm[ə]n   taxm[æ]n
strawb[ə]rry   bush-b[e]rri

In the left-hand side column the compounding elements *-land*, *-man* and *-berry* behave as if they were suffixes since the vowel in them is reduced. As Allen observes, however, from the morphological point of view these are not suffixes but words, since the plural form of *-man* is irregular, for example

     firemen not *firemans   postmen not *postmans

In other words, *-man* in the examples above functions as a compounding element in morphology, but as a suffix in phonology. We are thus dealing here with yet another instance of the lack of isomorphy between morphology and phonology.

Let us restate the major observations made in the previous pages. We have analysed numerous cases of morphophonological discrepancy in English. They occur both within the so-called dual class affixes and, less frequently and less systematically, within Class I and Class II derivatives. Moreover, the phenomenon under scrutiny appears to affect some compounds as well. So far it has been assumed that the lack of morphophonological isomorphy invalidates the lexical framework and undermines its basic claims. No attempt has been made to find ways of accounting for such cases within lexical phonology. In other words, it is worth considering whether the framework under criticism provides some means of handling problematic forms, i.e., whether our counter-examples are as strong as they appear to be.

Generally speaking, the issue has so far received very little attention and we can only speculate what solutions would be adopted in specific instances. Nevertheless, there are some indications as to how such problems can be dealt with. Halle and Mohanan (1985) present, for instance, the case of the superlative and comparative suffixes -er and -est, which, being stress-neutral, are members of Class II and, consequently, induce such processes as g-deletion after the velar nasal. However, when such suffixes are attached to three adjectives, i.e.,

   young   long   strong

the voiced velar plosive is not deleted, but preserved

   youn[g]er/youn[g]est   lon[g]er/lon[g]est
   stron[g]er/stron[g]est

What we are dealing with here is an instance of suffixes which, although morphologically Class II, in these specific examples have the phonological features of Class I. It is evident that in such cases the level approach does not work. The adjective *longest*, for example, cannot be properly derived if -*est* were appended at level 2, to which it normally belongs. This is shown in the derivation below, where the relevant rules are nasal assimilation before the velar plosives, and g-deletion, both applying at level 2 (after Halle and Mohanan). G-deletion operates in the following context

$$g \rightarrow \phi / \eta \text{ —\,]}$$

	[long] [ist]
level 1	— —
level 2	[[long] [ist]]
Nasal assim.	ŋ
G-deletion	φ
	*[lonŋist]

No rules of importance apply at level 1. At level 2 both nasal assimilation and g-deletion can operate leading thus to the incorrect form.

To avoid such derivations, Halle and Mohanan suggest that with the three adjectives in question the suffixes -er and -est are exceptionally attached at level 1 and that the subsequent bracket erasure, which operates at the end of each level, makes the deletion of the velar plosive impossible at level 2.

	[long] [ist]
level 1	[[long] [ist]]
bracket erasure	[longist]
level 2	[longist]
Nasal assim.	ŋ
G-deletion	–
	[loŋgist]

This approach is consistent with the lexical model and quite acceptable, particularly in view of the fact that only three adjectives are involved – it is clear that under any framework they have to be regarded as exceptions. Nevertheless, it is doubtful whether this procedure can be applied to other cases as well. Notice that -er and -est basically belong to Class II and only under special circumstances become Class I affixes. It does not mean, however, that they automatically acquire morphological features of Class I since, despite the change of class membership, the forms with -er and -est do not undergo any affixation processes of level 1. In other words, the assignment of the suffixes in question to level 1 has phonological, but not morphological consequences, which is surprising, because a derivational level is meant to represent a unity of morphological and phonological properties.

The real problems begin with those affixes which from the morphological point of view must be regarded as members of Class I, but phonologically have the features of both classes. Let us recall that such cases are very frequent and involve, for instance, such suffixes as -ize and -ant/-ent, i.e., whole classes of items. If a procedure similar to the one suggested by Halle and Mohanan for -er and -est is employed in those situations in which

-*ize* and *-ant*/*-ent* are stress-neutral, these suffixes should be appended not at level 1, but rather at level 2 so as to account for their failure to undergo certain phonological rules. This, however, is not a possible solution. First of all, assigning such formatives to level 2 incorrectly predicts that they cannot be subject to any level 1 affixation; as has been shown, all these items do undergo such processes (for example, the *-ation* and *-ial* affixations). Therefore, they must be attached at level 1, since it is not possible to go back from level 2 to level 1.[19] In short, an adequate phonological description requires the attachment of such affixes at level 2, which is incompatible with morphological facts calling for their assignment to level 1. Clearly, lexical phonology cannot handle such cases.[20]

We hope that the material gathered in the preceding pages is sufficient to demonstrate that lexical phonology suffers from significant shortcomings since, by integrating phonology and morphology in the lexicon, it rules out cases of the discrepancy between the two types of structures. Instances in which no morphophonological isomorphy can be observed are frequent in English and involve open classes of words. Nor has the lexical framework found any support in Polish, where no derivational level can be isolated, and where lexical mechanisms in themselves are incapable of accounting for the phonological properties of prefixes. This is indeed unfortunate since, as Aronoff and Sridhar (1983:5) point out, models based on the affix ordering generalization possess intuitive appeal and have led to some very elegant analyses.

We consider it therefore justified to reject the lexical integration of phonological rules with morphology in favour of a separational approach in which morphology and phonology are viewed as two distinct components. In such a model morphological strings can be modified before they are subject to the operation of phonological rules, hence morphological and phonological structures may, but need not always, be identical.

Interestingly enough, similar conclusions as to the relation of both components and based mostly on the analysis of 'bracketing paradoxes' have recently been arrived at by other researchers as well. For example, Halle (1986), a former proponent of lexical phonology, has abandoned the direct link between morphology and phonology. He states, 'we must return to the traditional view that morphology and phonology are distinct and separate components of a grammar'. Similarly, Halle and Vergnaud (1987:53) give up combining the two types of rules and claim that, 'for us, as for SPE, morphology is distinct and separate from phonology. Morphology interacts with phonology in that it creates the objects on which the rules of phonology operate'.

In the remaining parts of this book we shall endeavour to specify the details of a separational model which can handle the problematic cases discussed so far in a more satisfactory fashion. We shall start with a brief examination of the issue of rule cyclicity.

2.3 Strict cyclicity

Our commitment to the separational approach necessitates a reconsideration of the ways in which phonological rules can employ the information provided by the morphological component. As has been mentioned in Chapter 1, one of the basic grammatical prerequisites to phonological analysis is morphological brackets. It is largely uncontroversial that in models of abstract phonology, which are morphophonological in character, phonological rules are frequently morphologized and need to refer to lexical and grammatical categories delimited by morphological bracketing. Since this type of morphophonological dependencies is well-known, we shall not dwell on it here. Nevertheless, this is not the only function of morphological brackets; as pointed out earlier, they are often claimed to fulfil yet another significant role – that of determining the manner of application of phonological rules. Some processes, known as cyclic, are supposed to be sensitive to the constituent structure of words reflected by means of brackets, and apply several times in the course of one derivation. Other rules do not make use of bracket information, apply only once and are therefore non-cyclic.

In what follows we intend to examine briefly whether in a separational model such use of morphological bracketing is justified. We shall concentrate on one possible approach to the reapplication of rules which involves the principle of strict cyclicity. The discussion is not meant to be comprehensive, as a detailed presentation of all the consequences of adopting strict cyclicity, with its strong points and weaknesses, would require a separate study. Rather we shall focus our attention on some selected, but in our view crucial, aspects of cyclicity.

In the earlier sections of this chapter it has been mentioned that in the models of lexical phonology the cyclicity of phonological rules is, in a sense, a natural consequence of integrating them with morphology. To put it differently, cyclicity falls out mechanically from the way the grammar is organized; every process of affixation (at a cyclic level) is accompanied by the application of phonological rules which reapply with the next affixation, and so on. In a framework in which phonology is separated from morphology cyclicity has no such external motivation, and must be stipulated by additional principles, for example, the strict cyclicity principle.

Within a non-integrational framework two approaches to rule cyclicity deserve at least a brief mention. In models of cyclic phonology, suggested by Mascaró (1976) and outlined in Chapter 1, phonological rules are organized into two blocks, which cannot be intermingled, with cyclic rules invariably preceding the postcyclic ones. Cyclic rules apply in accordance with strict cyclicity, while postcyclic rules operate across the board, i.e., whenever their context is met. In cyclic phonology the cyclicity (or the non-cyclicity) of phonological processes is viewed as their inherent property. In other words, every process must be individually marked as to its cyclic/non-cyclic character.

A different approach to cyclicity is represented by Halle (1986) whose proposal on the phonology side is largely based on Halle and Mohanan (1985). While abandoning the idea of integrating phonology and morphology, Halle maintains that phonological rules are assigned to a number of strata, of which some are cyclic and others non-cyclic. Clearly, in this framework cyclicity is no longer regarded as a property of individual rules, but of strata (now understood as phonological rather than morphological constructs). This means that it is possible for one and the same rule to apply both in the cyclic and in the non-cyclic fashion, provided that its domain extends beyond one stratum. Consequently, cyclicity refers here not so much to the nature of phonological rules themselves, but rather to the manner of their application, which is not always a constant factor.

What these two approaches have in common is the acceptance

of strict cyclicity as the principle that governs the application of cyclic rules in Mascaró's model, and the operation of phonological processes at a cyclic level in Halle's proposal. Let us recall that strict cyclicity requires that rules apply either when the morpheme boundary is present or when the application of another cyclic rule has created the conditions for the operation of a later rule.[21] It is important that this feeding change takes place on the same cycle, i.e., a cyclic rule cannot use information provided on an earlier cycle. One of the consequences of strict cyclicity is that rules are barred from applying morpheme-internally.

In the next pages we intend to analyse some consequences of adopting strict cyclicity. Towards this purpose, we shall examine two selected processes: trisyllabic laxing in English and palatalization in Polish. The former is commonly regarded as a typical example of a cyclic rule in all cyclic/lexical descriptions of English (for example, Kiparsky 1982a; Rubach 1984b; Halle and Mohanan 1985) and, as a matter of fact, served Kiparsky (1973) as a basis for formulating the principle of rule application in a derived environment (see Chapter 1). Palatalization is also viewed as one of the most firmly established cyclic rules, on whose cyclic character the whole cyclic/lexical description of Polish (Rubach 1981 and 1984a) is based.

2.3.1 Trisyllabic laxing in English

Trisyllabic laxing (TSL) is a well-known rule of English which states that a vowel is shortened when followed by two or more vowels of which the first one is unstressed (metrically weak) (Kiparsky 1982a:147),

$$V \rightarrow [\text{-long}] / \underline{\quad} C_o V_i C_o V_j$$
where V_i is not metrically strong

Numerous examples can be given to illustrate the operation of TSL, for example

serēne – serĕnity   profāne – profănity
derīve – derĭvative   provōke – provŏcative

grāde – grădual   suprēme – suprĕmacy
līne – lĭnear   compāre – compărison
impēde – impĕdimental   crīme – crĭminal
profoūnd – profŭndity   grāteful – grătitude
decīde – decĭsion   revīse – revĭsion

TSL appears to have some lexical exceptions (SPE:123, 181), for example

obēse – obēsity   connōte – connōtative
        denōte – denōtative

As noted by Kiparsky (1982) as well as Halle and Mohanan (1985), TSL takes place only on the attachment of Class I affixes and is blocked by Class II affixes, for example

rain-i$_{II}$-ness$_{II}$ grate-ful$_{II}$-ly$_{II}$
might-i$_{II}$-ly$_{II}$ grace-ful$_{II}$-ness$_{II}$

Nevertheless, the assignment of TSL to Class I affixation is not sufficient to ensure its proper application. As shown in Chapter 1, TSL fails to affect long vowels in morphologically simple words, for example

Ōberon   īvory   dȳnamite
rōdeo   Ōedipus   nīghtingale
āpricot (BE)   Ābraham (BE)   Ābury (BE)

Such items, under the presented formulation of TSL, must be treated as exceptions. However, as Kiparsky (1973:71) correctly observes, 'to mark the words as exceptions misses the generalization that *all* non-derived words subject to trisyllabic laxing rule fail to undergo it, and it furthermore wrongly claims that such words are irregularities, and should tend to get "regularized" by shortening their first syllable, which does not appear to happen'. Clearly, the failure of TSL in morphologically simple words must be handled in a systematic rather than an *ad hoc* manner.

One possibility is to claim that the process under consideration has become to some extent morphologized, i.e., it is contingent in its application on the presence of the morpheme boundary. This observation necessitates an amendment of the formulation of TSL – 'writing in' the plus symbol into the structural description of the rule. According to Kiparsky, however, this procedure should not be allowed and the morpheme boundary symbol cannot be simply 'written in' at some place in the rule since what matters is not the exact placement of the boundary, but merely its presence somewhere after the vowel to be shortened. Thus, TSL takes place in such words as (Kiparsky 1973:71)

    trĭ+meter   grăn+ular   pĕnal+ty   ŏmin+ous

in which the morpheme boundary is located at different places. Kiparsky (1973:71) argues that, 'restricting the rule to apply only across morpheme boundaries requires in the present theory of phonology a complex disjunction of pluses in the environment of the rule, viz.

$$\underline{\quad\quad} \langle + \rangle_a \; C_o \; \langle + \rangle_b \; V \; \langle + \rangle_c \; C_o \; \langle + \rangle_d \; V \; C_o$$

condition: *a* or *b* or *c* or *d'*. In brief, it seems that within the traditional generative approach it is impossible to formulate TSL in a simple and general fashion.

As demonstrated in Chapter 1, a solution to the problem in focus is provided by strict cyclicity. Kiparsky (1973) argues that the fact that TSL applies only within morphologically complex items, and never within morphologically simple words, can be generalized to state that the rule operates in derived environment only. To put it differently, TSL is strictly cyclic and this property accounts for its failure to affect morpheme internal structures. Thus, if the strict cyclicity principle is adopted, all facts concerning TSL can be explained in a straightforward manner. Consequently, the cyclic analysis of TSL must be seen as superior to the non-cyclic approach, in which no general formulation of the process under consideration seems possible. To conclude, were all this reasoning correct, TSL would constitute one of the strongest arguments for the cyclic application of phonological rules.

Levels and cycles

Nevertheless, we believe that Kiparsky is wrong in his assumptions concerning the cyclic nature of TSL. Consider again the examples illustrating the operation of the rule. A closer scrutiny reveals that all of them are cases of laxing in which the vowel subject to TSL is followed by one or two consonants and then the morpheme boundary, for example

    serĕn+ity   suprĕm+acy   profŭnd+ity   derĭv+ative

In the case of

    trĭ+meter   trĭ+colour

the morpheme boundary is located directly after the shortened vowel. In sum, in all these instances the morpheme boundary is placed not in an arbitrary, but in a clearly defined position; TSL affects the last vowel in the morpheme:

$$\underline{\quad} C_o + C_o V C_o V$$

This observation is strikingly confirmed by numerous failures of TSL, which have been curiously overlooked by past research, for example

hȳphen – hȳphenate	dānger – dāngerous
mōment – mōmentary	feāture – feātural
flāvour – flāvorous	ōpaque – ōpacate
ōvule – ōvular	envīron – envīronment
ōdour – ōdorous	ōdour – ōdorate
dīet – dīetary	vāpour – vāporous
mōtor – mōtorist	ālien – ālienate

In these examples the antepenultimate vowel does not undergo TSL in spite of the fact that all such words are morphologically complex, i.e., they fulfil the derived environment condition:

īsol+ate	annīhil+ate	vīol+ate	hībern+ate
dānger+ous	ōvul+ar	mōment+ary	flāvor+ous

Furthermore, in all cases we are dealing with Class I suffixes (see section 2.2.2). It should be noted, however, that the problematic vowel is not the last one in the morpheme and is separated from the morpheme boundary by a longer string of ___ C_1^2VC+. Evidently, TSL is not applicable in this context.

Note that in the approach that treats TSL as a strictly cyclic rule all the items above have to be treated as unmotivated exceptions despite their apparent regularity. To paraphrase Kiparsky's comment on the failure of TSL in morphologically simple words, regarding the words such as *hyphenate* as exceptions misses the generalization which concerns the non-application of TSL in this context, and falsely predicts the tendency to shorten the antepenultimate vowel in such cases. In brief, although treating TSL as a strictly cyclic rule allows us to regard morphologically simple words such as *nightingale* as regular, it also forces us to view a large group of items such as *hyphenate* as exceptions. This is a dubious achievement since it consists in the arbitrary regularization of one part of English at the cost of making another part irregular. In other words, the alleged superiority of the cyclic approach to TSL is not only questionable, but downright non-existent.

It should be clear by now that an adequate approach to TSL must assume that all three groups of items, i.e., the '*sanity*', the '*nightingale*' and the '*hyphenate*' type, are regular. The following autosegmental formulation of TSL can reflect that:

$$[\text{-cons}] \rightarrow [\text{-cons}] / \underline{\qquad} + [\text{-cons}][\text{-cons}]$$
$$\underset{X \ X}{\wedge} \qquad \underset{X}{|} \qquad \qquad \underset{X}{|}$$

The rule refers only to the vocalic tier and states that the antepenultimate vowel is shortened when followed by two more vowels, of which the first one is short. Moreover, the vowel subject to the rule belongs to a different morpheme than the vowels found in rule environment.[22] To put it differently, TSL is morphologized and requires the presence of the morpheme boundary for its proper application. Nevertheless, the boundary in question must be placed not in an arbitrary, but in a clearly defined position. The suggested formulation covers all the cases which have been discussed so far. Thus, it predicts the application of TSL in the *'sanity'* type since the morpheme boundary appears in the proper place here. The items such as *nightingale* and *hyphenate* remain unaffected, since in these instances the structural description of the rule is not met. In short, all the relevant facts are accounted for without resorting to the cyclic mode of rule application.

What remains to be discussed are those cases which led Kiparsky (1973, 1982a) to the unwarranted conclusions, i.e., examples of TSL in contexts different from the one specified in the suggested formulation of the rule. Generally speaking, the number of such cases is low and they do not seriously invalidate the approach proposed here. Let us consider the major potential counter-examples.

pēnal – pĕnalty: this example ceases to be an exception to TSL if *-al* is regarded as an adjectival suffix found also in such cases as *pap+al* and *nas+al*. Under this assumption *penalty* can be claimed to have the structure: *pen+al+ty*, particularly when the noun is viewed as related to *pen+ance*.

hōly – hŏliday: since the synchronic relatedness of these words is dubious, restructuring can be claimed to have taken place, i.e., the first vowel of *holiday* can be viewed as phonologically short.

pōllen – pŏllinate: this is clearly a wrong example since both Jones (1982) and Kenyon and Knott (1953) give *pŏllen* and *pŏllinate* as the only possible pronunciations. Thus, the vowel in question appears to be phonologically lax and therefore not subject to TSL.

ōmen – ŏminous: in this case there are two possible pronunciations of the adjective: *ōminous* and *ŏminous* (Jones 1982).

At this point some other fluctuating forms should be mentioned, for example

prīvacy – prĭvacy   pīracy – pĭracy   dȳnasty – dy̆nasty

Such examples show that occasionally the scope of the rule may be broadened so as to allow for laxing in other contexts as well. Similarly, the requirement of the unstressed penultimate vowel in the context of the rule sometimes appears to be relaxed as, for instance, in American English -*ization* words, for example

palatalīze – palatalī'zation   organīze – organī'zation
civilīze – civilī'zation   nasalīze – nasalī'zation

These observations lead to a definite conclusion: 99 per cent of all cases of TSL refer to the last vowel in the morpheme. The remaining examples are marginal and should be viewed as positive exceptions to the rule.[23]

We shall conclude by emphasizing the theoretical importance of our analysis. TSL, which is frequently regarded as a typical example of a strictly cyclic rule, under closer scrutiny has appeared to be indeed morphologized to some extent, i.e., contingent on the presence of the morpheme boundary. However, Kiparsky's contention that the rule in question applies whenever the morpheme boundary is present somewhere in the input string has turned out to be incorrect. Consequently, no gains are achieved if TSL is treated as a strictly cyclic rule. On the contrary, this approach makes false predictions and has to be abandoned.[24]

2.3.2 *Palatalization in Polish*

Palatalization is the central rule of Polish consonantal phonology and comprises several changes which can jointly be summarized (Gussmann 1980a:20) as

$$[+\text{cons}] \rightarrow [-\text{back}] \: / \: \underline{\quad} \: [-\text{back}]$$

As Gussmann observes, this basic phonological modification is augmented in different ways by several more specific rules (such as two kinds of velar palatalization, two kinds of anterior palatalization, affricate palatalization, etc.) which determine the phonetic reflexes in individual instances. Some examples of palatalization are given below.

króli[k] rabbit – *króli[č]ek* id. dim.
bo[g]a god, gen. sg. – *bo[ž]ek* id. dim.
ko[s]a scythe – *ko[ś]ić* to scythe
ra[d]a advice – *ra[dź]ić* advise

po[t] sweat, noun – *po[ć]ić* to sweat
dob[r]y good – *wydob[ž]eć* get better
ma[m]a mother – *ma[m']e* id. dat. sg.
tysią[c] thousand – *tysią[č]ek* id. dim.

According to Rubach (1981, 1984a) palatalization in Polish is a cyclic rule. Its cyclicity can be seen in the fact that it applies only when the consonant subject to the rule and the conditioning front vowel (or the palatal glide) are found on the opposite sides of the morpheme boundary, i.e., when the derived environment condition is fulfilled. Furthermore, there are many instances of unpalatalized consonants followed by front vowels morpheme internally both in native words as well as in borrowings, for example

[se]rce heart   *[de]ptać* tread
[be]z without   *[te]raz* now
[ke]l[ne]r waiter   *[ge][ne]rał* general

Such sequences do not show any tendency to undergo palatalization, which can be explained under the assumption that the rule is strictly cyclic.

These claims can be illustrated with the word *temacie* subject, loc. sg. Its phonological structure

/temat+e/

contains two sequences of the dental plosive followed by the front mid vowel. In the first case /te/ is found inside a morpheme, whereas in the second instance the consonant and the vowel are separated by the morpheme boundary. The prediction of the cyclic analysis is that palatalization should affect the second, but not the first dental. This is indeed borne out by the facts; in the phonetic form

[temaće]

the first /t/ emerges as unpalatalized, while the second /t/ surfaces as the palatal fricative [ć].

Thus, a great advantage of the cyclic treatment of palatalization is that through disallowing the application of the rule on the first cycle, the lack of morpheme internal palatalizations is accounted for. It should be added that under the traditional non-cyclic framework such cases would either be treated as exceptions or the offending forms would have to have very abstract phonological representations (with non-palatalizing vowels). Clearly, the approach which involves strict cyclicity scores noticeably in the treatment of palatalization.

Nevertheless, there are many cases in which the cyclic analysis leads to less desirable and less felicitous consequences. First of all, as observed by Szpyra (1985), palatalization fails to apply in a number of derived environments with the front vowel, for example

pięk[n]y beautiful, masc. – *pięk[n+e]* id. fem. pl.
dob[r]y good, masc. – *dob[r+e]go* id. gen. sg.
ły[s]y bald – *ły[s+e]mu* id. dat. sg.
ma[w]a small, fem. – *ma[w+e]j* id. dat. sg.
ko[t] cat – *ko[t+e]m* id. instr. sg.
szan[s]a chance – *szan[s+e]* id. nom. pl.

In these examples palatalization does not take place although the necessary requirements, i.e., the presence of the front vowel and the morpheme boundary, are satisfied. Such cases cannot be ignored since they are by no means isolated; the suffixes -*e*, -*ego*, -*emu*, -*ej*, -*em* never trigger palatalization. In brief, what we have here is an allegedly cyclic rule, which, strangely enough, fails to operate in the cyclic environment.

To make the situation worse, the cyclic analysis appears to have no convincing solution to the failure of palatalization in the cases under consideration. Rubach (1984a), in order to make his analysis work, is forced to postulate an abstract, phonetically non-occurring vowel /ɤ/ as the initial segment in non-palatalizing suffixes. The vowel, which is mid, back and unrounded, blocks palatalization to be later converted unconditionally into [e]. In other words, a very costly mechanism of absolute neutralization has been introduced (Polish lacks the phonetic contrast between the mid back rounded and unrounded vowels) for the mere purpose of salvaging the cyclic analysis of palatalization.[25] This solution has been heavily criticized as highly arbitrary and totally unconvincing, and rejected by several researchers (Bochner MS; Spencer 1985; Szpyra 1985; Gussmann 1985c).

Furthermore, it seems that the restriction of palatalization to derived environments is not valid since there are cases in which the rule applies even if no morpheme boundary is found between the consonant and the front vowel. The following examples can be given to illustrate the phenomenon

ma[žec]   March – *ma[rc]a*   id. gen. sg.
kobie[žec]   carpet – *kobie[rc]a*   id. gen. sg.
ko[žec]   bushel – *ko[rc]a*   id. gen. sg.

The proof that palatalization is responsible for the occurrence of [ž] in these items is the fact that this consonant undergoes depalatalization when [c] follows. As noted by Gussmann (1978), depalatalization affects only those [ž] consonants which come from underlying /r/ since phonological /ž/ is not depalatalized in this context, for example

tę[žec]   tetanus – *tę[šc]a*   id. gen. sg.

In other words, the rule of depalatalization distinguishes between underlying /ž/ and derived [ž], affecting the latter, but not the former.[26] In order for the cyclic treatment of palatalization to work, it is necessary to claim that the sequence *ec* in the examples above is a separate morpheme. This, however, is totally arbitrary from the morphological point of view. Polish does possess the suffix *-ec*, which attaches to adjectives (for example *mądr+y* 'wise' – *mędrz+ec* 'wise man') nouns (for example *taśm+a* 'tape' – *tasiemi+ec* 'tape worm') and verbs (for example *wędr+owa+ć* 'wander' – *wędr+owi+ec* 'wanderer'), but it cannot be regarded as a suffix in words such as *marzec* 'March' since this item is a single morpheme.

The same argumentation holds true of the following examples

ka[žew]   dwarf – *ka[rw]a*   id. gen. sg.
o[žew]   eagle – *o[rw]a*   id. gen. sg.

which are opposed to

wy[žew] pointer – *wy[žw]a* id. gen. sg.

The possibility of depalatalization in the former words points to the underlying /r/, which undergoes palatalization in nominative forms. Yet *karzeł* and *orzeł* must be viewed as monomorphemic since there exist no roots such as *kar* and *or*. Nor can *-eł* be treated as a suffix. However, the only possibility of maintaining the cyclicity of palatalization is to introduce the morpheme boundary before *-eł* – a solution which has no morphological justification and, as such, has to be rejected.

It should be clear by now that strict cyclicity cannot fully account for all the facts pertaining to palatalization in Polish. Although it is capable of handling the lack of palatalization in the '*teraz*' type, it fails to provide a satisfactory explanation for its non-application in derived environments of the '*kotem*' type. Moreover, there are items such as *marzec*, in which palatalization applies morpheme internally, contrary to the predictions of strict cyclicity. In brief, the connection between the process under scrutiny and its allegedly strictly cyclic application can be seriously questioned.

So can, for that matter, the relation between palatalization and the frontness of the triggering vowels since, as Gussmann (1985c:618) points out, palatal reflexes can be found in a variety of contexts: in derived and non-derived environments, before front and back vowels alike, for example

le[ć+i] 'it flies' – before front vowels in derived environments
[ći]cho 'silently' – before front vowels in non-derived environments
bu[ć+o]r 'shoe, augm.' – before back vowels in derived environments
[ćo]cia 'aunt' – before back vowels in non-derived environments

The same is true of non-palatal consonants, which appear in exactly identical contexts,

pros[t+e] 'straight, nom. pl.' – before front vowels in derived environments
[te]raz 'now' – before front vowels in non-derived environments

>   *pros[t+o]* 'straight, adv.' – before back vowels in derived environments
>
>   *[tu]* 'here' – before back vowels in non-derived environments

These facts demonstrate that palatalization has nothing to do with either the derived/non-derived distinction or with the frontness/backness of vowels.

Various solutions which incorporate these observations can be offered without any appeal to strict cyclicity. Spencer (1985), for instance, proposes to handle the facts of Polish palatalization in terms of Lieber's (1980) morpholexical rules. A more promising line of research has been developed by Gussmann (in press) within the autosegmental framework. He suggests that palatalization should be viewed as independent of segmental features, i.e., as autosegmentalized. This means that both front and back vowels can trigger the rule in derived as well as non-derived environments as long as they have a palatalizing autosegment associated with them.

In summary, our analysis of what are frequently considered the most typical and the best-documented cases of strictly cyclic rules, i.e., of trisyllabic laxing in English and palatalization in Polish, has revealed that their allegedly cyclic character can be seriously put into doubt. In both cases adopting strict cyclicity does not ensure an adequate description of the relevant facts and, moreover, frequently leads to incorrect predictions. In English the cyclic analysis assumes that TSL should apply whenever the morpheme boundary is present somewhere in the input string; this leaves the failure of TSL in numerous morphologically complex words such as *hyphenate* unaccounted for and forces us, unjustifiably, to treat them as unmotivated exceptions. In Polish strict cyclicity disallows morpheme-internal palatalization, which is contrary to the observed facts, and necessitates arbitrary boundary assignments. Furthermore, to account for the frequent failure of palatalization in derived environments, the cyclic description must introduce an absolutely neutralized vocalic contrast not needed anywhere else in Polish phonology. In consequence, the evidence for treating TSL and palatalization as cyclic is flimsy and tenuous at best or downright non-existent. Moreover, it appears that in both cases more adequate accounts of the data can be construed, none of which makes use of strict cyclicity.

In view of these observations, in the remaining parts of this book strict cyclicity will not be employed as a principle of rule application. Although rejecting it on the basis of two rules only might appear premature, we should like to point out that both processes have been carefully selected as the most representative examples of 'cyclic' rules. If such seemingly well-established cases raise numerous serious doubts, there is good reason to believe that even more objections can be levelled at less firmly grounded instances of strictly cyclic rules. As a matter of fact, more evidence against the cyclic analysis of Polish and English can be found in Szpyra (1985, in press a and b) and Gussmann (1985a) as well as in the following chapters.

The rejection of the strict cycle does not mean, however, that a different, less mechanical and more sophisticated understanding of cyclicity cannot be adopted. We examine such a possibility in Chapters 3 and 4.

Chapter three

The cycle revisited – the multiple application of phonological rules

The preceding chapter can be viewed as downright reactionary in character since it attempts to refute some of the proposals which depart from the standard generative framework. First, it has been demonstrated that the integration of phonological rules with morphology suggested by lexical phonology should be abandoned in favour of the separational approach of the traditional model. Secondly, we have endeavoured to show that cyclic phonology also raises numerous doubts, and concluded that phonological rules ought to be regarded as non-cyclic rather than strictly cyclic.

This does not mean, however, that the standard generative framework is viewed as fully adequate and is accepted here in its totality. As a matter of fact, the present as well as the following chapters will provide justification for significant departures from it. In what follows we shall discuss some morphological and phonological problems involved in the formation of complex verbs and their derivatives in Polish. It will be argued that neither the traditional nor the cyclic/lexical frameworks are capable of accounting for all the relevant data. This necessitates the introduction of an additional mechanism, i.e., that of the multiple application of phonological rules as well as the total reanalysis of the relationship between the morphological and the phonological components. We shall defend the view that although morphology and phonology should be treated as separate and distinct parts of the grammar, there are many instances in which it is necessary to go back from the output of phonological rules to word formation processes. Both phonological and morphological arguments will be adduced in favour of this proposal. In this chapter we shall provide phonological evidence for it; the multiple application of rules will be shown to be indispensable for the correct derivation of complex verbs and items based on them as well as for some exceptional forms.

3.1 Complex verbs

In this section we shall examine some aspects of the formation of Polish verbs and their derivatives. Our analysis will demonstrate that such items pose numerous problems for both the traditional (separational) and the lexical (integrational) frameworks. The major difficulty concerns the operation of two rules: verb suffix truncation (VST), which is a part of the adjustment apparatus, and the process of derived imperfective tensing (DI tensing). We shall argue that the peculiar properties of these rules derive from the multiple phonological processing of complex verbs.

3.1.1 Primary verbs and their derivatives

We shall start with outlining the Polish verb system. It is extremely complex and characterized by a considerable amount of suppletion. Therefore, our presentation will of necessity be brief and largely simplified. For a fuller discussion of the Polish verb and deverbal forms the reader is referred to the traditional descriptions by Tokarski (1951), Schenker (1954), Szober (1962), Fokker (1965), Saloni (1976), Grzegorczykowa and Puzynina (1979), Zaron (1976), Grzegorczykowa, Laskowski and Wróbel (1984 – hereafter *Morfologia*) and to the generative analyses by Paulsson (1974), Lubaszewski (1982), Laskowski (1975), Gussmann (1978, 1980a) and Rubach (1984a). The latter three authors are also to be consulted with regard to the details of Polish phonology, to which frequent references will be made throughout this chapter.

The most significant fact about the structure of Polish verb stems is that they consist of

ROOT + VERBALIZING SUFFIX

The root is the carrier of the lexical meaning of the verb and is unspecified with respect to syntactic category. The verbalizing suffix (VS) introduces the root to the category of verbs.

The cycle revisited

Verbalizing suffixes are of several kinds (-*ć* is the infinitival ending).[1]

-*i* (as in *nos*+i+*ć* carry, *chodz*+i+*ć* walk)
-*a* (as in *pis*+a+*ć* write, *łap*+a+*ć* catch)
-*e* (as in *wisi*+e+*ć* hang, *krzycz*+e+*ć* shout)
-*aj* (as in *woł*+aj+*ą* they call, *szuk*+aj+*ą* they look for)
-*ej* (as in *lini*+ej+*ą* they shed hair, *grabi*+ej+*ą* they grow numb)
-*ną* (as in *puch*+ną+*ć* swell, *pło*+ną+*ć* burn)
-*owa* (as in *ład*+owa+*ć* load, *częst*+owa+*ć* treat)

Moreover, there is a class of verbs which take the zero verbalizing suffix, i.e., where

ROOT = STEM

for example *nieś*+*ć* carry, *pleś*+*ć* weave, *kłaś*+*ć* put.

We will follow the well-established morphological tradition (for example Laskowski 1975) in claiming that simple or primary verbal stems are not formed by any WFRs; the verbalizing suffix is a part of the verb and occurs with the root in the lexicon. To put it differently, the lexical representation of verbs consists not of roots, but of verbal stems.

Several arguments can be brought forward to support this claim. First of all, no description of Polish provides any rules for forming verbal stems of the type under discussion, since it is impossible to predict which suffix will attach to a given root. Consider, for example, several verbs which contain the roots of the same segmental structure (obstruent – vowel – voiceless dental spirant), all of them taking a different verbalizing suffix,

pisać write $[pis+a]_V$ *kisić* pickle $[kis+i]_V$
wisieć hang $[vis+e]_V$ *ciosać* hew $[ćos+aj]_V$
paść graze $[pas+\phi]_V$ *pasować* fit $[pas+ova+ć]_V$

Clearly, no productive WFRs can be formulated to derive such verbs since every root would have to be idiosyncratically marked as to which verbalizing suffix it takes.

The assumption that verbalizing suffixes are present in the lexical representation of verbs is strongly supported by the fact that suffixes determine the type of the derivational and inflectional paradigm that a given verb enters (Laskowski 1975; *Morfologia*). Thus, WFRs which operate on verbs make reference to VSs. For instance, verbal nouns (substantiva verbalia) are productively formed from almost all verbs by means of three suffixes: *-anie*, *-enie* and *-cie*. The distribution of these suffixes entirely depends on the verb suffix (Grzegorczykowa 1979:31; *Morfologia*:336): *-anie* attaches to verbs in *-a*, *-aj* and *-owa*, for example

pis+a+*ć* write → *pis+anie* writing
czyt+aj+*ą* they read → *czyt+anie* reading
mal+owa+*ć* paint → *mal+ow+anie* painting

-enie is added to verbs in *-i*, *-e*, *-ej* and C-stems, for example

pal+i+*ć* smoke → *pal+enie* smoking
drętwi+ej+*ą* they grow numb → *drętwi+enie* growing numb
krzycz+e+*ć* shout → *krzycz+enie* shouting
gryź+*ć* bite → *gryzi+enie* biting

-cie combines with those consonantal stems that terminate in the palatal glide (the glide is itself deleted before a consonant), for example

pij+*ą* they drink → *pi+cie* drinking
myj+*ą* they wash → *my+cie* washing

Another example of a WFR that must refer to VSs is the nominalization by means of the suffix *-iciel* (with its retracted vowel allomorph *-yciel* after hard consonants), which operates almost exclusively on verbal stems in *-i*, for example[2]

dus+i+*ć* strangle → *dus+iciel* strangler
donos+i+*ć* inform → *donos+iciel* informer
odkup+i+*ć* redeem → *odkup+iciel* redeemer
czc+i+*ć* worship → *czc+iciel* worshipper
doręcz+y+*ć* deliver → *doręcz+yciel* deliverer

The cycle revisited

If we assumed that the suffix *-iciel* attaches not to verbal stems but to roots, we would not be able to account for the fact that it regularly fails to occur with those verbs which have different verbalizing suffixes, for example

leci+e+*ć* fly → **lec+iciel*
pis+a+*ć* write → **pis+yciel*
bad+aj+*ą* they examine → **bad+yciel*

If, however, verbal suffixes form parts of verbs, the problem does not arise; *-iciel* is appended only to verbs in *-i* and that is why it never nominalizes such verbs as *leci*+e+*ć* and *pis*+a+*ć*.

Many other examples of WFRs which crucially refer to verbalizing suffixes are given in Grzegorczykowa and Puzynina (1979). We conclude that it is justified to claim that primary verbs in Polish are polymorphemic lexical structures which serve as input to further WFRs.

Nevertheless, this does not mean that in all cases the verb suffix must accompany roots in the lexicon; many verbs can be productively derived from other grammatical categories. The bases for verb formation are mostly nouns (for example *pędzel* 'brush' → *pędzl+owa+ć* 'paint') and adjectives (for example *piękn+y* 'beautiful' → *u+piękn+i+ć* 'beautify'), but also, though less frequently, numerals (for example *dw+a* 'two' → *dw+o+i+ć* 'double'), adverbs (for example *tak* 'yes' → *po+tak+iwa+ć* 'assent'), pronouns (for example *ty* 'you' → *ty+k+a+ć* 'address someone by his first name'), interjections (for example *miau* 'miaow' → *miau+cz+e+ć* 'to miaow') and even conjunctions (for example *gdyby* 'if' → *gdyb+a+ć* 'to keep repeating if, to complain'). Furthermore, even more complex bases can be verbalized, for example

mądr+y$_{Ad}$ wise → *mędr+ek*$_N$ know-all →
*mędr+k+owa+ć*V act the know-all
robak$_N$ worm → *robacz+yw+y*$_{Ad}$ worm-eaten →
robacz+ywi+e+ć$_V$ verminate
szydł+o$_N$ pricker → *szydeł+k+o*$_N$ crotchet-needle →
szydeł+k+owa+ć$_V$ to crochet

Both underived and derived verbs can serve as inputs to further morphological processes. Nouns based on verbs, as has already been demonstrated, are formed by the attachment of nominalizing suffixes to verbal stems. In the case of consonantal stems the procedure is straightforward

myj+ą they wash → *myj+nia* washer
nieś+ć carry → *niesi+enie* carrying

When the stem contains the verbalizing suffix, nominalization is accompanied by the truncation of the VS, for example

dźwig+aj+ą they lift → *dźwig+nia* lever
pis+a+ć write → *pis+mo* writing

An interesting fact about the truncation rule is that it applies only before derivational suffixes; when inflection follows, the verbalizing suffix is preserved, for example

dźwig+aj+ą they lift (*-ą* – 3rd person pl. present tense suffix)
dźwig+aj+my let's lift (*-my* – 1st person pl. imperative suffix)

Clearly, Polish needs a rule of the following form (Laskowski 1975:62)

Verb suffix truncation (VST):

VS → φ / ____ derivational suffix

The rule of verb suffix truncation plays an important role in deverbal derivation and its status should be considered in some detail.

First of all, it is evident that VST is needed only under the assumption that WFSs take verbal stems rather than roots as their input. If morphological processes are allowed to operate on roots, then the need for VST disappears altogether.

At this point Lieber's (1980) analysis of Latin verbs should be recalled as it seems to resemble the situation in Polish. Lieber claims that verbal stems must be listed in the lexicon since Latin roots differ arbitrarily and unpredictably in the stem vowel which they take – a suggestion that is true of Polish as well. Apart from stems, however, roots should also be lexical entries. The reason why the inclusion of roots is necessary in Lieber's view is that they can also serve as derivational bases for WFRs. For example, the root *am-*, which takes the suffix *-ā*, is represented in the lexicon as

$$\left\{ \begin{array}{l} \text{root: am} \\ \text{stem: amā} \end{array} \right.$$

and the morpholexical rule of the form

$$X \sim X\bar{a}$$

serves to relate the two items. The root combines with the suffix *-or*, for instance, to produce the noun *am+or* 'love', while the attachment of *-tor* to the stem yields the form *ama+tor* 'lover'. As Lieber fails to see anything regular in these phenomena, the listing of both stems and roots seems unavoidable. Consequently, in this approach a rule such as verb suffix truncation is not needed.

The question, naturally, arises whether a similar analysis could be adopted for Polish verbs as well, i.e., whether both roots and stems should be listed in the lexicon so that they can be inputs to WFRs. Nominalizations, it can be claimed, simply operate on roots, which eliminates the need for VST.

It seems that Lieber's solution should not be applied to Polish data. First of all, as has already been pointed out, derivation based on roots is untenable because such an approach does not allow for formulating any WFRs at all. It is therefore not surprising that this possibility has not been seriously entertained by any existing morphological descriptions of Polish. As we have shown, these are stems rather than roots that must be subject to WFRs, since the latter frequently refer to verbalizing suffixes. Yet deverbal nouns do not contain such suffixes, which shows that they must have been removed in the course of derivation. Consequently, verb suffix truncation must be postulated.

More evidence can be provided for the necessity of VST. Consider two nouns *myśliciel* thinker   *równacz* plane

These items are derived from the verbs

myśleć think   and   *równać* to smooth

respectively. Under the assumption that nominalizing suffixes attach to roots, the claim would be that *-iciel* is appended to *myśl-*, and *-acz* to *rown-*. What matters here is the fact that these roots are independent words in Polish

myśl thought   *równ+y* smooth, adj.

In other words, if the suffixes in question attached directly to these items, the following derivations would result

$[myśl]_N \rightarrow [[myśl]_N + iciel]_N$
$[równ]_{Ad} \rightarrow [[równ]_{Ad} + acz]_N$

i.e., we would be dealing with a denominal and a deadjectival noun.

This is not, however, an acceptable approach. In the first case *-iciel* cannot be attached to nouns as it is a deverbal suffix (Grzegorczykowa and Puzynina 1979:218), which is additionally supported by the deverbal meaning of *myśliciel*, i.e., 'somebody who thinks, a thinker'. Thus, the correct derivation of this word involves first the verbalization of the noun *myśl*, then the nominalization of the verb *myśleć*,

$myśl_N$ thought $\rightarrow$ $myśleć_V$ think $\rightarrow$ $myśliciel_N$ thinker

In the second case, the noun *równacz*, 'plane' cannot be derived directly from the adjective *równy* 'smooth' either. This time the reason is slightly different than in the previous case. The suffix *-acz* can occasionally attach to adjectives (Grzegorczykowa and Puzynina 1979:100 note only eight such formations), for example

bogaty rich → *bog+acz* richman
włochaty pily → *włoch+acz* plush

Such nouns have the meaning of a person or an object characterized by the base adjective. *Włochacz*, for instance, denotes something that is pily. *Równacz*, however, does not mean something which is smooth, but a tool for smoothing things out, i.e., a plane. The meaning of this noun is clearly deverbal, which can only be explained if the derivation proceeds in the following fashion,

rown+y$_{Ad}$ smooth → *równ+a+ć*$_V$ smooth out → *równ+acz*$_N$ plane

In short, both nouns under discussion are uncontroversially deverbal formations. Nevertheless they do not contain verbalizing suffixes in their surface structure. The suffixes are apparently truncated.[3]

$[[[myśl]_N + e]_V + iciel]_N$ → *myśl+iciel* thinker
              ↓
              φ

$[[[równ]_{Ad}] + aj]_V + acz]_N$ → *równ+acz* plane
                ↓
                φ

We conclude that verb suffix truncation is necessary to account for the morphology and semantics of deverbal formations in Polish.

Having established the need for VST, we should like to consider its placement with respect to other rules. At first glance, one might be tempted to treat VST as a part of WFRs which form deverbal derivatives. This, however, would have most infelicitous consequences. It would mean that there are as many truncation rules as there are WFRs which operate on verbs, and the unity of the process would be lost. It seems more justified to regard VST as a modification of the output of various WFRs, i.e. as an adjustment rule in the sense of Aronoff (1976).[4]

Before we turn to the discussion of the phonological aspect of forming verbs and their derivatives, let us repeat briefly the major morphological conclusions of our analysis. Morphological adequacy requires that primary verbs be listed in the lexicon together with verbalizing suffixes. WFRs operate not on roots, but on verbal stems, which necessitates the rule of verb suffix truncation.

It appears that these requirements cannot be satisfied by the cyclic/lexical description as they lead to phonological consequences undesirable in this framework. As has already been mentioned, cyclic phonological rules are supposed to follow the application of WFRs. Under the assumption that primary verbs are underived, i.e. not produced by any WFRs, we should expect no cyclic phonological rules to affect them. Yet this is clearly false; some VSs consist of, or begin with, a front vowel, which invariably palatalizes the root final consonant, for example

zwi[s] hang, noun – *wi[ś+e]ć* hang, verb
wi[d]ać can be seen – *wi[dź+e]ć* see

Let us remind ourselves that palatalization is regarded as a cyclic rule, which applies in derived contexts only (see Chapter 2, section 2.3.2). In the examples that have just been given, the environment of palatalization is 'derived' in the sense that it results from the combination of morphemes (the morpheme boundary is present). On the other hand, it is 'underived' since the sequence of morphemes does not arise in the process of derivation or inflection. Yet the rule does apply. Thus, what we have here is a cyclic phonological rule which *precedes* rather than *follows* WFRs. Since such an analysis constitutes a clear violation of the lexical principles, it obviously has to be rejected in this model, in which it must be claimed that VSs are attached to roots by means of WFRs, i.e. that underived verbs must, in fact, be derived. This is explicitly admitted by Booij and Rubach (1984:10).

The claim that nominalization operates on verbal stems also appears problematic for the lexical framework. Study deverbal nouns given below

chodz+i+ć walk – *chod+ak* clog (*chodziak)
wierc+i+ć drill – *wiert+ark+a* driller (*wierciarka)

tocz+y+ć turn – *tok+arz* turner (*toczarz)
szydz+i+ć scoff – *szyd+erc+a* scoffer (*szydzierca)
lecz+y+ć treat – *lek+arz* physician (*leczarz)

The starred ungrammatical forms are items derived lexically. Let us clarify this conclusion with a sample derivation.[5]

tokarz turner
WFR $[[tok]+i]_V$

Cycle 2
Palatalization   č
_____

WFR $[[toči]_V +až]_N$

Cycle 3
VST   ϕ
_____

Postcyclic rules $[točaž]_N$

Final devoicing   š
                       [tocaš]

The problem which the lexical derivation faces here is that on Cycle 2 the verbalizing suffix *-i* incorrectly induces the palatalization of the root-final consonant since it is not truncated until Cycle 3 (when the nominalizing suffix becomes available). To avoid such incorrect forms, the lexical analysis must claim that the nominalizing suffix *-arz* attaches not to the verbal stem, but to the root *tok-*. As we have demonstrated, this approach is completely untenable from the morphological point of view.

Within the lexical framework, derivations based on roots seem also inevitable in the case of numerous back-formed nouns. In contrast to English, where they are mostly of diachronic relevance (Marchand 1969), back-formations are very much alive in modern Polish (Satkiewicz 1969). Deverbal back-formed nouns are derived by the truncation of the verbalizing suffix and the subsequent attachment of inflection. Satkiewicz notes that such formations are productive, and even appear to replace synonymic suffixal items.

The issue at stake is the correct derivation of back-formed nouns. No problems occur with nouns derived from back vowel verbal stems; in such situations VSs do not have any significant phonological effect on the base, for example

ście[k]+aj+ą they flow down – *ście[k]* drain	/aj → ɸ/
napi[s]+a+ć write – *napi[s]* inscription	/a → ɸ/
utar[g]+owa+ć gain – *utar[k]* takings	/owa → ɸ/
udźwi[g]+ną+ć lift – *udźwi[k]* lifting	/ną → ɸ/

Many items suggest, however, that back formation must take place before the front vowel VSs manage to affect the roots, for example

spuś[ć+i]+ć release – *spus[t]* trigger	(*spuś[ć])
ukło[ń+i]+ć bow – *ukło[n]* bow, noun	(*ukło[ń])
wsa[dź+i]+ć put in – *wsa[t]* batch	(*wsa[dź])
obro[ć+i]+ć turn – *obró[t]* turn, noun	(*obró[ć])
uchwy[ć+i]+ć seize – *uchwy[t]* handle	(*uchwy[ć])

If the lexical derivation proceeds as follows:

ROOT → VS attachment → phonological rules /palatalization/ → back formation → phonological rules

then there is no way to prevent palatalization from affecting the root-final consonants, which results in ungrammatical (starred) forms. Note that the unpalatalized character of the final consonants in back-formed nouns cannot be explained by any depalatalization rule since in the word-final position palatalized consonants can occur freely. As a matter of fact, the items marked as incorrect actually do appear in Polish not as nouns, but as imperative forms of verbs, for example

obró[ć] turn   *spuś[ć]* release   *wsa[ć]* put in

In order to avoid the undesirable application of palatalization, the lexical description is forced to assume that back-formed nouns are derived from roots and not stems. This assumption is highly implausible, however. Apart from the arguments against derivations based on roots which have been given so far, there are other reasons why it cannot be maintained. Deverbal back-formed nouns are almost exclusively created from prefixed verbs. Since the relevant prefixes occur only with verbs, roots (which lack grammatical category) must first be verbalized before prefixes can be attached to them. Thus, the processes under discussion ought to be ordered in the following way:[6]

ROOT → VS attachment → prefixation → back-formation

Such an ordering of WFRs means in effect that VS attachment takes place on an earlier cycle than back formation and that, consequently, VSs can affect the phonology of the roots prior to their truncation. This obviously entails the incorrect application of palatalization.

In brief, the lexical framework, in order to handle phonological facts, is forced to adopt solutions which are totally arbitrary and therefore unacceptable from the morphological point of view. In other words, it gives up morphological adequacy to accommodate phonological phenomena. This conclusion supports our criticism of lexical phonology (see Chapter 2) as a model which represents an oversimplified approach to morphology.

No such problems arise in a framework that separates morphological and phonological rules. WFRs operate on verbal stems and create structures subject to adjustment processes such as VST. The strings thus formed then undergo phonological rules. For instance, the noun *wiertarka* 'driller' from the verb *wiercić* 'drill' is derived as follows:

	$[vert+i]_V$
WFR	$[[vert+i]_V +ark]_N$
Inflection	$[[vert+i]_V +ark+a]_N$
	↓
VST	φ
Phonological rules	/vert+ark+a/
Palatalization	v'
	[v'ertarka]

In this derivation the nominalizing WFR attaches the suffix *-arka* to the verbal stem. Then VST removes the verbalizing suffix *-i*, and the form in question is further modified by phonological rules. The prephonological truncation of *-i* prevents the suffix from affecting the preceding consonant, and in this fashion the correct phonetic form is produced.

The formation of deverbal back-formed nouns is not problematic either. The word *utrata* 'loss', from the verb *utracić* 'lose', is derived in a similar way as the items discussed previously.[7]

	$[trat+i]_V$
Prefixation	$[u+[trat+i]]_V$
Back-formation	$[u+[trat]]_N$
Inflection	$[u+[trat+a]]_N$
Phonological rules	/u+trat+a/
	–
	[utrata]

Here the verbal stem undergoes prefixation and the prefixed form is then subject to back formation. Thus, the palatalizing *-i* is truncated before the application of phonological rules without leaving any reflexes on the noun.

We conclude that a separational and not the integrational lexical approach is capable of deriving deverbal words in the manner which is both morphologically and phonologically adequate. Nevertheless, the next section will demonstrate that this statement also requires further revision.

3.1.2 Secondary verbal stems and derived imperfective tensing

In this section we shall be concerned with the formation of more complex verbs known as derived imperfectives (DIs). The issue which will be of our particular interest is the vocalic alternations that accompany imperfectivization.

According to the most up-to-date and, at the same time, the most comprehensive survey of Polish morphology (*Morfologia*), DIs, or secondary verbal stems, are formed from prefixed perfective verbs by means of DI suffixes *-aj* and *-ywa*.[8] The distribution of DI suffixes is largely predictable and depends on the nature of VSs and, to some extent, on the segmental structure of the root (*Morfologia*:217).

The suffix *-ywa* usually appears with the following VSs:

-*a* (for example *pod+pis+a+ć* sign – *pod+pis+ywa+ć*)
-*aj* (for example *wy+gr+aj+ą* they will win – *wy+gr+ywa+ć*)
-*owa* (for example *wy+prac+owa+ć* work out –
  wy+prac+ow+ywa+ć)

The suffix *-aj* occurs with the remaining VSs, for example

-*i* (for example *wy+rzuc+i+ć* throw out – *wy+rzuc+aj+ą* id. 3rd person pl.)
-*e* (for example *wy+trz+e+ć* wipe off – *wy+cier+aj+ą* id. 3rd person pl.)
C-stems (for example *wy+kraś+ć* steal – *wy+krad+aj+ą* id. 3rd person pl.)

Although some verbs (for example the majority of verbs in *ej*) do not form DIs, the process of secondary imperfectivization displays a high degree of regularity and productivity, which, according to some researchers (Piernikarski 1970; Grzegorczykowa 1979) points to its almost inflectional character. The structure of DI stems can thus be schematically presented as

PREFIX + ROOT + VERB SUFFIX + DI SUFFIX

The fact that the nature of the VS determines the choice of the DI suffix clearly shows that imperfectivization operates on verbal stems rather than roots. In other words, derived imperfectives confirm our earlier assumption concerning the derivation of deverbal formations from the structures ROOT + VS.

It should be noted, however, that on the surface the verbalizing suffixes are absent in DIs. This is, in fact, to be expected in view of the operation of VST; VSs are truncated in the context of the following derivational morphemes *-ywa* and *-aj*, for example

$$pod+pis+a+ć \rightarrow pod+pis+a+ywa+ć \rightarrow pod+pis+ywa+ć$$
$$\text{sign} \qquad\qquad \downarrow \qquad\qquad\qquad \text{id. DI}$$
$$\phi$$
$$do+tk+nǫ+ć \rightarrow do+tk+nǫ+aj+ć \rightarrow do+tyk+aj+ǫ$$
$$\text{touch} \qquad\qquad \downarrow \qquad\qquad \text{they touch, DI}$$
$$\phi$$

(we bypass, for the time being, the application of phonological rules in the derivation of DIs).

As in the cases discussed in the preceding section, there is evidence that in DIs verb suffix truncation must take place before the application of phonological rules. Consider the verbs below

$wy+patrz+e+ć$ look out – $wy+pat[r]+ywa+ć$ (*$wypat[š]ywać$)
$do+gorz+e+ć$ die out – $do+go[r]+ywa+ć$ (*$dogo[ž]ywać$)
$za+służ+y+ć$ deserve – $za+słu[g]+iwa+ć$ (*$zasłu[ž]ywać$)

Here the perfective verbs on the left contain front vowel VSs, which, if not removed, induce the palatalization of the root-final consonants (the starred forms on the right). Since no effects of palatalization can be observed in DIs (the middle column), the VSs must be truncated prephonologically.

$$do+gor+e+ywa+ć \rightarrow do+go[r]+ywa+ć \text{ die out}$$
$$\downarrow$$
$$\phi$$

Note that if the relevant processes are allowed to apply cyclically (as a result of being intermingled), the incorrect forms are yielded.

WFR	$[[gor]+e]_V$
Palatalization	$[[goż]+e]_V$
WFR	$[do+[[goż]+e]]_V$
Phonology	–
WFR	$[[do+[[goż]+e]]_V +iva]_V$
	$\downarrow$
VST	ϕ

WFR	$[[do+[gož]]_V +\text{i}va+ć]_V$
Phonology	–
	*[dogoživać]

In such instances palatalization applies on an earlier cycle than VST, which leads to incorrect outputs.

We shall now pass to the discussion of the major phonological processes that accompany secondary imperfectivization. The suffix *-ywa* induces few changes within the bases to which it is appended; its front vowel allomorph occurs after velar consonants and triggers the process known as surface velar palatalization (Gussmann 1980a:11), for example

zako[x]ać fall in love – *zako[x'iva]ć* id. DI
zamiesz[k]ać start living – *zamiesz[k'iva]ć* id. DI
zestru[g]ać whittle away – *zestru[g'iva]ć* id. DI

The retracted centralized vowel suffix [ɨva] appears after the remaining consonants without affecting them in any radical way, for example

zawią[z]ać tie – *zawią[zɨva]ć* id. DI
zatrzy[m]ać stop – *zatrzy[mɨva]ć* id. DI
omo[t]ać tangle up – *omo[tɨva]ć* id. DI

Gussmann (1980a:11) suggests that these distributional facts point to one underlying suffix. He proposes that it should be the more frequently occurring variant, i.e., [ɨva]. The subsequent rule of fronting changes [ɨ] to [i] after velar consonants so that they can be subject to surface velar palatalization.[9] Schematically,

	/-k+ɨva/	/z+ɨva/
Fronting	i	–
Surface velar palatalization	k'	–
	[k'iva]	[zɨva]

In brief, the phonological processing of -*ywa* imperfectives is largely unproblematic.

Nevertheless, DIs with the suffix -*aj* are considerably more complex in terms of their phonology. First of all, those verbs which have the palatalizing suffix -*i* in their perfective forms, show the effects of palatalization also in the corresponding DIs, for example

wyża[ż]yć anneal – *wyża[ż]ać* (cf. *ża[r]* heat)
zaciem[ń]ić darken – *zaciem[ń]ać* (cf. *ciem[n]y* dark)
osu[š]yć dry – *osu[š]ać* (cf. *su[x]y* dry, adj.)

There is evidence, however, that the type of palatalization which operates in DIs is different from the rule that applies in perfective verbs as in some cases the phonetic reflexes vary, for example

wyrzu[ć]ić throw away – *wyrzu[c]ać* (cf. *rzu[t]* throw, noun)
zmu[ś]ić force – *zmu[š]ać* (cf. *mu[s]* must, noun)
zara[ź]ić infect – *zara[ž]ać* (cf. *zara[z]a* plague)

Here the perfective verbs contain the palatal fricatives and affricates, whereas the DIs contain the dental and postalveolar consonants (as shown in related items the underlying segments are the same in both cases). It is usually assumed (Gussmann 1978; Rubach 1984a) that in the first instance we are dealing with palatalization which is triggered by front vowels, while in the second case the rule at work is J-palatalization, which is induced by the palatal glide. What is more, the effect of both processes is the same with all consonants except dental obstruents. To accommodate these facts, it can be assumed that the VS-*i* does not delete, but undergoes gliding to [j] and subsequently evinces J-palatalization. Gliding can be formulated in the following way

$$i \rightarrow j \: / \: \_\_\_ \: aj$$

It can be considered an allomorphy rule which applies before VST restricted now to syllabic VSs.[10] To clarify the situation, let us present a sample derivation of the verb *zarażać* infect (from *zarazić*)

The cycle revisited

WFRs	$[[za+[raz+i]]_V +aj+ć]_V$
Gliding	j
VST	–

Phonology	/za+raz+j+aj+ć/
J-palatalization	ž
J-deletion	ɸ ɸ
	[zarażać]

(the rule of J-deletion removes the palatal glide both after and before consonants – Gussmann 1980a:134). In brief, the consonantal changes within DIs can be accounted for in a fairly straightforward manner by means of well-established rules of Polish phonology.

These are vocalic modifications within DIs which appear more troublesome. The following presentation of data will provide the necessary perspective (the right-hand column contains DI equivalents of the verbs on the left).

1. *ze[rv]ać* tear – *z[riv]ać*
   we[tk]nąć stick in – *w[tik]ać*
   ode[tx]nąć breathe – *od[dix]ać*

2. *ze[br]ać* gather – *z[b'er]ać*
   ze[dž]eć tear off – *z[dz'er]ać*
   wy[tš]eć wipe off – *wy[ćer]ać*

3. *zapi[ō]ć* button – *za[p'in]ać*
   wygi[ō]ć bend – *wy[g'in]ać*
   nad[ō]ć puff out – *na[dim]ać*

4. *zapr[o]sić* invite – *zapr[a]szać*
   wyr[o]bić shape – *wyr[a]biać*
   odmł[o]dzić rejuvenate – *odmł[a]dzać*

5. *zagni[e]ść* knead – *zagni[a]tać*
   zapl[e]ść weave – *zapl[a]tać*
   wymi[e]ść sweep out – *wymi[a]tać*

6. *wypl[e]wić* weed out – *wypl[e]wiać*
   naj[e]żyć bristle up – *naj[e]żać*
   ośmi[e]szyć ridicule – *ośmi[e]szać*

7. *powr[u]cić* return – *powr[a]cać*
   zam[u]wić order – *zam[a]wiać*
   skr[u]cić shorten – *skr[a]cać*

8. *przerz[u]cić* throw over – *przerz[u]cać*
   wykł[u]cić argue – *wykł[u]cać*
   przybr[u]dzić soil – *przybr[u]dzać*

9. *zakr[a]ść* sneak – *zakr[a]dać*
   wyp[a]rzyć scald – *wyp[a]rzać*
   wys[a]dzić put down – *wys[a]dzać*

10. *wyp[i]ć* drink – *wyp[i]jać*
    zab[i]ć kill – *zab[i]jać*
    zak[i]sić pickle – *zak[i]szać*

11. *uch[i]bić* transgress – *uch[i]biać*
    wyż[i]wić feed – *wyż[i]wiać*
    przyskrz[i]nić pinch – *przyskrz[i]niać*

The data show that some vowels do not undergo any change ([a], [i], [ɨ]), while other vowels sometimes are modified and in some cases remain the same in DIs ([e], [u]). The vowel [o] is regularly lowered to [a], whereas consonantal clusters of the perfective forms are broken by the vowels [i] and [e] in DIs. The nasal vowel [õ] alternates with [i] and [ɨ].[11] Thus, on the surface the facts pertaining to the vocalic modifications within DIs appear to be very complex and seem to escape any generalization.

It is only the examination of the whole phonological system of Polish vowels which reveals that we are dealing here with regularities rather than completely random changes. Therefore, at least a cursory presentation of Polish vowels is indispensable.

According to all major descriptions of Polish phonology (Laskowski 1975; Gussmann 1980a, Rubach 1984a), it is crucial to recognize the distinction between tense and lax vowels at the underlying level. The vowel system can be claimed to have the following shape (Gussmann 1980a:74)[12]

ĭ ī   ɨ̆ ɨ̄ ū
ĕ ē   ŏ
         ā

Moreover, all the mentioned authors maintain that the vocalic changes which take place in DIs can be regarded as the process consisting in the tensing of root vowels in the context of the DI suffix *-aj*. The rule in question can be formulated as follows (Gussmann 1980a:74)

Derived imperfective tensing (DI tensing)

$$\begin{bmatrix} +\text{syll} \\ \langle -\text{high}\rangle \end{bmatrix} \rightarrow \begin{bmatrix} +\text{tense} \\ \langle +\text{low}\rangle \end{bmatrix} / \underline{\quad} \text{aj}_{DI}$$

Let us explain how DI tensing works in various types of verbs. The simplest case is with the vowels which are phonologically tense, i.e., (ī, ɨ̄, ū, ā); the rule applies vacuously to them and no alternations are observed on the surface – examples 8, 9, 10 and 11. Lax /ĕ/ when tensed merges with the underlying /ē/ and surfaces as [e] unless it is followed by a coronal anterior consonant. In the latter case /e/ undergoes the process of backing (and lowering) to [a]. The context of backing is met in 5, but not in 6, hence the emergence of [a] and [e] respectively. The derivations below illustrate the cases discussed so far (prefixes, for the sake of clarity, are ignored).

	wypijać drink /pij+aj+ć/	*przerzucać* throw over /žut+j+aj+ć/	*zagniatać* knead /gnĕt+aj+ć/
DI tensing	vacuous	vacuous	ē
Palatalization	p'	c	ń
Backing	–	–	a
J-deletion	ɸ	ɸ ɸ	ɸ
	[p'ijać]	[žucać]	[gńatać]

Let us now pass to the discussion of other vowels. Lax /ŏ/ surfaces as [a] in DIs. Interestingly, [a] is found also in DIs in 7, even though the perfective forms contain [u] and not [o]. What is more, [u] in 8 does not display any similar change. This apparent irregularity finds a simple explanation in terms of rule interaction; [u] in the perfectives in 7, but not in 8, is derived from /ŏ/, as the following alternations indicate

powr[o]ty returns – *powr[u]t* id. nom. sg.
obr[o]ty turns – *obr[u]t* id. nom. sg.

The rule responsible for the o → u change is known as raising (Gussmann 1980a:125). Thus, the verbs in 4 and 7 all comprise the underlying /ŏ/, which emerges as [a] in DIs, and is raised in the perfectives in 7. The relevant rules operate as follows

	zapraszać invite /prŏs+j+aj+ć/	*powracać* return /vrŏt+j+aj+ć/
DI tensing	a	a
Palatalization	š	c
J-deletion	ɸ ɸ	ɸ ɸ
	[-prašać]	[-vracać]

Finally, we are left with the examples in 1, 2 and 3. In the first two cases the vowels [i]/[ɨ] and [e] alternate with zero. Gussmann (1980a) assumes that these are high lax vowels that underlie such changes. If a high lax vowel (frequently referred to as a yer) is followed by a similar vowel in the next syllable, it is lowered to [e]. If this condition is not met, the yer is deleted. The rule which effects these modifications is lower (Gussmann, 1980a:90). Its operation can be seen in the nouns such as

pi[e]s dog – *[ps]a* id. gen. sg.
m[e]ch moss – *[mx]u* id. gen. sg.

interpreted phonologically as[12]

	pies /pĭs+ĭ/	psa /pĭs+a/	mech /mĭx+ĭ/	mchu /mĭx+u/
Palatalization	p'	p'	–	–
Lower	e ɸ	ɸ	e ɸ	ɸ
Depalatalization	–	p	–	–
	[p'es]	[psa]	[mex]	[mxu]

According to Gussmann, the items in 1, 2 and 3 all comprise high lax vowels, which are deleted in perfective forms (unless they are nasalized – examples 3) and are subject to DI tensing in

DIs. Additionally, tense vowels change to [e] when followed by [r] (the so-called r-lowering).

	zrywać tear /-rĭv+aj+c/	*zbierać* gather /-bĭr+aj+ć/	*zapinać* button /-pĭn+aj+ć/
DI tensing	ɨ	ī	ī
R-lowering	–	e	–
Palatalization	–	b'	p'
J-deletion	ɸ	ɸ	ɸ
	[-rɨvać]	[-b'erać]	[-pinać]

To summarize, the effects of DI tensing can be observed in the case of four phonologically lax vowels, which are modified in the following way: /ŏ/ → [a], /ĕ/ → [e] *or* [a], /ĭ/ → [i] *or* [e], /ɨ̆/ → [ɨ] *or* [e]. It should be added that the rule under consideration is morphologized; it applies only in DIs with the suffix *-aj*. Thus no tensing takes place when the DI suffix *-ywa* is attached, for example

zak[o]chać fall in love – *zak[o]chiwać* (*zak[a]chiwać*)
przech[o]wać store – *przech[o]wywać* (*przech[a]wywać*)

Nor is tensing triggered by the VS *-aj*, for example

wyw[o]ł+aj+ą they will call (*wyw[a]łają*)
pok[o]n+aj+ą they will defeat (*pok[a]nają*)

Nevertheless, it appears that the formulation of DI tensing which has been given is not fully adequate, as it fails to account for phonological changes in many verbs that contain high lax vowels. Nykiel-Herbert (1984) observes that the rule under discussion does not work in such cases as

u+skrzy[dl]+i+ć provide with wings – *u+skrzy[dl]+aj+ą* DI. 3rd person pl. (cf. *skrzyd[e]ł* wings, gen.) – *uskrzydylać*
na+my[dl]+i+ć soap – *na+my[dl]+aj+ą* DI. 3rd person pl. (cf. *myd[e]ł* soaps, gen.) – *namydylać*
roz+wi[dl]+i+ć fork – *roz+wi[dl]+aj+ą* DI. 3rd person pl. (cf. *wid[e]ł* forks, gen.) – *rozwidylać*

z+wę[gl]+i+ć carbonize – *z+wę[gl]+aj+ą* DI. 3rd person pl.
(cf. *węgi[e]l* coal) – *zwęgilać

z+wa[lč]+y+ć fight – *z+wa[lč]+aj+ą* DI. 3rd person pl.
(cf. *wal[e]cz+n+y* brave) – *zwaliczać

The problem is that all these verbs contain a high lax vowel in the syllable that precedes *-aj* (as shown by the presence of [e] in related forms) and yet this vowel deletes instead of being tensed in DIs. The verb *namydlać* 'soap', for example, has the following phonological structure

/na+mɨdɨł+j+aj+ć/

If the lax vowel of the root is tensed, the incorrect form

*namyd[ɨ]lać

is created.

Consider now another group of examples, also brought to attention by Nykiel-Herbert (1984).

wy+k[o]ńcz+y+ć finish off – *wy+k[a]ńcz+aj+ą* DI. 3rd person pl. (cf. *koni[e]c* end) – *wykoniczać

za+kr[o]pl+i+ć put drops – *za+kr[a]pl+aj+ą* DI. 3rd person pl. (cf. *krop[e]l* drops, gen.) – *zakropylać

u+pod[o]bn+i+ć resemble – *u+pod[a]bni+aj+ą* DI. 3rd person pl. (cf. *podobi[e]ń+stw+o* resemblance) – *upodobyniać

These items resemble the preceding group of examples in that they all have the high lax vowel in the root (see the related words with the vowel [e]), which fails to undergo DI tensing. Instead, tensing is assigned to the preceding vowel /o/. The latter surfaces as [a]. The verb *wykańczać* 'finish off' has the structure

/vɨ+konic+j+aj+ć/

If DI tensing applies in accordance with the formulation given earlier, the impossible form *wykon[i]czać

is produced.

There are also verbs which contain not only one, but two yers, none of which appears to be affected by DI tensing, for example

    s+pożytecz+ni+a+ć make use – /zɨ+požitɨk+ɨn+j+aj+ć/
      (cf. *pożyt[e]k* use, noun – *pożyt[tk]u* id. gen. sg.)
    u+darem+ni+a+ć thwart – /u+darɨm+ɨn+j+aj+ć/
      (cf. *dar[e]mny* futile – *da[rm]o* in vain)
    s+piekiel+ni+a+ć make infernal – /zɨ+pekɨł+ɨn+j+aj+ć/
      (cf. *pieki[e]ł* hells, gen. – *pie[kw]o* id. nom. sg.
    s+karczem+ni+a+ć make vulgar – /zɨ+karčɨm+ɨn+j+aj+ć/
      (cf. *karcz[e]mny* vulgar – *kar[čm]a* inn)

In these cases the verbs are derived from deadjectival nouns with yer vowels (see the forms given in parentheses). The adjectives, in turn, are formed by means of the suffix *-n(y)*, which also contains the high lax vowel. Several arguments can be brought forward to show that *-n(y)* phonologically starts with /ɨ/:
– the lax vowel induces palatalization, for example in

    uli[c]a street – *uli[č]+ny* id. adj.

– it brings about the emergence of the preceding yer, for example

    pożyt[tk]u use, gen. sg. – *pożyt[e]cz+ny* useful

– it occurs on the surface when another high lax vowel suffix (such as *-stwo*) follows, for example

    podo[b+n]y similar – *podobi[e]ń+stw+o* resemblance

Thus, the verbs in question possess a sequence of two lax vowels: one in the noun, another in the adjectival suffix. If DI tensing affected the last yer, forms such as

    *spożytcz[i]niać

would be yielded. If it skipped the last stem vowel and applied to the preceding one, an equally incorrect

*spożyt[i]czniać

would arise.

There are also verbs with the sequence of three lax vowels, all of which fail to undergo DI tensing. The verb *osłoneczniać* 'shine', for instance, phonologically can be presented as

/o+słonĭc+ĭn+j+aj+ć/

(cf. *sło[ńc]e* 'sun' – *słon[e]czny* 'sunny'). Here neither the two yers, nor the lax /ŏ/ appear to be subject to DI tensing; one of the high lax vowels is lowered to [e] before another one in the next syllable and the second yer is deleted, while nothing happens to /o/.

	/o+słonĭc+ĭn+j+aj+ć/
DI tensing	does not apply /?/
Palatalization	č ń
Lower	e ϕ
J-deletion	ϕ ϕ
ł → w	w
	[oswonečńać]

It should be clear now that the formulation of DI tensing which has earlier been provided does not cover all the facts concerning the vocalic modifications (or the lack of them) in DIs.[13] What is more, in all instances we are dealing not with isolated examples, but with whole classes of words, which requires systematic rather than an *ad hoc* treatment.

Before we suggest a solution to the problem in focus, we shall summarize the major observations that refer to DI tensing. For convenience the relevant types of changes are repeated here.

a) *ze[rv]ać* tear off – *zr[i]vać*
   za[br]ać take – *zabi[e]rać*
   we[tk]nąć stick in – *wt[i]kać*

b) *zar[o]bić* earn – *zar[a]biać*
   zagni[e]śś knead – *zagni[a]tać*
   powr[u]cić return – *powr[a]cać*

c) *wyk[o]ńczyć* finish off – *wyk[a]ńczać*
um[o]cnić strengthen – *um[a]cniać*
upod[o]bnić resemble – *upod[a]bniać*

d) *osł[o]n[e]cznić* shine – *osł[o]n[e]czniać*
sp[o]kr[e]wnić relate – *sp[o]kr[e]wniać*
ub[u]stwić worship – *ub[u]stwiać*

DI tensing in a) and b) operates in a straightforward manner – it tenses the last vowel preceding the suffix *-aj*. Note that the rule refers here both to yers and non-yer vowels in agreement with Gussmann's (1980a:74) formulation. The problem begins with the items in c); here DI tensing seems to skip the last yer and apply to the preceding vowel. The forms in d) show that the rule must have yet another clause which says that, 'if the verb contains a sequence of two yers, DI tensing does not apply at all'. In sum, DI tensing in some cases affects all vowels including yers, while in others the yer must be skipped. Moreover, only one but not two high lax vowels can be omitted. In this situation formulating one general rule of DI tensing seems virtually impossible.

Let us try to pinpoint the source of difficulty. All verbs appear to fall into two types with respect to DI tensing: those in a) and b), in which tensing applies in a regular fashion and those in c) and d) which require additional clauses and conditions. This division seems to suggest that the peculiar properties of DI tensing might be attributed to the differences between these two types of verbs. Indeed, the items in a) and b) differ rather strikingly from those in c) and d) in terms of their mophological structure; the former are based on primary verbal stems, whereas the latter are derived from nouns and adjectives, i.e., from morphologically more complex bases, for example

type a) and b) *type c) and d)*
zarabiać earn *osłoneczniać* shine
$[[za+[rob+i]]_V+aj+ć]_V$ $[[[o+[[słońc]_N+in]_{Ad}+i]]_V+aj+ć]_V$

Now the rule of DI tensing can be formulated in such a way as to make use of the distinction between the two kinds of verbs: in DIs based on primary verb stems tensing is assigned to the vowel in the syllable preceding *-aj*. In DIs based on de-nominal and de-adjectival verbs, one yer is skipped and the preceding vowel is tensed. Tensing does not affect denominal and deadjectival verbs which contain more than one yer.

Nevertheless, such a formulation of DI tensing is not particularly attractive. First of all, it is difficult to formalize. Secondly, it is very complex. Finally, it endows a phonological rule with access to the internal structure of words (i.e., their derivational history) in which it operates. In other words, DI tensing must be able to distinguish between DIs formed from primary verbs on the one hand, and denominal as well as deadjectival verbs on the other. Consequently, the power which one phonological rule possesses increases to the extent generally not admitted in phonology. In brief, the latter formulation of DI tensing is highly unsatisfactory. A more adequate solution must therefore be looked for.

Consider the process of DI tensing in denominal and deadjectival verbs once again. We suggest that only phonetic structures of such verbs be examined this time

a) *osłon[e]cznić* shine – *osłon[e]czniać*
   ub[u]stwić worship – *ub[u]stwiać*
   nam[i]dlić soap – *nam[i]dlać*
   rozw[i]dlić fork – *rozw[i]dlać*
   zah[a]czyć hook – *zah[a]czać*

b) *wyp[o]cić* sweat out – *wyp[a]cać*
   zamr[o]zić freeze – *zamr[a]żać*
   ochł[o]dzić cool down – *ochł[a]dzać*
   odmł[o]dzić rejuvenate – *odmł[a]dzać*
   um[o]cnić strengthen – *um[a]cniać*

Even a superficial examination reveals that the perfective and imperfective verbs in a) do not differ in terms of their root vowels, which in both cases are identical; it seems as if the process of DI tensing had not taken place here at all. The same, however, cannot be said about the items in b), in which the vowel [o] of the perfective form regularly corresponds to [a] in their imperfective counterparts.

Let us assume now that DI tensing (in its original formulation) is allowed to operate not on the phonological, but rather on the phonetic forms of denominal and deadjectival verbs, i.e., that the DI suffix *-aj* affects perfective verbs after they have been subject to the operation of phonological rules. This means that at the stage when DI tensing applies, the vowels which precede *-aj* in a) are already in their phonetic shapes [e, u, i, ɨ, a]. It is clear that the rule in question has no effect on them as their phonetic reflexes correspond closely to the underlying segments, i.e., /ĩ/ → [i], /ɨ̃/ → [ɨ], /ũ/ → [u], /ã/ → [a]. Nothing happens to the vowel [e] either as the context for backing is not met in these examples. Informally, DI tensing in *osłoneczniać* 'shine' and *zahaczać* 'hook' operates in the following way.

	[o+swoneč+ń+j+aj+ć]	[za+xač+aj+ć]
DI tensing	ē	ā
J-deletion	ɸ ɸ	ɸ
	[oswonečńać]	[zaxačać]

The verbs in b) contain the vowel [o] in perfective forms (phonetically). DI tensing predicts that in DIs the mid back vowel emerges as [a]. This is exactly what happens in b). The application of DI tensing in the verbs *wykańczać* 'finish off' and *umacniać* 'strengthen' is illustrated below

	[vɨ+końč+aj+ć]	[u+moc+ń+j+aj+ć]
DI tensing	a	a
J-deletion	ɸ	ɸ ɸ
	[vɨkańčać]	[umacńać]

In short, if the perfective denominal and deadjectival verbs were processed by the phonology prior to the application of DI tensing, its simple, general formulation could be retained and all the relevant facts could be accounted for.

Thus, what we would like to propose is that there is one rule of DI tensing of the following form.

DI tensing

$$\begin{bmatrix} +\text{syll} \\ -\text{nasal} \\ \langle -\text{high} \rangle \\ +\text{back} \end{bmatrix} \rightarrow \begin{bmatrix} +\text{tense} \\ \langle +\text{low} \rangle \end{bmatrix} / \underline{\quad} \text{aj}_{\text{DI}}$$

which applies to all types of verbs. What is different is the mode of processing them; DIs based on primary verbal stems are derived in the traditional fashion: the WFRs attach the DI suffix and the whole structure is subject to the linear application of adjustment and phonological rules. Below we present a sample derivation of the verbs *dotykać* 'touch' (from *dotknąć*) and *zarabiać* 'earn' (from *zarobić*).

WFRs	$[[do+[tɨk+nɨn]]_V +aj+ć]_V$	$[[za+[rob+i]]_V +aj+ć]_V$
Gliding	–	j
VST	ɸ	–
	/do+tɨk+aj+ć/	/za+rob+j+aj+ć/
DI tensing	ɨ	a
Palatalization	–	b'
J-deletion	ɸ	ɸ ɸ
	[dotɨkać]	[zarab'ać]

If, however, the verb is denominal or deadjectival, i.e., it has the structure

$$[[\quad]_{Ad}]_V \qquad [[\quad]_N]_V$$

the strings delimited by such bracket configurations are derived first, and only then is the DI suffix added. Once this has taken place, the whole word undergoes the operation of adjustment and phonological rules once again. In other words, we are advocating here a two-step processing of DIs based on denominal and deadjectival verbs; first of the perfective forms and then the imperfective verbs. This procedure is clarified with a sample derivation of the verbs *wykańczać* 'finish off' (from *wykończyć*) and *zamrażać* 'freeze' (from *zamrozić*)

WFRs	$[vɨ+[[konic]_N+i]]_V$	$[za+[mroz]_N +i]]_V$
Palatalization	ń č	ż
Lower	ɸ	
Vowel adjustment	ɨ	

(continued overleaf)

The cycle revisited

WFRs	$[[[vɨ+[konč]_N +i]]_V +aj+ć]_V$	$[[[za+[mroź]_N +i]]_V +aj+c]_V$
Gliding	—	j
VST	ɸ	—
DI tensing	a	a
Palatalization	—	ž
J-deletion	ɸ	ɸ ɸ
	[vɨkańčać]	[zamražać]

First the perfective verbs *wykończyć* and *zamrozić* are derived. In the former the lax vowel in the root is deleted by the rule of lower and in both verbs the root-final consonants are palatalized. Then the DI suffix *-aj* is appended creating the context for DI tensing. Adjustment rules modify VSs through gliding and VST and the verbs are subject to another application of phonological rules. Since the suffix *-aj* is preceded now by [o], the vowel is tensed to [a]. This, together with the remaining rules, produces the correct phonetic forms.

Thus, we would like to suggest that there are situations in which it is necessary for the output of phonological rules to return to the WF component and then undergo the operation of phonology for the second time. It might seem that the procedure proposed here is exactly the same as the methods of lexical phonology, in that WFRs may apply both before and after phonological processes, which are also allowed to operate more than once. The resemblance, however, is only superficial. In our view, as argued in Chapter 2, phonology and morphology are separate and distinct components and the two types of rules are not interspersed, as is the case with the lexical framework. What is more, in the lexical model only some phonological rules interact with morphology, whereas in our approach the output of all word-level rules is available to WFRs. Finally, while the lexical description suggests the intermingling of morphological and phonological rules in the derivation of every multimorphemic item, we propose to employ this procedure in some cases (such as denominal and deadjectival verbs). Schematically, both approaches can be presented in the models shown on p. 115.

Before we provide more evidence for the model on the right, we should like to demonstrate that the cyclic application of DI tensing does not bring the correct results with complex DIs. Consider the lexical derivation of *wykańczać* 'finish off'.

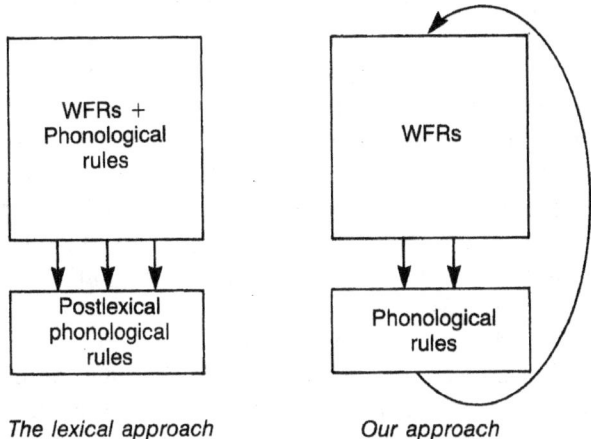

The lexical approach   Our approach

	[końic]$_N$
WFR	[[końic]$_N$ +i]$_V$
Palatalization	č
WFR	[vɨ+[końič+i]]$_V$
Phonology	–
WFR	[[vɨ+końič+i]$_V$ +aj]$_V$
VST	ɸ
DI tensing	ī
WFR	[vɨ+końič+aj+ć]$_V$
Phonology	–
Postcyclic rules	/vɨkońičać/
	–
	*[vɨkońičać]

The source of the incorrectness of this derivation lies in the fact that the high lax vowel which is present in the root cannot be deleted until the postcyclic stage; this is due to splitting the rule of lower into cyclic lower and postcyclic yer deletion (Rubach 1984a:185), crucial for the lexical description of Polish. Since the high lax vowel is preserved until almost the end of the derivation, it follows that DI tensing should affect it, contrary to the observed facts.

Let us briefly restate the findings of this section. We have demonstrated that the attachment of the DI suffix -*aj* is accompanied by vocalic modifications within the verbal base known as the process of DI tensing. It appears, however, that formulating one general rule of tensing is impossible both in the traditional linear and the cyclic/lexical approach, since DI tensing operates in two different fashions depending on the morphological structure of perfective verbs. Consequently, a distinction has been introduced between primary verbal stems on the one hand, and perfective verbs formed from nouns and adjectives on the other, both of which serve as inputs to DI formation. We have suggested that denominal and deadjectival verbs should be processed by phonological rules prior to the attachment of -*aj*. Then the imperfective verb is subject to another application of phonology. This amounts to saying that, in the case of derived verbs, we must go back from phonology to morphology and then to phonology again. This procedure allows us to retain the simple formulation of DI tensing without having to refer to the derivational history of words. Moreover, in all cases which are problematic for both the traditional as well as cyclic/lexical models we are able to obtain the correct results.

We are aware of the fact that our suggestion is open to objection on grounds of its arbitrariness since it introduces a novel and powerful mechanism into the grammar for the mere purpose of regularizing and simplifying one phonological rule. If the suggested procedure of going back from phonology to morphology, and the multiple application of phonological rules, is a genuine linguistic mechanism, we should be able to find more support for it. In what follows we hope to provide more evidence for this hypothesis.

3.1.3 *Items based on DIs and verb suffix truncation*

Derived imperfectives, just like simple verbs, can serve as an input to various nominalization processes. Below we present some deverbal nouns based on DIs in -*aj*, which are formed by means of the suffixes -*alnia*, -*arka* and -*acz*. The attachment of these suffixes appears to have different effects upon the verbal bases.

-alnia
spie[k]+alnia sintering plant – *rozcień[č]+alnia* diluting plant
  (cf. *cien[k]o* thinly)
rozmo[t]+alnia reeling mill – *skrę[c]+alnia* twisting plant
  (cf. *skrę[t]* twist, noun)
ście[r]+alnia pulp mill – *wyża[ž]+alnia* annealing plant
  (cf. *ża[r]* heat)

-arka
nakła[d]+arka glue spreader – *wygła[dz]+arka* smoothing
  machine (cf. *gła[t]ki* smooth)
wstrzą[s]+arka shaker – *odwła[š]arka* unhairing machine
  (cf. *wło[s]* hair)
zgnia[t]+arka plodder – *narzu[c]+arka* sand slinger
  (cf. *narzu[t]* fling, noun)

-acz
obcią[g]+acz honing tool – *nawil[ž]+acz* moistener
  (cf. *wil[g]oć* moisture)
przepy[x]+acz push broach – *osu[š]+acz* drier (cf. *su[x]y* dry)
opie[k]+acz toaster – *zmięk[č]+acz* softener
  (cf. *mięk[k]o* softly)

Superficially it seems that the suffixes in question are of two kinds: one group is 'palatalizing', i.e. it triggers the palatalization of the root-final consonant, the other is 'non-palatalizing', i.e. it does not affect the segment under consideration. However, when one examines the verbs these nouns are derived from, it becomes clear that associating these phenomena with the appended suffixes is the wrong approach. Thus, if a DI verb contains a palatalized consonant in the stem-final position, this feature is directly reflected in deverbal nouns derived from them, for example

wytra[v']+ać pickle → *wytra[v']+alnia* pickling plant
wygła[dz]+ać smooth → *wygła[dz]+arka* smoothing machine
utwar[dz]+ać harden → *utwar[dz]+acz* hardener

If, on the other hand, a DI stem ends in an unpalatalized consonant, the same is true about nouns derived from such stems, for example

zamia[t]+ać sweep → *zamia[t]+arka* sweeping machine
wstrzą[s]+ać shake → *wstrzą[s]+acz* shaker
zmy[v]+ać wash up → *zmy[v]+alnia* scullery

These observations hold true also of the vowels in DI stems, which are not modified when nominalizing suffixes are appended, for example

ści[e]r+ać wipe off → *ści[e]r+alnia* pulp mill
skr[a]pi+ać sprinkle → *skr[a]pi+arka* sprinkler
przep[i]ch+acz push → *przep[i]ch+acz* push broach

Such facts show that neither the palatalization of the root-final consonant, nor the quality of the root vowel are connected with nominalizing suffixes, but with the structure of the base DIs. In other words, whatever changes occur within the roots, these are DI suffixes rather than nominalizing formatives which are responsible for them.

Take the noun *przepychacz* 'push broach' from the DI verb *przepychać* 'clean out', which, in turn, is derived from the perfective form *przepchać* (/pše+pĭx+aj/). First the root vowel must be tensed

/pĭx/ → /pīx/

in the context of the DI *-aj*, and then the suffix *-acz* can be appended. This is necessary since *-acz* does not trigger DI tensing (cf. *tkacz* weaver from *tkać* weave – /tĭk+aj/ and *tracz* sawyer from *trzeć* saw – /tĭr+e/, which do not become *tykacz* and *cieracz*).

Two significant consequences follow from these remarks. The first one is that the suffix *-aj* is absent from the phonetic structure of nouns based on DIs (i.e. *przepychacz* is not *przepychajacz*), hence it must be truncated. Note that *-aj* has double function in DIs: it is both an imperfectivizing suffix and the verb suffix for DIs. Since it is a verb suffix, it is subject to VST before derivational affixes. Thus, its absence on the surface can be easily accounted for.[14] The second, more important consequence is that *-aj* can be deleted only after it has triggered DI tensing. In other words, it cannot be truncated prephonologically. To clarify this point, consider the derivation of *przepychacz* 'push broach', in which VST applies before the operation of phonological rules.

WFRs $\quad$ $[[[pše+[pïx+aj]]_V+aj]_V+ač+ï]_N$
VST $\quad\quad\quad\quad\quad\quad$ φ $\quad$ φ
DI tensing $\quad\quad\quad\quad$ —
Lower $\quad\quad\quad\quad\quad$ φ $\quad\quad\quad\quad$ φ
$\quad\quad\quad\quad$ *[pšepxač]

The first rule to apply in this derivation is VST. Note that two morphemes are subject to it: the verb suffix of the verb *pchać* 'push', i.e. *-aj*, and the verb suffix of the DI verb *przepychać* 'push through', i.e. the second *-aj*. Now phonological rules can apply. The only process that is applicable to this string is lower which deletes both yers. This produces the incorrect form

przepchacz

The problem we envisage here concerns the operation of VST; if the DI suffix *-aj* is truncated prephonologically, then the context for DI tensing is removed and the root vowel is deleted rather than tensed. Clearly, if the correct form is to be yielded, *-aj* cannot be deleted before the application of DI tensing. To put it differently, *-aj* must be truncated not *before* but *after* the relevant phonological rules.

At this point it is significant to recall our analysis of verbs and deverbal derivatives in section 3.1.1, where we have provided arguments to show that it is crucial for VST to take place *before* the application of phonological rules. For instance, if the VSs are not removed prephonologically from the nouns such as *wiertarka* 'driller' (from *wiercić* 'drill'), and *tokarz* 'turner' (from *toczyć* 'turn'), the wrong forms **wierciarka* and **toczarz* are produced (see the derivations in section 3.1.1).

What we seem to have here is the problem of ordering VST with respect to phonological rules: in some derivations truncation must precede the phonology (the *wiertarka* type), in others it must be placed among phonological rules (the *przepychacz* type). Moreover, neither the traditional linear nor the cyclic/lexical approaches appear to be capable of solving the problem.

The cycle revisited

Consider the derivations of the verbal noun *polatanie* flying around (from *lecieć* fly → *polecieć* id. perf. → *polatać* id. DI) within these two frameworks.

WFRs   [[[po+[lĕt+e]]$_V$ +aj]$_V$ +an+e]$_N$
VST   ɸ   ɸ
Palatalization   ń
Backing   o
            *[polotańe]

Here the prephonological truncation of *-aj* makes the operation of DI tensing impossible. Consequently, the root vowel does not surface as [a], but as [o].

Study now a simplified lexical derivation of *polatanie* (we ignore the prefix cycle which has no bearing on the phonology of the root).

WFR	[po+[[lĕt]+e]]$_V$
Palatalization	ć
WFR	[[po+lĕć+e]$_V$ +aj]$_V$
VST	ɸ
DI tensing	ē
WFR	[[po+leć+aj]$_V$ +an]$_N$
VST	ɸ
WFR	[po+leć+an+e]$_N$
Palatalization	ń
Postcyclic rules	/polećańe/
	—
	*[polećańe]

The fault in the incorrectness of the cyclic application of VST is exactly the same as in the case of nouns of the *wiertarka* type – the front vowel VS evinces palatalization before it is truncated since the context for the former rule is created prior to the context for the latter process.

Thus, neither of these two approaches appears to be capable of handling the phenomenon under analysis: the traditional generative approach fails since VSs in all cases must be deleted prephonologically, the lexical approach is inadequate since it does not allow for prephonological truncation, while the facts indicate that VST must apply both before and after phonological rules. To obtain the correct form of the noun *polatanie*, for instance, /e/ should be removed prior to the phonology, while *-aj* must be preserved until the application of DI tensing.

Observe that the point at which the VS is truncated closely depends on the structure of verbs on which it operates: when the base is a primary verbal stem, VST takes place before phonological rules (for example *wiertarka* 'driller'), while in items formed from more complex bases, i.e. from secondary verbal stem, VST must refer to more surface-like strings (for example *przepychacz* push broach). The situation clearly resembles the peculiar application of DI tensing, which also makes a distinction between simple and complex verbs.

This suggests a solution to the problem, which is the same as the one proposed for denominal and deadjectival verbs in the preceding section; primary verbal stems are processed together with the nominalizing suffixes in the traditional manner, whereas secondary verbal stems, i.e., deverbal verbs, undergo phonological rules before any affixes are attached to them, then return to the WF component to be subject to affixation, and then are processed by the phonology again. We shall illustrate this procedure with the noun *polatanie* 'flying around', whose derivation is problematic under previous approaches.

WFRs	$[[po+[lět+e]]_V +aj]_V$ (*polatać*)
VST	φ
DI tensing	$\bar{e}$
Backing	a
WFRs	$[[[po+[lat]]_V +aj]_V +an+e]_N$
VST	φ
Palatalization	ń
	[polatańe]

Since *polatać* is based on a primary verbal stem, it is processed in the traditional fashion and VST applies prephonologically in it. The noun *polatanie*, however, derives from a complex deverbal verb, hence the nominalizing suffix -*anie* is attached to the already processed form and -*aj* is truncated after the relevant changes have taken place in the root.

In brief, we are suggesting that if the verb is deverbal, i.e. it has the structure

$$[[\ ]_V]_V$$

it is subject to the operation of adjustment and phonological rules before it undergoes any further morphological processes. Due to this procedure the problem with the placement of VST disappears altogether; the rule need not be complicated and can be treated as an adjustment process, which modifies the output of WFRs before it can serve as the input to the phonological component. In brief, there is nothing peculiar about VST, which applies in a regular fashion, and whose properties derive from the mode of processing deverbal verbs.

Nouns back-formed from DIs provide additional support for the line of reasoning pursued here. Consider the examples below.

zr[i]v severance (*ze[rv]ać* tear away – *zr[i]vać* id. DI) *zer[e]w*
przeł[i]k gullet (*prze[wk]nąć* swallow – *przeł[i]kać* id. DI)
  przeł[e]k
st[i]k joint (*ze[tk]nąć* connect – *st[i]kać* id. DI) *zet[e]k*

These nouns must be formed directly from DIs, i.e. after the verbal stems have undergone DI tensing. If VST takes place before tensing, ungrammatical starred forms are obtained, as shown in the derivation of *styk* joint.

	$[zi+[tik+nin]]_V$
Back formation	$[zi+[tik]]_N$
Inflection	$[zi+[tik+i]]_N$
Lower	e e ɸ
	*[zetek]

To conclude, our analysis has demonstrated that the following structures

$$[[\ ]_N]_V \quad [[\ ]_{Ad}]_V \quad [[\ ]_V]_V$$

i.e. denominal, deadjectival and deverbal verbs must be processed by phonological rules before they undergo any further WFRs. These three cases can be generalized to state that the suggested procedure is needed for complex verbs

$$[[\ ]_X]_V \quad \text{where } X = N, \text{Ad or } V$$

Before we pursue further consequences of our proposal, it is worth considering whether an alternative solution to the problem of complex verbs can be offered. An obvious candidate is the claim that all verbs, both simple and complex, are listed in the lexicon so that they can be available for further morphological processes. What is more, the assumption would have to be that complex verbs are stored in their phonetic rather than their phonological shapes. This approach seems untenable if only because it denies the productive nature of the rules which form such verbs. If complex verbs are listed in the lexicon, this means that there is something irregular about them. This conclusion does not appear justified in many cases; as has already been mentioned, derived imperfectives, for instance, are productively derived from their perfective counterparts in a manner that resembles inflectional processes in terms of its regularity. Therefore, we reject the listing solution.

We should like to conclude our discussion of complex verbs with a brief presentation of a class of verbs which has so far escaped notice. These verbs are limited in number, but fairly regular. They take not one, but two imperfectivizing suffixes, *-aj* and *-ywa*, and can therefore be termed 'double' derived imperfectives or tertiary verbal stems. Such verbs have the following structure

PREFIX + ROOT + VERB SUFFIX + DI SUFFIX *-aj*
+ DI SUFFIX *-ywa*

The cycle revisited

for example

perfective verb	DI with -aj	DI with -aj and -ywa
wy+pleś+ć weave	→ wy+plat+a+ć	→ wy+plat+ywa+ć
wy+mieś+ć sweep out	→ wy+miat+ać	→ wy+miat+ywa+ć
wz+leci+e+ć fly up	→ wz+lat+a+ć	→ wz+lat+ywa+ć
przy+skocz+y+ć jump up	→ przy+skak+a+ć	→ przy+skak+iwa+ć
przy+kro+i+ć cut out	→ przy+kraj+a+ć	→ przy+kraw+ywa+ć

At first glance it may seem that we are dealing here not with double imperfectives, but with verbs that form two kinds of DIs: one with -aj and another with -ywa, for example

$$wy+pleś+ć \text{ weave} \begin{cases} wy+plat+aj+ą \text{ they weave} \\ wy+plat+ywa+ć \end{cases}$$

This approach, however, has to be rejected on phonological grounds. As noted earlier, only -aj, but never -ywa, induces the tensing of the root vowel. If -ywa were attached directly to the stems of verbs such as

wypleść weave   *wyskoczyć* jump out

we would get incorrect forms such as

*wypl[o]tywać   **wysk[o]kiwać*

The only way to obtain the vowel [a] in the imperfectives is through the attachment of -aj and subsequent DI tensing. We conclude that such verbs contain not one but two DI suffixes: -aj and -ywa, the first of which conditions DI tensing and is then deleted by VST.[15]

Thus, the verb *wyskakiwać* 'jump out' can be morphologically presented as

$$[[[vi+[skok+i]]_V +aj]_V +iv+a+ć]_V$$

i.e. it is a verb which comprises two other verbs in its structure

The cycle revisited

$[[\ ]_V]_V]_V$

Since the multiple application of phonological rules affects complex verbs, it follows that the structure of this sort will be subject to two passes through the phonology. The verb, *oblatywać* test a plane will then be derived in the following way

WFRs	$[[obi+[lĕt+e]]_V +aj]_V$
VST	φ
DI tensing	ē
Lower	φ
Backing	a
WFRs	$[[[ob+[lat]]_V +aj]_V +iv+a+ć]_V$
VST	φ
Phonology	–
	[oblativać]

First the verb suffix is deleted prephonologically. Then DI tensing affects the root vowel, which after backing emerges as [a]. The whole form returns then to the morphological component, where the remaining suffixes are appended. The attachment of *-ywa* triggers the truncation of *-aj*, so that phonetically the only trace of the latter suffix is the tense root vowel.

Just like the remaining verbs, double imperfectives can be used to form deverbal nouns, for example

wyplatywać weave – *wyplatywacz* weaver
oblatywać test a plane – *oblatywacz* test pilot

Consider now the noun *oblatywacz* test pilot

$[[[[obi+[let+e]]_V +aj]_V +iv+a]_V +ač+i]_N$

It is based on the complex verb *oblatywać* 'test a plane', which, as has been demonstrated, requires two passes through the phonology. In the case of *oblatywacz*, the last bracket with the label 'verb' is

125

followed by the nominalizing as well as the inflectional suffixes, which must also be phonologically processed. This necessitates the third pass through the phonological rules

WFRs $\quad [[[ob+[lat]]_V +iv+a]_V +ač+i]_N$

VST $\qquad\qquad\qquad\qquad\qquad\quad \phi$

Lower $\qquad\qquad\qquad\qquad\qquad\quad \phi$
$\quad$ [oblativač]

We can thus draw the conclusion that there are as many passes through the phonology as there are proper bracket configurations. In the derivation of *oblatywacz* the third pass was not induced by the complex verb, but logically follows from the necessity of the phonological processing of the material which follows the last label 'verb'.

In this chapter we have examined some morphological and phonological aspects of the formation of Polish verbs which display different degrees of morphological complexity (i.e. primary, secondary and tertiary verbal stems) as well as words derived from them. It has appeared that processing them correctly involves numerous problems within both the traditional and the lexical frameworks, mainly because of the seemingly unusual properties of two rules: verb suffix truncation and DI tensing. The former applies in two different fashions depending on the type of verbal stems: prephonologically in items based on primary verbs, and postphonologically in words derived from deverbal verbs. The rule of DI tensing also appears to distinguish between simple verbs, in which case it operates on their underlying structures, and more complex verbal stems, to whose phonetic forms DI tensing must refer. We have suggested that these facts can be accounted for if complex verbs are processed by adjustment and phonological rules before they are subject to any further affixation.[16] This amounts to going back from the input of phonological rules to the word formation component and then back to the phonology.

Thus, what we are advocating here is some kind of a cyclic mechanism, according to which, under special circumstances, phonological rules can apply more than once in the derivation of one item. Our understanding of cyclicity, however, differs considerably from the way this concept is treated in the cyclic/lexical model. We argue against the mechanistic cyclic approach in which the attachment of every single affix brings about the application of phonological rules – a doctrine that Polish data seriously call into question. We claim that only certain lexical items, in this case complex verbs, possess cyclic structure, whereas others do not, and in the latter instances evoking the cyclic application of rules is not only totally unnecessary, but often counterproductive. Thus, cyclicity is a property of certain structures rather than individual rules.[17]

3.2 Other cases

We hope that enough evidence has been provided to justify the multiple application of phonological rules in the case of complex verbs. A significant question is whether other morphologically complex items should also be processed in the modified way suggested here. It appears that this is not possible. Thus, if other items are derived in the same fashion as complex verbs, incorrect forms are produced. Below we present some examples of words based on morphologically complex items, where the multiple application of phonological rules creates wrong outputs.

$[[\ ]_V]_N$

$kop+a+ć_V$ dig → $kop+ark+a_N$ digging machine →
   $kop+arecz+k+a_N$ id. dim. (*$koparczka$)

$[[\ ]_N]_N$

$lal+a_N$ doll → $lal+k+a_N$ id. dim → $lal+ecz+k+a_N$ id. dim.
   (*$lalczka$)

$[[\ ]_{Ad}]_{Ad}$

$mał+y_{Ad}$ small → $mal+eńk+i_{Ad}$ tiny → $mal+eniecz+k+i_{Ad}$
   id. dim. (*$maleńczki$)

$[[\ ]_V]_{Ad}$

$za+pal+i+ć_V$ rouse → $za+pal+on+y_{Ad}$ enthusiastic →
   $za+pal+eni+ec_N$ enthusiast (*$zapaloniec$)

$[[\ ]_V]_{Ad}]_N$

pleś+ć$_V$ weave → *pleci+on+y*$_{Ad}$ woven → *pleci+on+k+a*$_N$
plaitwork → *pleci+on+ecz+k+a*$_N$ id. dim. (*plecionczka*)

$[[\ ]_N]_N]_N$

szynk$_N$ pub → *szynk+arz*$_N$ bar-keeper → *szynk+ar+k+a*$_N$
female bar-keeper → *szynk+ar+ecz+k+a*$_N$ id. dim.
(*szynkarczka*)

$[[\ ]_{Ad}]_{Ad}]_{Ad}$

biał+y$_{Ad}$ white → *biel+utk+i*$_{Ad}$ id. dim. →
biel+ut+eńk+i$_{Ad}$ id. dim. → *biel+ut+eniecz+k+i*$_{Ad}$ id.
dim. (*bieluteńczki*)

Although examples can be multiplied, the general picture will probably not change: the modified processing is not applicable to other morphologically complex bases and is restricted to derived verbs only.

A significant issue that arises is the following: what makes complex verbs so special that they are treated in a different way by the grammar? Unfortunately, we do not have any definite and clear answer to this question. Apparently verbs occupy a special position in the grammatical system of Polish, which may be due to their considerable morphological complexity. If some principle is at work here, it is yet uncovered. Hence complex verbs must be marked as cyclicity triggers as soon as they are created. This means that the morphological component contains some kind of a convention, which can, informally, be presented as

$[[\ ]_X]_V$ → [+processed by phonological rules]

It will ensure that complex verbs are subject to the operation of phonological rules before they take part in further morphological processes.

The multiple application of phonological rules can also be employed in the derivation of some idiosyncratic forms. Examples of this sort are discussed by Gussmann (1980a:69–70).

He observes that words such as *kwiaciarnia* 'flower shop' behave as if the root *kwiat* 'flower' were processed by phonological rules before it combined with the suffix *-arnia*. The reason for this assumption is the irregular application of backing. Usually the distribution of the vowels [e] and [a] in alternating morphemes follows a clear pattern: [e] occurs before palatal sounds, [a] in the context of the following back coronals, for example

mi[as]to town – *mi[eś]cie* id. loc. sg.
ci[as]to cake – *ci[eś]cie* id. loc. sg.

This holds true also of several forms that contain the root *kwiat* 'flower'.

kwi[at]+ek id. dim. *kwi[eć]+e* id. loc. sg.
kwi[at]+uszek id. dim. *kwi[eć]+ist+y* flowery
kwi[at]+ow+y flowery *kwi[eć]+ak* fleuron

Some words, however, violate this regularity for no apparent reason. In such cases the vowel [a] occurs before palatal consonants, for example

kwi[ać]+arz florist *kwi[ać]+ast+y* flowery
kwi[ać]+arni+a florist's *kwi[ać]+ark+a* flower-girl

These items can be properly derived if the multiple application of phonological rules is employed. The procedure is illustrated with the derivation of the noun *kwiaciarka* 'flower-girl'.

WFRs	$[kfet]_N$
Palatalization	f'
Backing	a
WFRs	$[[kf'at]_N +erik+a]_N$
Palatalization	ć
Lower	φ
Backing	a
	[kf'aćarka]

On the first pass the root-vowel is subject to backing since the consonant which follows it is coronal. On the next pass the consonant undergoes palatalization, but the effect of backing is preserved as a result of which we obtain the correct phonetic form.

As the examples given earlier show, the root *kwiat* cannot be marked as cyclic, i.e. as inducing the multiple application of phonological rules, since it does not display this property throughout the whole paradigm (for example in forms such as *kwiecień* April). It is only in combination with specific suffixes that the suggested mechanism becomes activated. Thus, the noun *kwiaciarka* flower-girl will have to be idiosyncratically marked as

$[[kf\widetilde{et}]_N +er\dot{i}k+a]_N$
↓
[+processed by phonological rules]

To conclude, complex verbs and forms of the *kwiaciarka* type provide evidence for the multiple application of phonological rules, which results from postulating the phonology–morphology loop. In the following chapter we intend to provide more arguments in favour of this organization of the grammar, based on fully regular and productive processes in Polish as well as in other languages.

Chapter four
Phonetic inputs to WFRs – morphological evidence for the cycle

In the preceding chapter we have argued that in some cases it is necessary to return from the output of the phonological component to word formation rules and then to the phonology again. This procedure has been motivated by the need to account for the peculiar behaviour of some phonological rules which take part in the formation of complex verbs and their derivatives in Polish.

The present chapter provides more evidence for the proposed organization of the grammar. We discuss three very productive morphological processes in Polish: comparative degree formation, imperative formation, and augmentative back-formation, and demonstrate that, contrary to the assumptions of the linear and the lexical models, these rules must operate not on underlying or intermediate structures, but on the output of all word-level rules, i.e. on phonetic forms. This hypothesis finds additional confirmation in some WFRs of English and Dutch. Finally, we argue that the phonology–morphology loop is not an exceptional grammatical mechanism, since a similar device is needed in the case of phrase-level syntax and word formation.

A few remarks on the existing approaches to the nature of inputs to WFRs will facilitate the subsequent discussion.

In the traditional generative framework WFRs operate on morphological structures, which are identical with phonological representations. This means that both derivational bases as well as affixes occur in their underlying shapes and the concatenation of morphemes is performed on phonological strings. Such an approach follows from the strict separation of the morphological and the phonological components, from the ordering of the former before the latter.

As demonstrated by Szpyra (1987), in the lexical model, in which the processes of word formation are interspersed with phonological rules, the first WFR that attaches an affix to an underived form operates on the phonological structure of both the base and the affix. If a derived, i.e. morphologically complex form, serves as an input to a WFR, then the morphological operation is carried out not on the phonological, but rather on the intermediate (lexical) representation of lexical items, i.e. on the structures obtained as a result of the application of lexical phonological rules. In other words, in this model underlying forms act as inputs to word formation for every first attachment of affixes, while lexical representations enter every further affixation.

Positing the loop from the phonological component to WFRs creates yet another possibility, i.e. that of morphological rules taking phonetic inputs derived by the application of all word-level rules.

In what follows we shall examine some WFRs in Polish in terms of the exact nature of input forms, of which three possibilities will be considered: phonological, lexical and phonetic.

4.1 Comparative degree formation

Polish, similarly to English, employs two ways of forming the comparative degree of adjectives: analytic, by means of the adverb *bardziej* 'more', for example

    przekonywujący convincing – *bardziej przekonywujący* more convincing
    niebieski blue – *bardziej niebieski* more blue

and suffixal, through the addition of one of the suffixes: *-sz* [š], and *-ejsz* [ejš], for example[1]

a) *głup+i* silly → *głup+sz+y*
    czuł+y tender → *czul+sz+y*
    dług+i long → *dłuż+sz+y*
    dzik+i wild → *dzik+sz+y*
    mił+y nice → *mil+sz+y*

b) *mądr+y* wise → *mądrz+ejsz+y*
   smukł+y slim → *smukl+ejsz+y*
   ładn+y pretty → *ładni+ejsz+y*
   ciepł+y warm → *ciepl+ejsz+y*
   ciemn+y dark → *ciemni+ejsz+y*

It is the latter case that will be of our interest here. To be more exact, we shall be concerned with the factor which determines the occurrence of either the syllabic or the non-syllabic comparative degree suffix.[2]

As noted by several traditional grammars (for example Szober 1962; *Morfologia*), the distribution of the comparative suffixes depends on the segmental structure of the adjectival stems: *-ejsz* occurs after consonant clusters, *-sz* after single consonants. Both types are illustrated in b) and a) respectively.

This generalization, although undoubtedly true in the majority of cases, occasionally appears to be false, since there are adjectives whose stems terminate in consonant clusters, and yet they combine with the suffix *-sz* and not *-ejsz*, for example

prost+y simple → *prost+sz+y* (**prościejszy*)
tward+y hard → *tward+sz+y* (**twardziejszy*)

These examples show that what matters is not just the presence of the cluster, but also the quality of the consonants involved.

Let us, then, consider different types of adjective-final consonantal clusters and their influence on the choice of the comparative suffix.

It appears that a sequence of sonorants in the stem-final position invariably requires the syllabic suffix, for example

uprzejm+y polite → *uprzejmi+ejsz+y*
skromn+y modest → *skromni+ejsz+y*
wiern+y faithful → *wierni+ejsz+y*

The same is true also about the adjectives terminating in the cluster obstruent + sonorant, for example

chytr+y cunning → *chytrz+ejsz+y*
bystr+y clever → *bystrz+ejsz+y*
korzystn+y advantageous → *korzystni+ejsz+y*

The situation is less uniform with clusters ending in obstruents. The syllabic suffix is used with the sequences obstruent + spirant, for example

trzeźw+y sober → *trzeźwi+ejsz+y*
łatw+y simple → *łatwi+ejsz+y*

However, with the cluster sonorant + obstruent *-sz* is used, for example

tward+y hard → *tward+sz+y*
żółt+y yellow → *żółt+sz+y*

The adjectives which end in *st*, i.e. in the sequence spirant + plosive, usually combine with the shorter suffix, for example

oczywist+y obvious → *oczywist+sz+y*
puszyst+y fluffy → *puszyst+sz+y*
wyrazist+y expressive → *wyrazist+sz+y*

In some instances both the shorter and the longer comparative forms can occur after *st*, for example[3]

tłust+y greasy → *tłust+sz+y* / *tłuści+ejsz+y*
gęst+y thick → *gęst+sz+y* / *gęści+ejsz+y*
czyst+y clean → *czyst+sz+y* / *czyści+ejsz+y*

An interesting question is what happens with the adjectival stems that end in other obstruents. Unfortunately, no decisive evidence can be found in such cases. Simply, those adjectives which could be used as diagnostic material, form periphrastic comparatives. For instance, of the items that end in affricates, none appears to form suffixal comparatives, for example

obc+y strange – *bardziej obcy*
oszczercz+y slanderous – *bardziej oszczerczy*
władcz+y masterful – *bardziej władczy*

As to the adjectives that end in plosives, apart from *st* clusters, only consonant + the voiceless velar plosive can be found in adjectival stems. Curiously enough, the addition of the comparative suffix causes the truncation of *-k*, for example[4]

słod+k+i sweet → *słod+sz+y*
krót+k+i short → *krót+sz+y*
szyb+k+i fast → *szyb+sz+y*

To summarize, the suffix *-ejsz* appears in fewer contexts than *-sz*, i.e. after stems ending in CR (consonant + sonorant) and CS (consonant + spirant), while *-sz* occurs elsewhere, i.e. after single consonants and after the remaining clusters. Stems terminating in CP (consonant + plosive) admit both *-ejsz* and *-sz*. These observations lead to the rule of comparative degree formation, which, in a simplified form (that disregards the semantic and morphological constraints on forming comparatives – as is well known, many adjectives are not gradable at all) can be presented as

Comparative degree formation

$$[X]_{Ad\ Comp.} \rightarrow \begin{cases} /a/\ [[X]_{Ad} + ej\check{s}],\ \text{if}\ [X]_{Ad}\ \text{ends in CR, CS,} \\ \quad CCC,\ CP\ \text{(optionally)} \\ /b/\ [[X]_{Ad} + \breve{\imath}\check{s}]\ \text{in other cases} \end{cases}$$

Observe that our analysis of comparative forms has been carried out without assuming any specific descriptive framework. In other words, the rule of comparative degree formation has been established on the basis of uncontroversial facts valid under any approach. Nevertheless, this relatively simple process appears to cause problems for both the traditional and the lexical models.

Consider, for example, the adjective *pożyteczny* useful. Its structure has the following form

$[[po\check{z}it\breve{\imath}k]_N + \breve{\imath}n + i]_{Ad}$

Evidence can be brought up to show that both the root and the adjectival suffix *-n(y)* contain high lax vowels. The former is motivated by the vowel-zero alternation in the noun *pożyftek]* use, noun – *pożyftk]u* id. gen. sg.

the latter by the fact that it brings out the root-yer and palatalizes the preceding consonant

pożyfteč+n]+y useful

(see also the discussion of *-ny* in the preceding chapter). Assume now that the phonological form of the adjective, i.e.

[[požitĭk]$_N$ +ĭn]$_{Ad}$

is subject to comparative degree formation. As the stem ends in a single consonant, clause b) of the rule attaches *-sz* to it. This, however, disagrees with the facts since the comparative form

pożyteczni+ejsz+y more useful

contains *-ejsz* and not *-sz*. The attachment of *-sz* produces the following derivation

	/požitĭk+ĭn+ĭš+ɨ/
Palatalization	č ń
Lower	e e ɸ
	*[požɨtečeńsɨ]

The lexical analysis fares no better. At the cycle at which comparative degree formation operates, the adjective has already undergone the application of phonological rules such as palatalization and lower, and the relevant structure is the following

[požiteč+ĭn]$_{Ad}$

Note that the yer of the adjectival suffix is preserved since the rule of yer deletion, as explained in Chapter 3, does not apply until the postcyclic stage. As the stem ends in a single consonant, again only clause b) of comparative degree formation is applicable. This means, of course, the attachment of *-sz* instead of *-ejsz* and the incorrect derivation such as

	[požitĭk]$_N$
WFR	[[požitĭk]$_N$ +ĭn]$_{Ad}$
Palatalization	č
Lower	e
WFR	[[požiteč+ĭn]$_{Ad}$ +ĭš]$_{Ad}$
Palatalization	ń
Lower	e
WFR	[požiteč+eń+ĭš+i]$_{Ad}$
Cycle 4	–
Postcyclic rules	[požitečeńĭsɨ]
Lower	φ
	[požitečeńsɨ]

In brief, under the assumption that the syllabic suffix *-ejsz* attaches only to adjectival stems that end in consonant clusters, no correct derivations of forms such as *pożyteczniejszy* can be produced within the traditional generative and the lexical frameworks. This is not, of course, an isolated example, but a representative of one of the most productive adjectival formations in Polish. Let us mention just a few other examples of the same sort

skutecz+n+y effective → *skutecz+ni+ejsz+y*
   (cf. *sku[tek]* result – *sku[tk]u* id. gen. sg.)
piekiel+n+y infernal → *piekiel+ni+ejsz+y*
   (cf. *pie[kw]o* hell)
liczeb+n+y numerous → *liczeb+ni+ejsz+y*
   (cf. *li[džb]a* number)
hanieb+n+y shameful → *hanieb+ni+ejsz+y*
   (cf. *ha[ńb]a* shame)

All these adjectives have stems that phonologically end in single consonants, i.e. /n/, and, as such, should combine with the shorter comparative degree suffix *-sz*. Yet, the suffix *-ejsz* appears to be attached to such adjectives.

To save both frameworks under criticism, the following clause should be added to the rule of comparative degree formation: '-*sz* attaches to single-consonant stems with the exception of those cases in which the consonant is preceded by a high lax vowel. In the latter instances the suffix -*ejsz* must be appended'. Such a formulation, however, destroys the validity of the otherwise firmly established generalization concerning the distribution of comparative suffixes. Furthermore, it lacks the explanatory power inherent in the approach that refers to consonantal clusters; under the formulation proposed earlier the syllabic suffix is appended in those cases in which the addition of a consonantal formative would lead to heavy clusters. No such reason can be provided for the occurrence of -*ejsz* after single consonants, unless we want to endow comparative degree formation with some kind of global power which would allow the rule to 'foresee' that as a result of yer deletion consonantal clusters would be created. This solution does not seem very attractive or feasible.

Notice that on the surface forms such as

pożyte[čń]+ejszy more useful   *skute[čń]+ejszy* more effective

licze[bń]+ejszy more numerous   *piekie[lń]+ejszy* more infernal

do not violate the distribution of comparative degree suffixes established earlier; the adjectival stems end in consonantal clusters (consonant + sonorant) and, as such, take the longer suffix -*ejsz*, in agreement with clause a) of the rule. In other words, comparative degree formation appears to 'know' that -*ejsz* should be appended since a cluster of consonants will arise in the derivation.

We should like to suggest that this 'global' power of the process under scrutiny results from the fact that comparative degree formation operates on inputs that have already been processed by phonological rules. To put it differently, adjectival stems that are subject to the attachment of comparative suffixes undergo the application of phonological rules, and then return to the word formation component. Now comparative degree formation appends the appropriate suffixes and the whole form enters the phonological derivation for the second time.

Let us illustrate this procedure with the derivation of the comparative degree adjectives *skuteczniejszy* 'more effective' and *pożyteczniejszy* 'more useful'. Before adjectival stems leave the morphological component, they acquire the label 'comparative degree', which indicates that such structures act as inputs to comparative degree formation and must return to WFRs via the phonology–morphology loop.

WFR	[[skutĭk]$_N$ +ĭn]$_{Comp. Degree}$	[[požĭtĭk]$_N$ +ĭn]$_{Comp. Degree}$
Palatalization	č	č
Lower	e ϕ	e ϕ
Comparative degree formation	[[skuteč]$_N$ +n+ejš]$_{Ad}$	[[požiteč]$_N$ +n+ejš]$_{Ad}$
Inflection	[[skuteč]$_N$ +n+ejš+i]$_{Ad}$	[[požiteč]$_N$ +n+ejš+i]$_{Ad}$
Palatalization	ń	ń
	[skutečńejsi]	[požitecńejsi]

On the first pass through the phonology the rule of lower affects the yer vowels in the adjectival stems; the root yer becomes [e] while the vowel in the suffix deletes. Now the adjectives return to the word formation component and are subject to comparative degree formation. Since at this stage the stems end in clusters of two consonants (more exactly CR), the upper expansion of the rule applies and *-ejsz* is appended. The second application of phonological rules brings about the palatalization of the nasal consonant in the adjectival suffix and the correct forms are yielded.

At this point it is worth considering the lexicalization approach, i.e. the assumption that adjectives are stored in the lexicon in their surface shapes, and that is why some WFRs, such as comparative degree formation, can have access to them. In our opinion such an approach is totally incorrect. First of all, many classes of adjectives are productively derived in Polish (Szymanek 1985) and there is no reason to assume that they should be present in the lexicon at all. Secondly, even if some items must be stored, this does not automatically mean that they are idiosyncratic from the phonological point of view, and should be listed in their phonetic form. In other words, some adjectives might be irregular in terms of their morphology or semantics, which provides justification for listing them in the lexicon, but perfectly regular with respect to their phonological properties. Such is the case with the adjective *piekielny*, only one meaning of which, i.e. 'infernal', is directly derivable from the base noun *piekło* 'hell'. The other meaning, i.e. 'terrible, awful', has no immediate relation to *piekło*, hence, the adjective must probably be stored in the lexicon. There is nothing peculiar, however, about its phonology; it can be derived by means of regular rules of Polish phonology. Therefore, recording its surface shape does not seem a plausible approach. Finally, there are cases in which the comparative degree adjective cannot be properly formed from the phonetic structure of the positive degree adjective.

Consider the adjective *lekki* light. If the form [lekk] were subject to comparative degree formation, after the attachment of *-ejsz* (motivated by the presence of the consonantal cluster), the derivation would proceed as follows:

	/lekk+ejš+ɨ/
k-truncation	ɸ
Palatalization	č
	*[lečejšɨ]

Clearly, this is the wrong result as the comparative degree form is *lżejszy*.

The derivation from the underlying structure

/lĭg+ĭk/

also leads to the incorrect output, since the stem ends in a single consonant, which induces the attachment of the suffix *-sz* instead of *-ejsz*.

Let us now employ the procedure suggested for the other adjectives.

WFR	$[lĭg+ĭk]_{Comp.\ Degree}$
k-truncation	φ
Lower	φ
WFR – comparative degree formation	$[[lg]_{Ad} +ejš]_{Ad}$
Inflection	$[[lg]_{Ad} +ejš+i]_{Ad}$
Palatalization	ž
	[lžejši]

The phonological form of the adjective *lekki* is assigned the label 'comparative degree' in the word formation component and enters the derivation. First, /-ĭk/ is truncated (by the rule which deletes it in comparative degree forms) and the root yer is removed by the rule of lower. Then the item [lg] re-enters the morphological component and undergoes comparative degree formation. Of course the longer suffix is appended and the whole adjective is processed again by the phonology. The suffix *-ejsz* triggers palatalization and *lżejszy* is created. Note that [lg] is a phonetically non-occurring form, which cannot exist independently, but only as an input to comparative degree formation.

To conclude, the analysis of the distribution of the comparative degree suffixes *-ejsz* and *-sz* has revealed that it is strictly connected with the segmental structure of the adjectival stems. Generally speaking, *-ejsz* is the variant which appears after consonantal clusters (with some classes of exceptions), whereas *-sz* occurs with the items that terminate in a single consonant. This generalization, however, cannot be maintained in either the linear or the lexical descriptions, since there are cases in which the longer suffix is appended to what at the phonological level (or at the lexical level) are single consonant stems. To put it differently, the distribution of the comparative degree suffixes can be stated in a simple and general fashion only in surface, and not underlying (or intermediate) terms. Moreover, reference to the phonetic structure of adjectival stems has more explanatory value: the assignment of the syllabic suffix is accounted for by the need to avoid heavy consonantal clusters. To accommodate these facts, we have suggested that comparative degree formation is a morphological process which operates on the strings that have already undergone phonological rules, which condition must be built into the rule itself. Due to this procedure we are capable of deriving all comparative degree adjectives without violating the constraints on the distribution of *-ejsz* and *-sz*.

In the next section we discuss a more complex process, i.e., that of forming imperatives, which also seems sensitive to the phonetic structure of the input strings.

4.2 Imperative formation

Imperative forms in Polish pose a number of interesting phonological and morphological problems. On the phonology side an issue of much interest is to account for several different manifestations of the imperative. They are the following.[5]

a) phonetic zero – in such cases the imperative form is identical with the verbal stem, i.e. ROOT + VS, for example[6]
czyt+aj+ą they read → *czyt+aj*
łysi+ej+ą they get bald → *łysi+ej*
myj+ą they wash → *myj*

b) the palatalization of the root-final consonant, for example
plo[t]+ę I weave → *ple[ć]*
pie[k]+ę I bake → *pie[č]*
pa[s]ę I graze → *pa[ś]*

c) the j-palatalization of the root-final consonant, for example
pi[s]+a+ć write → *pi[š]*
ka[z]+a+ć order → *ka[š]*
cze[s]+a+ć comb → *cze[š]*

d) the palatalization of the stem-final consonant which accompanies the attachment of the suffix *-ij*, for example
dotk+[n]ą+ć touch → *dotk+[ń]+ij*
klęk+[n]ą+ć kneel → *klęk+[ń]+ij*
potk+[n]ą+ć stumble → *potk+[ń]+ij*

According to two detailed generative descriptions of the imperative (Gussmann 1980b and Rubach 1985), there are two allomorphs of the imperative suffix: /ĭ/, which attaches to the forms in a), b) and c), and /ijĭ/, which is present in d). These suffixes are appended to verbal stems and induce the changes which have just been described. Without going into insignificant details, and ignoring certain differences between the linear and the cyclic descriptions, the phonology of the imperative in the types a), b) and c) can be interpreted in the following fashion.

a) The forms in a) contain stems which end in the palatal glide. Consequently, the imperative suffix /ĭ/ does not affect them in any important way. As /ĭ/ is a high lax vowel, which is not followed by another yer, it is eventually deleted by the rule of lower (or yer deletion), for example
/bad+aj+ĭ/ → *bad+aj* examine, imper.
/truj+ĭ/ → *truj* poison, imper.

b) The items in b) are characterized by the palatalization of the root-final consonants, which is induced by the imperative suffix /ĭ/, for example

	paś graze	*piecz* bake
	/pas+ĭ/	/pek+ĭ/
Palatalization	ś	p' č
Lower	ϕ	ϕ
	[paś]	[p'eč]

In those cases in which the verbalizing suffix intervenes between the root and /ĭ/, the VS must be deleted before the imperative suffix. This can be effected by the prephonological front vowel truncation of the following form (Rubach 1985:151)[7]

$$\begin{bmatrix} +\text{syll} \\ -\text{back} \end{bmatrix} \to \phi\ /\ \underline{\quad}\ \text{i}]_{\text{Imper.}}$$

The remaining rules operate in the same way as in the instances discussed previously. The imperative forms *leć* 'fly' (from *lecieć*) and *proś* 'ask' (from *prosić*) are derived as follows

	/let+e+ĭ/	/pros+i+ĭ/
Front vowel truncation	φ	φ
Palatalization	č	ś
Lower	φ	φ
	[leć]	[proś]

c) The imperative forms in c) display the effects of j-palatalization. The conditioning palatal glide is inserted before a sequence of two vowels, of which one is back (Gussmann 1980b:39). The derivation of *pisz* 'write, imper.' (from *pisać*) and *każ* 'order, imper.' (from *kazać*) proceeds as follows

	/pis+a+ĭ/	/kaz+a+ĭ/
J-insertion	j	j
Palatalization	p'š	ž
Vowel deletion	φ	φ
Lower	φ	φ
Final devoicing	—	š
	[p'iš]	[kaš]

d) Here the front vowel of the suffix *-ij* triggers the palatalization of stem-final consonants. The verbalizing suffix *-ną*, which can phonologically be interpreted as /nĭn/ (Gussmann 1980b:42), loses its lax vowel in the imperative form, and the cluster of two nasal consonants is subject to degemination. The imperative form *szepnij* 'whisper' (from *szepnąć*) can be derived in the following manner[8]

	/šep+nĭn+ijĭ/	
Palatalization	ń	
Lower	φ	φ
Palatal assimilation	ń	
Degemination	φ	
	[šepńij]	

We can conclude that the phonology of the imperative provides sufficient reasons for positing the suffixes /ĭ/ and /ijĭ/ as imperative markers, and that these suffixes, together with the presented rules, are capable of accounting for the phonological properties of imperative forms.

On the morphology side, an interesting question is to identify the factors responsible for the distribution of the two imperative suffixes. According to Gussmann (1980b) and Rubach (1985), the answer is straightforward: the choice from between /ĭ/ and /ijĭ/ crucially depends on the segmental structure of the stems, or, to be more exact, on the presence or absence of the yer in the verbal stem. Thus, /ijĭ/ attaches only to the verbs whose last vowel is a yer, for example

klń+ij swear, imper. from /klĭn+ijĭ/
kop+n+ij kick, imper. from /kop+nĭn+ijĭ/

whereas /i/, as the unrestricted variant, occurs elsewhere, i.e. with *-aj, -ej, -i, -e, -a* and C-stems (examples in a), b) and c)). In other words, the distribution of the suffixes in question seems complementary, and imperative formation appends the appropriate allomorph on the basis of the phonological structure of verbal stems.

Bethin (1987) observes, however, that serious doubts can be raised with regard to this analysis. The following objections can be levelled against it.

1. There are yer-stems with the suffix *-ną*, which do not take /ijĭ/, but /ĭ/, for example

to+ną+ć drown → *to+ń* id. imper. not **to+n+ij*
sta+ną+ć stand → *sta+ń* id. imper. not **sta+n+ij*
pły+ną+ć swim → *pły+ń* id. imper. not **pły+n+ij*
fru+ną+ć fly → *fru+ń* id. imper. not **fru+n+ij*
mi+ną+ć pass → *mi+ń* id. imper. not **mi+n+ij*

To account for this 'irregularity' in the distribution of /ijĭ/, both Gussmann (1980b) and Rubach (1985) postulate additional allomorphy statements. This, as Bethin notes, results in complex analyses which lack explanatory power. To put it differently, the fact that *-ij* fails to occur with such verbs is not explained, but treated as idiosyncratic (reduced to allomorphy).

Furthermore, there is evidence that neither of these two

approaches is fully correct and able to handle this group of verbs. According to Gussmann (1980b:43), forms such as *toń* 'drown, imper.' necessitate an allomorphy rule which deletes the vowel /ĭ/ of the imperative suffix *-ij* if *-nǫ* is appended to roots terminating in a non-consonantal segment

i → ɸ / [-cons] +nĭn + ___ jĭ

As Rubach (1985:148) points out, this leads to incorrect forms such as *[toneń]

	/to+nĭn+ijĭ/	
Allomorphy i-deletion	ɸ	
Palatalization	ń	
Lower	e	ɸ
J-deletion	ɸ	
	*[toneń]	

To amend the situation Rubach (1985:149) suggests another allomorphy rule, according to which a portion of /nĭn/ is truncated after non-consonantal roots:

nĭn → n / [-cons] ___ [-cons]

The verb *tonąć*, for example, is subject to this rule

/to+nĭn/ → /ton/

Now the process of imperative formation takes place and assigns the suffix /ĭ/ to such a stem since the yer vowel is absent from it. After the application of palatalization, the correct form [toń] is yielded. In verbs such as *szepnij* whisper, imper. from /šep+nĭn/, Rubach's allomorphy rule does not apply, since the root ends in an obstruent and the suffix *-ij* can be appended (the preceding vowel is lax).

Consider, however, the following type of imperative verbs

za+[mk]+n+ij shut   (cf. *za+[mik]+a+ć* id. DI)
po+[px]+n+ij push   (cf. *po+[pix]+a+ć* id. DI)

po+[wk]+n+ij swallow (cf. *po+[wĭk]+a+ć* id. DI)
wy+[sx]+n+ij dry (cf. *wy+[sĭx]+a+ć* id. DI)
za+[tk]+n+ij stick in (cf. *za+[tĭk]+a+ć* id. DI)

All these verbs contain yer roots: /mĭk/, /pĭx/, /łĭk/, /sĭx/, and /tĭk/, which end with obstruents. Therefore, the suffix /nĭn/, which occurs with such roots, is not subject to Rubach's *-nĭn-* allomorphy. This leads (both within the traditional and the lexical models) to the derivation of incorrect imperative forms. The verb *zamknij* 'shut', for instance, is subject to the following processing.

	/za+mĭk+nĭn+ijĭ/
nĭn-allomorphy	inapplicable
Palatalization	ń
Lower	e ɸ ɸ
Palatal assimilation	ń
Degemination	ɸ
	*[zamekńij]

The problem here is that both the root and the verb suffix contain yer vowels and, consequently, the first one is lowered to [e], which produces the incorrect result.[9]

In brief, in spite of the use of complex allomorphy mechanisms, neither of the analyses under scrutiny can handle the correct formation of imperative forms which involve the VS *-ną*.

2. There are non-yer stems that none the less take *-ij* and not /ĭ/, for example

dudn+i+ć rumble → *dudn+ij* id. imper.
nagl+i+ć urge → *nagl+ij* id. imper.
za+okrąg+l+i+ć round up → *za+okrąg+l+ij* id. imper.
u+ściśl+i+ć make precise → *u+ściśl+ij* id. imper.

Under the analysis that appends *-ij* only to yer-stems, such forms would have to be treated as exceptions, individually marked as to the imperative suffix which they take. This is suspicious since these are not isolated examples, and the list of such can be easily expanded.

3. The restriction of *-ij* to yer-stems also fails to account for the occurrence of such doublets as

zde+jm / *zde+jm+ij* take off, imper.
przy+jm / *przy+jm+ij* receive, imper.
obe+jrz / *obe+jrz+yj* look, imper.

Here the roots comprise high lax vowels and only longer imperatives are expected.

pastw się / *pastw+ij się* maltreat, imper.
u+wielb / *u+wielb+ij* adore, imper.
o+trzeźw / *o+trzeźw+ij* bring around, imper.

These items have no yers in the roots and, as such, should not combine with *-ij*.

4. The attachment of *-ij* is also problematic in such cases as

zw+a+ć name → *zw+ij* id. imper.
ss+a+ć suck → *ss+ij* id. imper.
sł+a+ć send → *śl+ij* id. imper.
sp+a+ć sleep → *śp+ij* id. imper.
rw+a+ć tear → *rw+ij* id. imper.

These roots are phonetically asyllabic, i.e. they contain a yer in their phonological structure. Nevertheless *-ij* should not be attached here, since the stems end in the VS *-a* and should be subject to the attachment of /ĭ/ (as, for example the verb *pis+a+ć* write – *pisz*, id. imper.).

To summarize, the fact that there are
yer-stems that take /ijĭ/, for example *kln+ij* swear, imper.
yer-stems that take /ĭ/, for example *to+ń* drown, imper.
non-yer stems that take /ijĭ/, for example *nagl+ij* urge, imper.
non-yer stems that take /ĭ/, for example *leć* fly, imper.
yer-stems that take both /ijĭ/ and /ĭ/, for example *zde+jm* / *zde+jm+ij* take off, imper.
non-yer stems that take both /ijĭ/ and /ĭ/, for example *u+wielb* / *u+wielb+ij* adore, imper.

clearly shows that the occurrence of a yer in the verbal stem is not a decisive factor in the distribution of the imperative suffixes. Consequently, an alternative explanation of the problem must be sought.

Bethin (1987), following the traditional descriptions of Polish (for example Szober 1962; Schenker 1954) claims that what determines the choice of the imperative marker is the presence as well as the nature of the stem- (or root-) final consonantal cluster. Bethin argues that even if Polish on the whole admits heavy consonantal clusters, some of them are marked as syllable codas. In such cases, to avoid impermissible or highly marked syllable structure, the imperative suffix *-ij* is attached. Take the imperative form *dudn+ij* 'rumble'. Without the suffix *-ij* the impossible structure [dudń] would be created since [dń] cannot be a coda in Polish (generally speaking, obstruent–sonorant clusters are highly marked as codas). Moreover, according to Bethin, Polish seems to have a hierarchy of tolerance with regard to consonant clusters as codas; some are unacceptable and rejected by all the speakers (for example [dń]), others are acceptable (for example the majority of obstruent clusters)

po+więk+sz+y+ć enlarge → *po+więk+sz* id. imper.
na+ostrz+y+ć sharpen → *na+ostrz* id. imper.

and as to some clusters (for example [lb], [źw], [stf]) there are no unambiguous acceptability judgements, which may differ from speaker to speaker. In the first case *-ij* must be obligatorily appended as a means of avoiding marked sequences in the coda position. In the second case the unrestricted variant /ĭ/ is attached as nothing necessitates *-ij*. In the third instance two possibilities are available: if a speaker finds a given cluster difficult to pronounce word-finally, he uses *-ij*; if he treats it as unmarked, he attaches /ĭ/.

This approach appears to have numerous strong points, and is capable of accounting for various issues inexplicable under previous descriptions. More specifically, it provides a solution for the four cases presented earlier. Let us return to them briefly.

1. Verbs with the VS *-ną* take either /ĭ/ or /ijĭ/. The first variant is used in those cases in which short imperative forms do not

violate any restrictions on codas, for example

płyń swim   *stań* stand   *fruń* fly

The longer suffix is employed in the situations where /ĭ/ would lead to impermissible syllable structure, for example

*krzyk+ń shout   *szep+ń whisper   *mok+ń get wet

(we bypass the problem of truncating part of -*ną*, which is discussed later). As a result of this analysis, -*ną* verbs cease to be idiosyncratic and appear to behave in a regular fashion.

2. The items in 2 take the longer imperative suffix, since their roots end in highly marked obstruent+sonorant sequences (which violate the hierarchy of sonority), such as [dń], [gl], [śl]. Thus, the attachment of -*ij* prevents the formation of such words as

*dudń rumble   *nagl urge

3. The variation displayed by the imperatives in 3 is motivated by the fact that speakers' judgements as to clusters such as [stf], [lb] and [źv] in the coda position are varied. Such sequences seem to occupy a place in the middle of the hierarchy of tolerance and, as such, admit both /ĭ/ and /ijĭ/, for example

u+wielb / *u+wielb+ij* adore

It should be added that because of considerable tolerance of consonantal clusters in Polish in general, as well as because of economy of expression, the shorter imperatives are used more frequently, particularly among younger generations.

4. Verbs in 4 must obligatorily combine with the syllabic imperative suffix, since after the deletion of the VS and the root-yer not only the structures of the coda but also of the whole syllable is violated; simply, with the removal of the only vowel, impossible forms such as [zv, ss, sw] are created. Thus, the attachment of -*ij* is needed here to allow for well-formed items.

Finally, as Bethin observes, reference to syllable structure makes it possible to predict the direction of language change, i.e. those cases in which the overt imperative desinence is likely to be retained and when it is likely to be lost. No such predictions are possible in an analysis in which the only factor that determines the occurrence of *-ij* is the presence of a yer in the verbal stem.

It seems that the arguments just expressed sufficiently demonstrate the superiority of the approach which refers to syllable structure to the one involving the use of yer vowels. What remains to be done is to incorporate this conclusion into a linguistic description.

While we accept the validity of Bethin's observations, the solution she proposes for handling the imperative forms appears less convincing. Bethin argues that there is just one imperative suffix *-ij*, which attaches to every verb stem. Rules that assign syllable structure apply and reapply in a cyclic fashion after the attachment of every affix. At the cycle where verbal stems are processed, syllabification takes place, and if the stem ends in a marked coda, *-ij* is syllabified with it. If there is no violation of the coda structure *-ij* is not syllabified with the verb and, as a result, it remains unpronounced.

The problem with Bethin's solution is that it lacks phonological adequacy. In other words, it does not explain how it is possible to obtain several different phonetic manifestations of the imperative, shown at the beginning of this section under a), b) and c). In these instances evidence can be given that the imperative morpheme is indeed /ĭ/, for example

it induces the palatalization of final consonants in
gry[ś] bite (cf. *gry[z]ę* I bite)
nie[ś] carry (cf. *nio[s]ę* I carry)
it brings about the emergence of the root yer in
bi[e]rz take (cf. *[br]ać* id. infinitive)
pi[e]rz wash (cf. *[pr]ać* id. infinitive)
it triggers the raising of /o/ to [u] in
r[o]b+ię I do – *r[u]b* id. imper.
o+zd[o]b+ię I will adorn – *o+zd[u]b* id. imper.

It is not clear how these facts would be handled by Bethin with her assumption that there is only one imperative suffix, i.e. *-ij*, which, when unsyllabified, has no phonological effect on the verbal stem. To put it differently, phonological facts require positing two imperative suffixes and not just one. Hence the speaker's choice is not whether he should syllabify -*ij* or not, but which suffix to select for a given verb stem.

What is also clear is the fact that the choice of either of the imperative markers must make reference to the syllable structure of the stem *after it has been subject to the operation of various allomorphy and phonological rules*. In other words, imperative formation appears to have access not to the underlying but rather to more surface-like structure.

Consider the verb

dudn+i+ć rumble

At the phonological level the stem of this item ends in a vowel (i.e., -*i*) and, if this form is available to imperative formation, the suffix /ǐ/ should be appended to it, as is the case with other -*i* verbs, for example

chodz+i+ć walk → *chodź* id. imper.
świec+i+ć light → *świeć* id. imper.

Nevertheless, it is not /ǐ/, but rather -*ij* that forms the imperative

dudn+ij rumble

which indicates that imperative formation has access to the verb in question after the verb suffix has been removed.

One may be tempted to claim that the process in focus simply ignores verb suffixes and is sensitive only to the structure of the root; it 'sees' that the root of *dudn+i+ć* ends in a consonant cluster and, therefore, attaches -*ij* to it. Note, however, that such an approach is not possible, since frequently VSs do have influence upon the choice of the imperative desinence. Compare, for instance, two pairs of verbs (the -*ną* verb expresses unreiterated action) and their imperative forms

pełz+aj+ą they crawl → *pełz+aj* id. imper.
pełz+ną+ć crawl → *pełz+n+ij* id. imper.

Although the roots are identical, in the first case /i/ is appended, while in the second case it is -*ij*, which can only be attributed to the presence of different verb suffixes. In other words, imperative formation seems to 'know' that [n] of -*ną* will be part of the consonantal cluster [wzn], undesirable in the word-final position, and whose emergence must be prevented by the addition of -*ij* to it. Similarly, imperative formation attaches -*ij* to such items as

śp+ij sleep, imper. (from /sɨp+a/)
zw+ij name, imper. (from /zɨv+a/)

as if it could foresee that once the VS and the root vowel are deleted, unacceptable items such as [sp] and [zv] would arise. As Bethin notes, imperative formation does not refer as much to the presence of yer vowels, as to their absence. To put it differently, the process under consideration seems to be endowed with some kind of global power, in the sense that it has access not to the underlying structures, but to the result of the application of phonological rules.

Note that the lexical approach, with its intermingling of morphological and phonological rules, is of little use here. As has already been explained, within this framework it is crucial for yers to be preserved until the post-cyclic stage. Consequently, they are all present throughout the operation of WFRs, which can refer to their presence, but not to their absence. This follows from the assumption that, as Booij and Rubach (1987:1) put it, 'cyclic rules interact with morphology, whereas postcyclic rules apply after morphology'.

To clarify the situation, consider the imperatives such as

śpij sleep   *zwij* name

once again. At the stage when imperative formation takes place, the relevant structures (after the removal of the VS) are the following

/sɨp/   and   /zɨv/

These forms are now subject to the -*ij* attachment, but only by virtue of the fact that they contain yers, and not because the deletion of the lax vowels would create impossible items. On the other hand, -*ij* is attached to the verb like

dudn+ij rumble

since the root terminates in a heavy consonantal cluster. Thus, in the lexical analysis, imperative formation must contain at least two independent clauses such as

assign -*ij* to yer-stems
assign -*ij* to those stems whose roots terminate in heavy consonantal clusters.

This is evidently an unsatisfactory solution, since two independent clauses fail to express the essence of the process under scrutiny, namely that in all instances -*ij* is added to verbs in order to prevent the rise of impermissible structures. In other words, an adequate formulation of imperative formation must express the unity of the process as well as its inherent nature.

We should like to suggest that imperative formation, just like comparative degree formation, discussed in the preceding section, does not operate on phonological strings, but on structures that have undergone the allomorphy and phonological rules. Such already processed forms return to WFRs, are subject to /i/ or /ij/ attachment, and then re-enter the phonological component. The claim thus is that imperative formation is a morphological rule which takes phonetic inputs and can refer to the surface syllable structure of verbal stems. It can be formulated as follows

Imperative formation

$$[X]_{Imper.} \rightarrow \begin{cases} /a/ \; [[X]_V +ij]_{Imper.}, \text{ if } [X]_V \text{ violates syllable structure} \\ /b/ \; [[X]_V +i]_{Imper.} \text{ in other cases} \end{cases}$$

condition: inputs processed by the phonology

Phonetic inputs to WFRs

Let us now illustrate this procedure with examples representing all types of Polish verbs. The simplest case is with -*aj*, -*ej*, and C-stems. Study the derivation of the imperatives *czytaj* 'read', *malej* 'become smaller', and *paś* 'graze'. The specification 'imperative' with verbal stems is assigned to input strings to imperative formation. Syllable structure is presented in a simplified fashion.

WFRs	[čit+aj]$_{Imper.}$	[mał+ej]$_{Imper.}$	[pas]$_{Imper.}$
Palatalization	–	l	–
Syllabification	[čit+aj] σ σ	[mal+ej] σ σ	[pas] σ
WFRs – imperative formation	[čit+aj+ï]	[mal+ej+ï]	[pas+ï]
Palatalization	–	–	ś
Lower	φ [čitaj]	φ [malej]	φ [paś]

Nothing of interest happens on the first pass through the phonology. Since the stems end in single consonants, imperative formation attaches the unrestricted imperative suffix in all three cases. On the second pass, /ï/ palatalizes the final consonant in /pas/ and is everywhere deleted by the rule of lower.

The verbs in -*e* and -*i* do not display the presence of these suffixes in imperative forms. Therefore, they necessitate an allomorphy rule such as

$$\begin{Bmatrix} -e \\ -i \end{Bmatrix} \rightarrow \phi \, / \, \underline{\quad}] \text{ Imper.}$$

This rule corresponds to Rubach's already mentioned front vowel truncation. Consider now the derivation of *leć* 'fly, imper.', *proś* 'ask, imper.', and *dudnij* 'rumble, imper.' (*σ means that in this case syllable structure is violated).

Phonetic inputs to WFRs

WFRs	[let+e]$_{\text{Imper.}}$	[pros+i]$_{\text{Imper.}}$	[dudn+i]$_{\text{Imper.}}$
Allomorphy -e/-i deletion	ϕ	ϕ	ϕ
Syllabification	[let] |/ σ	[pros] |/ σ	[dudn] |/ *σ
WFRs – imperative formation	[let+ĭ]	[pros+ĭ]	[dudn+ij]
Palatalization	ć	ś	ń
Lower	ϕ	ϕ	–
	[leć]	[proś]	[dudńij]

In these cases the rule of -e/-i deletion removes the VSs at the beginning of the derivation. Syllabification assigns unmarked syllable structure to the first two verbs, but specifies [dn] as an impossible coda in the third case. On return to the word formation component [let] and [pros] receive the suffix /ĭ/, while /ij/ is attached to [dudn]. All the appended suffixes palatalize the preceding consonants, and yers are deleted by lower. Note that many verbs which admit two imperatives, for example *wielb* / *wielbij* 'adore' will belong here as well. Those speakers who find clusters like [lb] 'heavy', will attach the longer suffix, while others will append /ĭ/.[10]

Verbs with the VS -a retain it in imperative forms, with the exception of those instances in which the root contains a high lax vowel. This is expressed by the following allomorphy statement

$$-a \rightarrow \phi \;/\; \begin{bmatrix} V \\ +\text{high} \\ -\text{tense} \end{bmatrix} C \underline{\quad}]_{\text{Imper.}}$$

Below we present the derivation of *śpij* sleep, imper. and *pisz* write, imper.

WFRs	[pis+a]$_{\text{Imper.}}$	[sĭp+a]$_{\text{Imper.}}$
-a-deletion	–	ϕ
Palatalization	p'	–
Lower	–	ϕ
Syllabification	[p'is+a] |/ |/ σ σ	[sp] |/ *σ

WFRs – imperative formation	[p'is+a+ĭ]	[sp+ij]
J-insertion	j	–
Palatalization	š	p'
Vowel deletion	φ	–
Lower	φ	–
J-deletion	φ	–
Palatal assimilation	–	ś
	[p'iš]	[śp'ij]

The derivation of *pisz* involves the attachment of /ĭ/, the insertion of the palatal glide before a sequence of two vowels, j-palatalization of [s], and the deletion of the glide as well as both vowels. In the case of the second verb, the loss of the VS and the root vowel on the first pass results in the assignment of the marked (in fact impossible) syllable structure, and consequently, the attachment of -*ij*.

Finally, we are left with -*ną* verbs. The following prephonological truncation rule is needed for them

nĭn → n / ——]$_{Imper.}$

The imperatives *toń* 'drown' (from *tonąć*), *klepnij* 'pat' (from *klepnąć*) and *klnij* 'swear' (from *kḷać*) are derived as follows.

WFRs	[to+nĭn]$_{Imper.}$	[klep+nĭn]$_{Imper.}$	[klĭn]$_{Imper.}$
nĭn-allomorphy	[to+n]	[klep+n]	–
Lower	–	–	φ
Syllabification	[to+n] \\/ σ	[klep+n] \\\/ *σ	[kln] \\/ *σ
WFRs – imperative formation	[to+n+ĭ]	[klep+n+ij]	[kln+ij]
Palatalization	ń	ń	ń
Lower	φ	–	–
	[toń]	[klepńij]	[klńij]

In these derivations *nin*-allomorphy removes part of the VS in the first two verbs, and makes the stem of *klepnąć* unacceptable in terms of syllable structure (an obstruent + sonorant coda). Consequently, the attachment of -*ij* is necessary in this case. The same is true of *kląć*, in which on the first phonological pass lower deletes the only vowel within the stem. No such need arises for *tonąć*, which returns to the morphological component with the stem ending in a single consonant. Hence /i/ and not /ij/ is attached to it.

Let us take stock of the analysis of imperative forms presented in this section. The examination of such items has revealed that the distribution of the imperative suffixes /i/ and /ij/ strictly depends on the syllabic structure of verbal stems. More important, it has turned out that what is of significance to imperative formation is not the underlying or some intermediate form of verbs, but the structure obtained due to the application of all word-level allomorphy and phonological rules. We have drawn the conclusion that none of the existing descriptions can be regarded as adequate with respect to the process under investigation. It has been suggested that, in order to handle imperative forms, use should be made of the phonology–morphology loop that has been argued for in Chapter 3 as well as in section 4.1 of the present chapter. We have demonstrated that the multiple processing of verbal stems yields the correct imperative forms of all types of verbs.[11] Furthermore, this procedure allows imperative formation to refer to the surface syllable structure of verbs.

The next section examines yet another morphological process which brings further support for the procedure suggested for comparative degree formation and imperative formation.

4.3 Augmentative back-formation

Polish possesses several very productive patterns of forming augmentative nouns, of which three, discussed by Szymanek (1986), will be of interest to us here. The first method consists in the truncation of the suffix -*k* /-ɨk/,[12] for example

1. *szpil+k+a* pin → *szpil+a*
   ścier+k+a cloth → *ścier+a*
   łap+ów+k+a bribe → *łap+ów+a*

ciot+k+a aunt → ciot+a
plot+k+a gossip → plot+a

Such augmentatives are very frequently used in colloquial Polish.

Another way of forming augmentatives is through the replacement of the stem-final sibilant with the voiceless velar spirant [x], for example

2. papiero[s] cigarette → papiero[x]
   mię[s]+o meat → mię[x]+o
   kiełba[s]+a sausage → kiełba[x]+a
   Ba[ś]+a fem. name → Ba[x]+a
   Ry[ś]+o masc. name → Ry[x]+o

Finally, there are augmentative nouns in which both k-truncation and consonant modification take place, for example

3. ty[šk]+a spoon → ty[x]+a
   kre[sk]+a line → kre[x]+a
   de[sk]+a board → de[x]+a
   pro[šk]+i pills → pro[x]+y
   ła[sk]+a favour → ła[x]+a

All three cases can be gathered into one rule (based on Szymanek 1986), which may be termed augmentative back-formation.[13]

Augmentative back-formation

$$[+ \ldots \ldots /S\ C_0^2/ \underset{[x]}{\overset{\overset{\phi}{\uparrow}}{\downarrow}} + /\text{ik}/]_N, \text{ where } S = \text{sibilant}$$

(semantics: augmentative)

The 'upper' expansion of the rule accounts for the forms in 1, for example

/špil+ĭk+a/ → /špil+a/ (*szpila* pin)
    ↓
    φ

the lower expansion for the items in 2, for example

/baś+a/ → /bax+a/ (*Bacha* fem. name)
    ↓
    [x]

and both clauses are responsible for the examples in 3,[14] for example

/kres+ĭk+a/ → /krex+a/ (*recha* line)
   ↓ ↓
   [x] φ

Augmentative nouns are very interesting from the morphological point of view (Szymanek 1986).[15] In what follows, however, we shall be concerned mostly with their phonological properties, i.e. with the problem of their correct derivation. Consider the following group of examples.

a) *groch+[u]w+k+a* pea soup → *groch+[u]w+a* id. augm.
    (cf. *groch[o]wy* of peas, adj. – **grochowa*)
    har+[u]w+k+a hard work → *har+[u]+w+a* id. augm.
    (cf. *har[o]wać* work hard – **harowa*)
    łap+[u]w+k+a bribe → *łap+[u]w+a* id. augm.
    (cf. *łap[o]wnik* bribe-taker – **łapowa*)
    mr[u]w+k+a ant → *mr[u]w+a* id. augm.
    (cf. *mr[o]wisko* ant hill – **mrowa*)
    dw+[u]j+k+a bad mark, two → *dw+[u]j+a* id. augm.
    (cf. *dw[o]j+e* two, of people – **dwoja*)

In these examples both the base nouns and the augmentative forms derived from them display the presence of the high round vowel [u]. As the items given in parentheses demonstrate, [u] is of the alternating kind since in related forms it emerges as [o]. As was pointed out in Chapter 3, in such instances it is usually assumed that the mid vowel is the underlying segment and [u] is derived from it through the rule of raising, which applies across a voiced consonant before a yer in the following syllable, for example

ogr[o]d+y gardens – *ogr[u]d+ek* id. dim. sg. (from /ogrod+ĭk+ĭ/)
k[o]z+a she-goat – *k[u]z+k+a* id. dim. (from /koz+ĭk+a/)

Clearly, the context of raising is met in the base nouns, in which it applies.

/mrov+ĭk+a/ → *mr[u]wka* ant

Curiously enough, raising takes place also in the augmentatives despite the fact that the conditioning high lax vowel is absent in their phonological shapes, for example

/mrov+a/ → *mr[u]wa* ant, augm.

and forms such as **mrova* are to be expected. It should be added that we are not dealing with any exceptions here; the raised vowel is present in all forms of type a).
Examine now another group of items.

b) *s[e]t+k+a* hundred → *s[e]t+a* id. augm.
    (cf. *[st]o* hundred) – **sta*
   ós[e]m+k+a eight → *ós[e]m+a* id. augm.
    (cf. *ó[sm]y* eighth) – **ósma*
   kump[e]l+k+a pal, fem. → *kump[e]l+a* id. augm.
    (cf. *kum[pl]ować* be pals) – **kumpla*
   rzodki[e]w+k+a radish → *rzodki[e]w+a* id. augm.
    (cf. *rzod[kf']i* radish, gen. sg.) – **rzodkwa*

These words display the 'e~o' alternation; the front mid vowel is present both in the semantically neutral and in pejorative nouns, and is absent in related forms (given in parentheses). This, as has many times been argued, points to the underlying high lax vowel and the operation of lower. The occurrence of [e] indicates the presence of another yer in the following syllable, as the latter brings out the emergence of the former. Thus, *setka* 'hundred' is derived as follows

/sĭt+ĭk+a/
Lower   e   ϕ
[setka]

The examples of interest, however, are augmentative nouns; here the vowel [e] appears on the surface although no high lax vowel can be found later in the word. The phonological structure of *seta* 'hundred, augm.' is thus

/sĭt+a/

and, consequently, the root-yer should be deleted to yield **sta*. Clearly, this does not happen and [e] is lowered rather than deleted.

The examples in c) confront us with yet another phonological problem.

c)   *ci[a]st+k+o* cake → *ci[a]ch+o* id. augm.
        (cf. *ci[e]ście* cake, loc. sg.) – **ciecho*
    powi[a]st+k+a story → *powi[a]ch+a* id. augm.
        (cf. *powi[e]ść* novel) – **powiecha*
    wi[o]s+k+a village → *wi[o]ch+a* id. augm.
        (cf. *wi[e]ś* village) – **wiecha*

In this case we are dealing with the alternations of front and back vowels; phonological /ē/ emerges as [e] before palatal consonants, and as [a] in the context of back coronals, while lax /ĕ/ surfaces as [e] and [o] respectively. This happens due to the rule of backing, briefly presented in the preceding chapter, for example

    mi[eść]e town, loc. sg. – *mi[ast]o* id. nom. sg.
    pl[eć]e he weaves – *pl[ot]ę* I weave

The effects of backing can be observed in both types of nouns in c). While this is the expected result with the neutral nouns, in which the vowel in question is followed by a dental consonant, the occurrence of [a] and [o] in the augmentatives, i.e. before the velar spirant, must be viewed as deviating from the regular pattern. In other words, the existing phonological rules lead to the following incorrect derivations

	/vex+a/
Palatalization	v'
Backing	–
	[v'exa]

Equally unexpected phonological phenomena can be observed in yet another class of words.

d) *wi[ó]z+k+a* bundle – *wi[ó]ch+a* id. augm.
    (cf. *wi[ę]ź* tie) – **więcha*
 pi[ó]st+k+a fist, dim. – *pi[ó]ch+a* id. augm.
    (cf. *pi[ę]ść* fist) – **pięcha*
 pami[ó]t+k+a keepsake – *pami[ó]ch+a* id. augm.
    (cf. *pami[ę]ć* memory) – **pamięcha*

Examples in d) contain alternating nasal vowels. As the discussion of the VS *-ną* has pointed out, in such instances the phonological high lax vowel is postulated at the underlying level. The vowel in question, roughly speaking, undergoes tensing and the subsequent backing to [o] in the context of the yer vowel in the suffix /-ĭk/, for example

g[ę]ś goose – *g[ó]s+k+a* id. dim.
cz[ę]ść part – *cz[ó]st+k+a* id. dim.

These changes are effected by two rules (Gussmann 1980a:105–6) that we shall jointly refer to as nasal tensing. In view of the generalizations expressed by the process under discussion, it is not surprising to find [ó] in the semantically neutral nouns in d) since they all contain the suffix -*k*. What has to be accounted for, however, is the application of nasal tensing in the augmentatives, in which the conditions for the rule are not met. To put it differently, although -*k* is absent in the augmentatives, nasal tensing takes place in them.

Let us recapitulate the observations made in the previous pages. We have examined four groups of nouns as well as augmentatives derived from them. In all cases the application of several phonological rules has been noted: regular in semantically neutral nouns and totally idiosyncratic in the augmentatives. This means that four independently motivated rules of Polish, i.e., raising, lower, backing and nasal tensing operate in pejorative nouns despite the fact that in none of the cases is their context satisfied. The issue undoubtedly calls for some explanation.

One possible approach to the issue in question is to assume that the context of all these rules should be expanded so as to cover such cases as well. This is to say that there should be added to all the rules involved a separate clause such as: 'apply rule X in augmentative back-formations'. A move of this sort is not advisable, however; the processes in question are phonologically conditioned and this fact would be considerably obscured by the addition of the morphological context. Furthermore, the same clause would have to be repeated four times, which means the loss of generalization inherent in the phenomenon under investigation. Evidently, this solution must be rejected.

Another possibility is to consider all four phonological changes as part of the process of augmentative back-formation. This amounts to claiming that the formation of pejorative nouns of the type under discussion, apart from consonantal modifications (such as the replacement of the sibilant with the velar spirant), consists in certain vocalic processes such as raising, backing, etc. In other words, it can be assumed that the occurrence of some vowels (for example [u]), is a marker of pejorativeness. This claim, however, can be easily refuted as there are numerous back-formed augmentatives in which no vocalic changes can be observed. For instance, raising does not take place in such items as

    ci[o]t+k+a aunt → *ci[o]t+a* id. augm. (*cióta)
    pl[o]t+k+a gossip → *pl[o]t+a* id. augm. (*plóta)
    dew[o]t+k+a bigoted woman → *dew[o]t+a* id. augm.
      (*dewóta)

The word *plota* 'gossip, augm.' is of particular interest since no raising occurs here even though the root vowel does undergo it in the related form *pl[u]t+ł* he talked nonsense

Clearly, there is no direct connection between the morphological process of augmentative back-formation and the application of individual phonological rules.

Without pursuing any further possibilities, let us point out that the vowels in the augmentative forms are identical with the vowels of the nouns from which they are derived, for example

w[u]d+k+a vodka → *w[u]d+a* id. augm.
s[e]t+k+a hundred → *s[e]t+a* id. augm.
ci[a]st+k+o cake → *ci[a]ch+o* id. augm.
wi[ō]z+k+a bundle → *wi[ō]ch+a* id. augm.

This clearly suggests that all the relevant phonological processes take place prior to the truncation of the suffix *-k* and the *s* → *ch* change. To put it differently, the correct results can be obtained only if augmentative back-formation is allowed to operate on nouns which have already been processed by phonological rules. Only then can the identity of root vowels in both neutral and augmentative forms be accounted for.

Below we present the derivation of the nouns *dwója* 'bad mark' and *seta* hundred.

WFRs	$[dv+oj]_N +ik]_{Augm.}$	$[[sit]_N +ik]_{Augm.}$
Raising	u	–
Lower	ɸ	e ɸ
WFRs	$[[dv+uj]_N +k]_{Augm.}$	$[[set]_N +k]_{Augm.}$
Augmentative back-formation	$[dv+uj]_N$	$[set]_N$
Inflection	$[dv+uj+a]_N$	$[set+a]_N$
Phonology	–	–
	[dvuja]	[seta]

When the forms marked as inputs to augmentative back-formation enter the phonological component, the yers present in

165

Phonetic inputs to WFRs

the suffix /-ɨk/ induce raising in the first case and the lowering of the root vowel in the second example. The yer vowels in both suffixes are deleted. On return to WFRs, augmentative back-formation removes -*k* and inflectional endings are appended. The second pass through the phonology does not bring any major changes.

Consider now the derivations of *wiącha* 'bundle'[16] and *ciacho* 'cake', which represent the two remaining types of augmentative nouns.

WFRs	$[[\text{vĭnz}+a]_V +\text{ĭk}]_{\text{Augm.}}$	$[[\text{ćēst}]_N +\text{ĭk}]_{\text{Augm.}}$
VST	φ	–
Nasalization	ĩ	–
Palatalization	v'	–
Backing	–	a
Nasal tensing	õ	–
Lower	φ	φ
WFRs	$[[\text{v'õz}]_V +k]_{\text{Augm.}}$	$[[\text{ćast}]_N +k]_{\text{Augm.}}$
Augmentative back-formation	$[\text{v'õx}]_N$	$[\text{ćax}]_N$
Inflection	$[\text{v'õx}+a]_N$	$[\text{ćax}+o]_N$
Phonology	–	–
	[v'õxa]	[ćaxo]

On the first phonological pass the root-vowel of *wiązka* is subject to nasal tensing and emerges as [o]. The phonological front vowel in *ciastko* undergoes backing since it is followed by a coronal consonant. Lower deletes the suffix yers. The forms thus produced re-enter the morphological component, where augmentative back-formation truncates -*k* and replaces the preceding consonants with [x]. After the attachment of inflection another pass through the phonology follows, yielding the correct forms *wiącha* and *ciacho*.

To conclude, augmentative back-formation appears to belong to those morphological processes which operate on inputs which have already been subject to the application of phonological rules.[17] Due to this approach augmentative nouns can be derived properly without the necessity of complicating four phonological rules of Polish.

4.4 Other cases

In the preceding sections of the present chapter we have examined three morphological processes of Polish: comparative degree formation, imperative formation and augmentative back-formation. It appears that considerable gains can be achieved if all these rules are allowed to refer not to the underlying or intermediate structures of their inputs, but to the forms which result from the application of all word-level rules. In the first two cases the suggested procedure enables simple, general formulations of WFRs, while in the third instance it allows for the correct derivation of augmentative nouns without the need to morphologize well-established phonological rules. This, coupled with the phonological arguments advanced in the preceding chapter, constitutes, in our view, sufficient evidence for the proposed organization of the grammar which involves the phonology-morphology loop.

Several significant questions arise in connection with the suggested procedure. One of them is the issue whether there are other WFRs in Polish which require surface-like inputs. No other morphological rules have been investigated in enough detail to justify any definite conclusions, but it seems that more examples of this sort can be found.

Polish, with its rich derivational and inflectional morphology, allows for the formation of several different kinds of diminutives. One type, frequently encountered in the so-called 'baby talk', resembles formally augmentative back-formation discussed in the previous section; it consists in the replacement of the hard consonant with the corresponding palatal, for example

no[s] nose – *no[ś]+o* id. dim.
brzu[x] belly – *brzu[ś]+o* id. dim.
Ró[ž]+a fem. name – *Ró[ź]+a* id. dim.

Moreover, the modification of the root-final consonants is

frequently accompanied by the truncation of the suffix /-ĭk/, for example

dzia[d]+ek grandfather – *dzia[dź]+o* id. dim.
kum+o[ś]+k+a crone – *kum+o[ś]+a* id. dim.
Zby[š]+ek masc. name – *Zby[š]+o* id. dim.

Consider now the following group of nouns

n[u]ż+k+a leg, dim. – *n[u]zi+a* id. dim.
  (cf. *n[o]ga* leg) – *nozia
t[u]ż+k+o bed – *t[u]zi+o* id. dim.
  (cf. *t[o]że* bed) – *tozio
w[u]z+ek pram – *w[u]zi+o* id. dim.
  (cf. *w[o]zić* drive sb) – *wozio

In these items the vowels in both the base nouns and the diminutives are high rounded and result from the raising of /o/, as the related forms indicate. Yet only in the bases is the context for raising met.

The items such as

pi[e]s+ek dog, dim. – *pi[e]si+o* id. dim.
  (cf. *[ps]a* dog, gen. sg.) – *psio
r[ō]cz+k+a hand, dim. – *r[ō]si+a* id. dim.
  (cf. *r[ę]ka* hand) – *ręsia

display the operation of lower and nasal tensing, although these rules appear to be applicable only in the case of base forms.

Again, as with augmentatives, these facts can be accounted for if the suffix /-ĭk/ is allowed to affect the root-vowels before it is truncated by diminutive back-formation, as the process in question might be dubbed. In other words, we seem to be dealing with another WFR which requires phonetic inputs.

Similar assumptions must probably be made in order to derive diminutive nouns such as

pi[e]si+ulek, pi[e]si+uni+o dog, dim. (cf. *[ps]y* dogs)
t[e]p+uś, t[e]p+ulek, t[e]p+uni+o head, dim.
  (cf. *[wb]y* heads)

s[e]t+uchn+a hundred, dim. (cf. *[st]o* hundred)

In these cases the presence of [e] in the diminutives can be explained if the items in question are derived from the phonetic forms of

pi[e]s+ek dog   *ł[e]p+ek* head   *s[e]t+k+a* hundred

with the subsequent truncation of *-/e/k*.

In view of the fact that more WFRs than those presented in the preceding sections appear to require access to the output of phonological derivation, a legitimate question is whether all these processes have any common denominator. Augmentative back-formation and diminutive back-formation might suggest that it is the expressive part of the vocabulary that is derived in the fashion proposed in this book. This generalization, however, is evidently false. The augmentative suffix *-isko*, for instance, requires phonological inputs as seen in

samoch[u]d car – *samoch[o]dz+isko* id. augm.
  (**samochódzisko*)
ł[e]b head – *[wb]+isko* id. augm. (**łebisko*)
mi[a]st+o town – *mi[e]ść+isko* id. augm. (**miaścisko*)
z[ó]b tooth – *z[ē]b+isko* id. augm. (**ząbisko*)

Here phonetic inputs result in the incorrect starred forms, since the root vowels are subject to raising, lower, backing and nasal tensing in the base nouns, but not in the augmentatives.

Also the diminutive suffix /ĭk/ must attach to underlying forms. Otherwise the presence of the vowel [e] in the diminutives below could not be accounted for, for example

książ[š+k]+a book – *książ+[e]cz+k+a* id. dim. (**książczka*)
wstąż[š+k]+a ribbon – *wstąż+[e]cz+k+a* id. dim. (**wstążczka*)
la[l+k]+a doll – *lal+[e]cz+k+a* id. dim. (**lalczka*)

In brief, not all WFRs which produce expressive forms operate on phonetic inputs.

It seems, however, that comparative degree formation, imperative formation, augmentative back-formation and diminutive back-formation have at least one feature in common, namely they all belong to what in the Slavic morphological tradition is known as modificational derivation (Grzegorczykowa 1979:28), i.e. processes which do not change radically the properties of the base, but which only modify its meaning by adding some features to it, such as size, masculinity, perfectiveness, etc. Nevertheless, as the examples involving *-isko* augmentatives and *-k/a/* diminutives demonstrate, not all WFRs of this type take surface-like inputs. This means that whenever this is the case, a given morphological rule will have to be marked with such a property.

A significant issue is whether the suggested method of deriving some classes of words constitutes an idiosyncratic property of Polish, or whether other languages employ it as well. It is the latter assumption which seems to hold true. Recall that in Chapter 2 it was mentioned that according to Siegel (1974) certain morphological processes in English are sensitive to the stress pattern of the base. The noun-forming suffix *-al*, for instance, requires that the final syllable of the verb to which it is appended be stressed. Other rules that appear to display sensitivity to stress are, in Siegel's view, *-ful* and *-(e)teria* suffixations. If stress in English is not treated as a lexical property of individual words, but as a productive phonological rule, the assumption can be that sensitivity to it points to the phonetic nature of inputs to a given WFR. This follows from the proposed organization of the grammar; if phonology and morphology are distinct components, the only way in which phonological information might become available to WFRs is through the phonology–morphology loop, activated primarily by the input conditions on morphological processes.

Another example of the applicability of the proposed procedure can be found in Dutch. Booij (1981) argues that in this language there are instances in which morphological and phonological rules must be intermingled in the derivation of some complex words. The relevant example is the word *ambassadrice* 'female ambassador', derived from *ambassadeur* 'ambassador' by replacing the suffix *-eur* with *-rice*. *Ambassadeur*, in turn, is derived from *ambassade* 'embassy'. An important phonological rule is schwa deletion, which removes the vowel schwa before another vowel. If all morphological rules precede all phonological rules, the incorrect form is created.

Phonetic inputs to WFRs

	[ambasadə]$_N$
WFRs	
-*eur* affixation	[[ambasadə]$_N$ +ör]$_N$
-*eur*/-*rice* substitution	[[ambasadə]$_N$ +risə]$_N$
Prevocalic schwa deletion	—
	*[ambasadərisə]

The problem with this derivation is that the schwa vowel fails to delete in spite of the fact that it is not found in the proper phonetic form [ambasadrisə]. Booij observes that the correct result can be obtained by placing prevocalic schwa deletion between the two morphological rules.

-*eur* affixation	[[ambasadə]$_N$ +ör]$_N$
Prevocalic schwa deletion	ɸ
-*eur*/-*rice* substitution	+risə
	[ambasadrisə]

This method is, of course, typical of the lexical framework.

We should like to point out that exactly the same result can be arrived at if -*rice* formation is allowed on phonologically derived inputs.

WFRs	[[ambasadə]$_N$ +ör]-*rice* formation
Prevocalic schwa deletion	ɸ
WFRs	
-*rice* formation	[[[ambasad]$_N$ +ör]$_N$ +risə]$_N$
-*ör* truncation	ɸ
Phonology	—
	[ambasadrisə]

We conclude that the phonology–morphology loop is needed not only in Polish, but also in other languages although, of course, more detailed studies are needed to achieve more evidence in this respect.

A comment on the content of the notions such as 'surface-like structures' and 'phonetic inputs' also seems in order. These terms might imply that we are dealing here with forms fully specified as to phonetic detail. This is not exactly true, however. For one thing, since phonological rules in our approach are allowed to refer to morphological brackets and categories (such as the presence of specific affixes), we assume that they are preserved throughout the whole derivation and, consequently, also in the structures we have termed 'surface-like'. Thus, bracket erasure will be treated as a convention which plays no significant role in the derivation, and which applies directly before the phonetic representations are formed.

Another issue concerns the nature of phonological rules that create 'phonetic inputs'. These are all word-level rules (where 'word' means 'phonological word' – for a discussion of this notion and its role in phonology see Chapter 5), which do not comprise those processes that affect larger strings. Voice assimilation in Polish, for instance, operates within the domain of the phonological phrase and does not apply in the derivation of surface-like structures. Consider, for instance, the following examples.

mró[f]ka ant → *mró[v]a* id. augm.
stó[f]ka hundred → *stó[v]a* id. augm.
wó[t]ka vodka → *wó[d]a* id. augm.

Here the augmentative nouns are pronounced with voiced obstruents, that is, the base nouns are devoiced due to the presence of the following [k] via voice assimilation. If the rule in question applied prior to augmentative back-formation, incorrect forms

**mró[f]a*   *stó[f]a   *wó[t]a

would result. Clearly, voice assimilation does not take part in the formation of the augmentatives, owing to the fact that it is a phrase-level rule. It should be added that these comments refer also to the nature of forms which are obtained from the multiple application of phonological rules suggested for complex verbs in Polish.

Let us go over the major results of the analysis presented in this as well as in the preceding chapter. We have examined the most important problems involved in the derivation of complex verbs in Polish and in the formation of several productive morphological processes. Two types of descriptions: the traditional generative and the cyclic/lexical have been applied with the conclusion that neither of them can be viewed as fully adequate. In some instances the SPE framework yields proper results, in other situations the lexical approach appears more satisfactory. Yet in the majority of cases under scrutiny, particularly those comprising the WFRs of the present chapter, neither of these two descriptive possibilities is capable of handling the relevant data. The principal source of difficulty is the mutual relationship between morphological and phonological rules: sometimes correct derivations require *the application of all WFRs prior to the phonology* (for example the '*wiertarka*' and the '*samochodzisko*' types), in other situations *morphological operations must take place after phonological processes* (for example, the '*seta*' and the '*klęknij* types). The lexical and the linear approaches fail exactly because they admit only one possibility: either the intermingling of *all WFRs with the phonology* (the lexical model), or the application of *all WFRs before phonological rules* (the traditional framework), while the facts appear to require a combination of both approaches. This requirement is satisfied by the suggested mechanism of returning from the output of phonological rules to the word formation component and to the phonology again, which procedure is carried out in certain cases only. This means that usually the processing of lexical items will proceed in the traditional generative fashion: from the morphological to the phonological component, i.e. unidirectionally. Such an ordering of both types of rules is a natural consequence of the proposed organization of the grammar; morphology and phonology are separate and distinct, with the former creating inputs to the latter. It follows that the modified processing of words proposed in this book will be employed only in specific cases. We have identified two such situations: when the return to morphology is required by certain types of structures (for example complex verbs in Polish, the '*kwiaciarka*' type) and when it is a WFR which must have access to the information supplied by phonological rules (for example three WFRs in Polish discussed in this chapter, English *-al* affixation, Dutch *-rice* formation).

At this point it might be useful to repeat the major advantages of the suggested procedure. First of all, due to it those WFRs which employ the information provided by the phonology obtain access to it, while those rules that do not, are not unnecessarily intermixed with phonological processes. Furthermore, by operating on phonetic structures WFRs can be formulated in a simple and general manner. The same is true of phonological and allomorphy rules such as verb suffix truncation, DI tensing, lower, backing, raising and nasal tensing, which do not have to refer to the derivational history of words, and apply in several different fashions depending on the lexical and grammatical category of words. In this way we can retain the position that while individual phonological rules interact with morphology only in a limited manner, there is no such restriction on the interaction of both components. To put it differently, our proposal amounts to reducing the power of individual rules at the cost of increasing the role of the whole components. Finally, owing to the proposed mechanism we are able to produce correct derivations of complex verbs, comparative degree adjectives, imperative verbs and back-formed augmentatives, which is non-trivial in view of the fact that other approaches frequently fail to handle this problem.

All this has been possible due to the loop from phonology to morphology, i.e. due to giving up the unidirectional relation between the two components. This proposal, viewed in isolation from the rest of the grammar, might be considered too radical and unnecessarily complex. There are reasons to believe, however, that more such 'loops' might turn out to be necessary.

Without aiming at a comprehensive analysis, we should like to present a case which indicates that it is sometimes necessary to go back from phrase-level syntax to morphology, a possibility that has been entertained by other researchers as well. In the traditional morphological descriptions of Polish (Grzegorczykowa 1979, *Morfologia*) a special derivational type is frequently isolated. These are items formed from prepositional phrases. Numerous examples of such formations can be given.

pod nog+ami under the feet → *pod+nóż+ek* footstool
za głow+ą behind the head → *za+głów+ek* bolster
przed wiosn+ą before spring → *przed+wiosni+e* early spring
między wojn+ami between the wars → *między+wojni+e* interwar period

An argument against treating such nouns as synchronically derived from prepositional phrases is their often unpredictable meaning. For instance, the noun

przed+szkol+e kindergarten

which can be traced back to the prepositional phrase

przed szkoł+ą before school, in front of the school building

does not denote anything that happens before one goes to school, or is placed in front of the school building, but a special kind of a pre-school institution, i.e. kindergarten. Similarly

za+plecz+e subsidiaries, base of supplies

does not necessarily mean the same as the phrase

za plec+ami behind the back

or *naręcze* armful, something which is found in one's arms (*na ręk+ach* in the arms). In brief, there is no doubt that in numerous cases we are dealing with lexicalized expressions which are characterized by various semantic idiosyncrasies.

This does not mean, however, that the formation of nouns from prepositional phrases is no longer productive in Polish. As a matter of fact, this type appears to be very frequently employed. For instance, the area behind a river can be named in a simple, if somewhat old-fashioned way, by nominalizing the sequence

za behind + name of the river

Nouns of this sort appear with the inflectional (palatalizing) suffix *-e*, for example

za Olz+ą → *Za+olzi+e*   *za Dniepr+em* → *Za+dnieprz+e*
za Dunaj+em → *Za+dunaj+e*   *za Don+em* → *Za+doni+e*

The meaning of such nouns is compositional and, hence, fully predictable. Moreover, it is possible to form many other nouns of this kind, which points to the productivity of the process in question, for example

za Wieprz+em → *Za+wieprz+e*   *za Bugi+em* → *Za+buż+e*
za Wolg+ą → *Za+woł+że*   *za Narwi+ą* → *Za+narwi+e*
za Nys+ą → *Za+nysi+e*   *za Wisł+ą* → *Za+wiśl+e*

These are not isolated examples. The majority of prepositional phrases can be nominalized when the noun refers to some location or a period of time, for example

przed mur+em before the wall → *przed+murz+e* bulwark
nad brzegi+em at the river bank → *nad+brzeż+e* river bank
przed bram+ą before the gate → *przed+brami+e* foregate
przed wiosn+ą before spring → *przed+wiośń+e* early spring

Apart from these items, which are attested in the dictionaries, many others can be easily formed, for example

przed dom+em in front of the house → *przed+domi+e* area in front of the house
nad staw+em at the pond → *nad+stawi+e* bank of the pond
za bram+ą behind the gate → *za+brami+e* area behind the gate
przed zim+ą before winter → *przed+zimi+e* early winter

These nouns are as yet unattested, but do not differ from those already found in the dictionaries; they are all well formed and easy to understand. This implies that prepositional phrases in Polish constitute an input to productive WFRs.

If our reasoning is correct, then the loop from phonology to morphology is not the only one – another from phrase-level syntax to morphology has to be postulated as well.

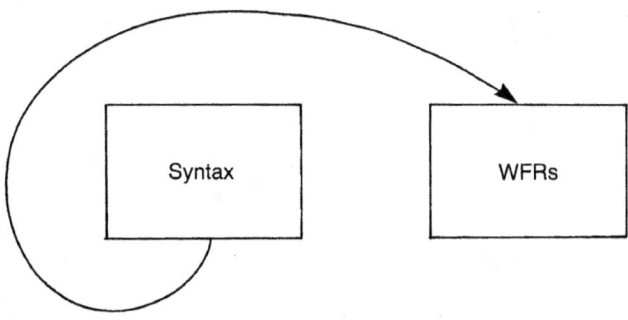

Chapter five

Words – the morphological hierarchy versus the phonological hierarchy

The previous two chapters have addressed the issue of morphological bracketing and its role in phonology. Nothing has been said, however, about an adequate description of English affixes as well as Polish prefixes outlined in Chapter 2. This is the problem which will be of our primary concern in the following pages. On the theoretical side, we shall consider the validity of various prosodic categories postulated by prosodic phonology. The focus will be on the relation between morphological and phonological words in English and Polish, i.e., between the morphological and the prosodic hierarchies.

In Chapter 2 we have attempted to demonstrate that the phonology of English affixation and Polish prefixation cannot be properly handled by reference to such morphological devices as the ordered levels of lexical phonology, since in many cases there is no one-to-one correspondence between morphological and phonological properties of whole classes of words. This has led us to conclude that the two components should be viewed as separate rather than integrated, so that morphological structures can be modified before entering phonological derivation, in those instances in which they diverge from the phonological structures. This is indeed necessary since, as noted by many researchers, phonological rules are sensitive not only to morphological, but, first and foremost, to phonological categories. In other words, phonological rules frequently need to refer to the units which are not identical with any morphosyntactic items.

Many processes appear to operate within the domain that is either smaller or larger than the morphological word. This necessitates isolating a unit of description which does not correspond to one morphological category. The unit in question can be referred to as the phonological word.

The need for the phonological word has been established for a number of languages: for Sanskrit by Selkirk (1980), Greek and Italian by Nespor (1985), Dutch and German by Booij (1985b), Polish by Rubach (1984a), Latin, Turkish, Hungarian and Yidiny by Nespor and Vogel (1986). All these linguists have noted that in the languages under investigation morphological words (roughly understood as terminal elements in syntactic tree structures) do not correspond to prosodic words, which act as the major domain of rule application.

These languages require a set of rules to relate the two types of units, i.e. a mechanism that maps morphological words onto phonological words. It has further been observed that mapping rules are language-specific. Thus, in some languages, such as Dutch (Booij 1985b), morphological information (concerning different types of affixes) is sufficient for the mapping rules. In other cases, for example in Italian (Nespor 1985), phonological information concerning the segmental and the syllabic structure of items is also necessary for the construction of the prosodic word.

In what follows, the concept of the phonological word will be employed in the description of English affixation and Polish prefixation. A set of mapping rules for both languages will be formulated. We shall argue that incorporating the phonological word, as well as other prosodic categories, into English and Polish phonology leads to analyses which are more adequate than those put forward within other existing approaches.

5.1 The phonology of English affixation

We shall start our discussion of English affixation with a brief summary of basic facts which have been considered in greater detail in Chapter 2. English affixes appear to fall into three distinct classes; these can be termed, respectively, Class I, Class II and dual class affixes.

Class I affixes seem to be the least problematic of all. Their attachment induces the application of all phonological rules except for those which refer to the word-final position. They condition such rules as

Stress shift, for example	'atom – a'tomic
Trisyllabic laxing, for example	sāne – sănity
Degemination, for example	in+numerable → i[n]umerable
Nasal assimilation, for example	in+proper → i[mp]roper

Class II affixes are different from Class I affixes in that they must frequently be blocked from triggering phonological rules. For instance, Class II affixation blocks all the rules just mentioned

Stress shift, for example	'citizen – 'citizenship
Trisyllabic laxing, for example	mīght – mīghtily
Degemination, for example	un+natural – u[nn]atural
Nasal assimilation, for example	un+popular – u[np]opular

On the other hand, Class II affixes condition the application of phonological rules typical of the word-final environment, for example

G-deletion, for example	si[ŋ] – si[ŋ]er
Cluster simplification, for example	bo[m] – bo[m]ing
Sonorant syllabification, for example	hind[ə] – hind[ə]rer

Dual class affixes have the properties of both classes in that their attachment to some forms results in the application of phonological rules, but in other cases in blocking them. For example, the suffix *-ize* has dual membership since it is both

stress-determining, for example	'synonym – sy'nonymize
and stress-neutral, for example	'skeleton – skeletonize

Moreover, *-ize* induces sonorant syllabification in

sob[ə]rize

and blocks it in

thea[tr]ize

Morphological versus phonological hierarchy

It has to be added that dual class affixes often have double nature only with respect to phonological rules, and are uniform from the morphological point of view, as demonstrated in Chapter 2.

Finally, there are less regular cases, which violate some generalizations concerning Class I and Class II affixes. Thus, some Class I affixes fail to induce phonological rules in certain words, for example

-*ify* in some cases blocks TSL, for example spēechify, tōwnify, stēelify
-*y* in some cases is stress-neutral, for example 'heterodox – 'heterodoxy

Similarly, there are words in which Class II affixes behave contrary to their morphological nature and display the properties of Class I affixes. For instance,

-*y* fails to trigger sonorant syllabification in
 an[gr]y   hun[gr]y
-*ly* evinces degemination in
 simple+ly → simp[l]y   bubble+ly → bubb[l]y
-*age* causes the shift of stress in
 'concubine – con'cubinage   e'quip – 'equipage

It is clear that any adequate description of English phonology must account for the phonological differences between Class I, Class II and dual class affixes in a systematic way. Let us recall that the lexical model has not provided solutions which would be fully satisfactory. Therefore, alternative descriptions have to be considered.

5.1.1 The SPE analysis

Before we present an analysis of English affixation which involves the use of prosodic categories, it is worthwhile examining the traditional generative approach to the issue in question.

As mentioned in Chapter 1, SPE proposes to handle the phonological properties of English affixes by means of several boundary markers. Thus, Class I affixes are associated with the morpheme boundary, while Class II affixes are associated with the word boundary. The morpheme boundary conditions, but never blocks, phonological rules, while the word boundary usually prevents them from applying.

The boundary approach has a number of strong points. First of all, it reflects the systematic difference between the two classes of affixes. It accounts for the fact that the majority of phonological rules are restricted to Class I affixation. It also explains why Class II affixes display phonological properties characteristic of the word-final position.

Another significant aspect of this analysis is that SPE suggests a mechanism which allows an affix to change its class membership for the sake of phonological rules. The device in question is boundary-weakening effected by readjustment rules. Leaving the technicalities of this proposal aside, it is seen to make the correct prediction that the change in class membership is brought about only to ensure the proper application of phonological rules, and has no impact on the rest of the grammar.

The SPE theory of boundaries, however, has been heavily criticized, which we noted in Chapter 1. The most relevant objection is that the phonological description of SPE was carried out without an adequate morphological analysis; morphological boundaries were arbitrarily postulated to accommodate phonological, but not morphological facts. Moreover, the assumption that all affixes are introduced with the word boundary could not be maintained since they appear to display divergent morphological properties. Hence, they must be differentiated in the morphological component.

The question that arises is whether the SPE approach to affixation can be maintained by enriching it with morphological analysis, i.e. by providing morphological justification of boundaries. It can be assumed, much in the sense of Aronoff (1976), that all affixes are listed in the lexicon together with the boundaries, which constitute their inherent properties. Under this assumption the SPE mechanism of rule conditioning and rule blocking could be preserved, provided it would be supplemented with the possibility of either boundary weakening (for Class II affixes which behave phonologically as Class I affixes) or boundary strengthening (in the case of Class I affixes which have phonological features of Class II affixes). Both boundary weakening and boundary strengthening can be effected by readjustment rules.

This approach appears problematic. Apart from theoretical objections that the use of boundaries raises, certain empirical inadequacies must be noted as well. Booij (1985a:25) observes, for
instance, that the single-word boundary does not always have the same phonological consequences; the presence of # results in different syllabifications of the expressions such as

##a#name## – a$name$
##an#aim## – anaim

(at least in lento speech). Clearly, the word boundary blocks syllabification. The same, however, cannot be said about other cases. In the words

##sleep#s## – $sleeps$
##sleep#er# – $slee$per$

#does not prevent the sounds on the opposite sides of the word boundary from being syllabified together.

Another problem is created by those items in which Class I affixes appear outside Class II affixes. In such cases the internal word boundary is present, for example

##standard#ize+ation##
##remove#abil+ity##

blocking the application of stress across it. Consequently, the stress pattern of these words (with the main stress on the affixes) cannot be properly derived.

In brief, the boundary approach, in spite of its many strong points, cannot be viewed as the most effective solution.

5.1.2 The phonological word, mapping and rebracketing

Many difficulties can be overcome if use is made of the units of the prosodic hierarchy. Following Aronoff and Sridhar's (1983) as well as Booij's (1985a) approach, it can be assumed that in English phonological words are not always identical with morphological words. For example, six morphological words given below

purity   unnatural
musician   bombing
hindrance   hinderer

can be considered as nine prosodic words

(purity)$_\omega$ (un)$_\omega$(natural)$_\omega$
(musician)$_\omega$ (bomb)$_\omega$(ing)$_\omega$
(hindrance)$_\omega$ (hinder)$_\omega$(er)$_\omega$

(where ω stands for the phonological word – Selkirk 1980). In other words, the claim is that the phonological status of Class I and Class II affixes is different; the former form prosodic words together with the base to which they are attached, whereas the latter are separate phonological words (p-words).

The further claim is that the majority of phonological rules of English operate within the domain not of the morphological, but rather the phonological word. To put it differently, usually they do not cross the boundaries of p-words. Such rules comprise basically all phonological processes which have traditionally been restricted to Class I or morpheme boundary affixation (for example stress, nasal assimilation, trisyllabic laxing, degemination, etc.). Furthermore, it seems that those phonological rules that in SPE refer to the morphological word boundary (for example sonorant syllabification, cluster simplification, G-deletion) can be reformulated now in such a way as to make use of the edges of the p-word. Post-nasal G-deletion, for instance, can be stated as

$$g \rightarrow \phi\ /\ \eta \underline{\ \ \ \ })_\omega$$

where $\underline{\ \ \ \ })_\omega$ means 'finally in the phonological word'.

A significant issue that should be addressed is how phonological rules 'know' which structures should be interpreted as separate p-words, and which should form p-words together with their bases. It seems that in the majority of cases it is morphology that decides the issue, i.e. the relevant information is encoded in the morphological structure of words. Since the two classes of English affixes have different morphological properties, it can be suggested that their lexical representations are different. They can be represented in the following way

	suffixes	prefixes
Class I	+ X	X +
Class II	[+ X]	[X +]

With Class I affixes the lack of brackets indicates that they are attached directly to the base. With Class II affixes the presence of brackets points to the fact that they behave like compounding elements.[1] Pluses in the lexical representation of affixes show that they are not independent items, but bound morphemes. Moreover, the placement of the plus indicates on which side of the base an affix is appended. Lexical morphemes differ from affixes in that they are specified with respect to their grammatical category, while affixes do not have any category of their own, but rather assign it to the base to which they are attached. This is in agreement with claims made, for example, by Selkirk (1984). Morphological structure of some basic types of English words can be presented as follows,

democracy	$[[\text{democrat}]_N +y]_N$
refusal	$[[\text{refuse}]_V [+al]]_N$
immoral	$[in+[\text{moral}]_{Ad}]_{Ad}$
unripe	$[[un+] [\text{ripe}]_{Ad}]_{Ad}$
naturalness	$[[[\text{natur}]_N +al]_{Ad} [+ness]]_N$
impoliteness	$[[in+[\text{polite}]_{Ad}]_{Ad} [+ness]]_N$
ungrammaticality	$[[[un+] [\text{grammatical}]_{Ad}]_{Ad} +ity]_N$
blackboard	$[[\text{black}]_{Ad} [\text{board}]_N]_N$

Fully bracketed structures produced by the morphological component are now subject to prephonological mapping conventions which assign phonological parentheses denoting the edges of phonological words. The basic mapping rule of English can be presented as

$$[\ ] \rightarrow ([\ ])_\omega$$

where [ ] can contain any number of left and right brackets, but no internal occurrences of][.

This convention will ensure the prosodic assignment of Class I affixes to either the preceding or the following item. Class II affixes will be interpreted as separate phonological words. Some of the words whose structure has been earlier presented will now acquire the following shape

$$([[democrat]_N +y]_N)_\omega$$
$$([[refuse]_V)_\omega ([+al]]_N)_\omega$$
$$([[[un+])_\omega ([grammatical]_{Ad}]_{Ad} +ity]_N)_\omega$$

Since in the approach advocated here morphologically and phonetically conditioned phonological rules can be intermingled, it follows that the assignment of phonological parentheses does not wipe off morphological bracketing. This means that rules can employ both bracket as well as parenthesis information. Thus, phonological rules fall into two classes: those which are morphologized and refer to brackets (and, sometimes, to grammatical categories), and those which do not require any morphological information, and make use of prosodic categories only. While the latter do not, as a rule, refer to brackets, the former might be sensitive to prosodic factors as well. An example of such a process is TSL in English, which, on the one hand, has the p-word as its domain of application (it is blocked by Class II affixes), but which also requires access to the placement of the morpheme boundary (see the discussion in Chapter 2).

Let us now turn to the problem of dual class affixes. As has earlier been mentioned, they do not form one homogeneous group and should, therefore, be handled in several different ways. The simplest case is affixes with two variants: one which is both morphologically and phonologically Class I, and another which has both morphological and phonological features of Class II affixation. The first type is introduced without any brackets and is, consequently, interpreted by phonological rules as forming one p-word with the base; the other type constitutes a separate prosodic unit. Such 'neat' cases, however, are rare.

An example of this sort is the suffix -*t*, which is used in forming abstract nouns. Consider the following forms.

a) contain – content b) complain – complaint
    conjoin – conjunct   pursue – pursuit
    produce – product   descend – descent
    conceive – concept   receive – receipt
    perceive – percept   deceive – deceit

Clearly -*t* suffixation is synchronically unproductive and full of idiosyncracies, but it serves well to illustrate the morphological and phonological differences between the two types of the suffix -*t*. In column a) -*t* induces the shift in stress as well as some allomorphic changes, and should be viewed as Class I or, in our terminology, a bracketless affix. The attachment of -*t* to the verbs in b) leaves the stress on the verbal base, while the preceding obstruent is additionally deleted, which points to its Class II nature. Morphological facts support the existence of two kinds of -*t*. Thus, some items in a) can be subject to stress-changing affixation processes, for example

'concept – con'ceptual   'conjunct – con'junctive

The nouns in b), in turn, can only be subject to Class II affixation, for example

de'ceit – de'ceitful   re'ceipt – re'ceiptor

In brief, there seem to be two kinds of -*t*, both in terms of phonology and morphology. In the framework proposed here this means that there are two suffixes, +t and [+t], with all the consequences discussed earlier.

Much more common are situations in which an affix has morphological properties of one class, but phonological features of both classes. The suffixes -*ize*, -*ant*/-*ent* and -*ance*/-*ence* belong to this group. From the morphological point of view, as argued in Chapter 2, they have to be regarded as Class I. Consequently, they enter morphological derivation as bracketless affixes. However, their behaviour with respect to phonological rules is not uniform and, consequently, they have to be differentiated for the purposes of phonology. The mechanism we suggest is rebracketing. Simply, in some lexically specified cases adjustment rules will add brackets to bracketless affixes so that they can function in phonology as separate p-words.

We shall now illustrate the suggested procedure with some examples. The suffix *-ize* in all cases must be viewed as morphologically Class I since the stress-changing suffix *-ation* attaches to it, for example

'synonym – sy'nonymize – synonymi'zation
'alcohol – 'alcoholize – alcoholi'zation

Clearly, in the first example *-ize* is stress-changing and its morphological structure

$[[\text{synonym}]_N + \text{ize}]_V$

is interpreted by the phonology as

$([[\text{synonym}]_N + \text{ize}]_V)_\omega$

In the second example *-ize* is stress-neutral and behaves as if it were a separate phonological word. What we need is the following bracket adjustment

$[[\text{alcohol}]_N + \text{ize}]_V \rightarrow [[\text{alcohol}]_N [+\text{ize}]]_V$

Since in the majority of cases *-ize* behaves as a Class II affix (it blocks stress shift and TSL), rebracketing can be treated as a property of this particular affix rather than of individual words. The appropriate rule can thus be formulated as

-ize → [-ize]

Those words in which *-ize* is Class I (for example *synonymize*) will have to be marked as not undergoing rebracketing. Returning to the verb *alcoholize*, its rebracketed form will now be subject to the automatic phonological parentheses assignment:

$$[[\text{alcohol}]_N\ [+\text{ize}]]_V \rightarrow ([[\text{alcohol}]_N)_\omega\ ([+\text{ize}]]_V)_\omega$$

which ensures the correct phonological derivation. In this way we express the essential fact of the morphological uniformity and the phonological diversity of the suffix in question.

It is interesting to see what happens when *-ation* is attached to *-ize* verbs. Obviously, when *-ize* is stress-determining, *-ation* is directly appended to it and forms one p-word together with *-ize* and the base

$$[[[\text{synonym}]_N\ +\text{ize}]_V\ +\text{ation}]_N \rightarrow$$
$$([[[\text{synonym}]_N\ +\text{ize}]_V\ +\text{ation}]_N)_\omega$$

In the second case, i.e. when *-ize* is stress-neutral, *-ation* forms one p-word with *-ize*,

$$[[[\text{alcohol}]_N\ [+\text{ize}]]_V\ +\text{ation}]_N \rightarrow$$
$$([[[\text{alcohol}]_N)_\omega\ ([+\text{ize}]]_V\ +\text{ation}]_N)_\omega$$

(As to the prosodic status of such strings, as well as rules affecting them, see section 5.1.3.)

Similar treatment can be extended to other morphologically Class I affixes which have phonological properties of both classes.

Apart from dual class affixes discussed so far, there are also cases of morphologically Class II affixes that sometimes behave phonologically as Class I formatives, although the latter instances are definitely less frequent than the former group. The adjective-forming suffix *-y* belongs to this type. In some cases it blocks sonorant syllabification, contrary to its morphological nature, for example

anger – angry   hunger – hungry

We can account for this phenomenon by means of rebracketing: in such adjectives the suffix [+y] undergoes a prephonological change to +y.

$$[[\text{angr}]_N\ [+y]]_{Ad} \rightarrow [[\text{angr}]_N\ +y]_{Ad}$$

Now parentheses can be assigned

$$[[\text{angr}]_N +y]_{Ad} \rightarrow ([[\text{angr}]_N +y]_{Ad})_\omega$$

and the whole item is subject to word-level phonological rules. Since /r/ is not found adjacent to the edge of the p-word, its syllabification is blocked.

The same procedure is applicable in other cases as well. Thus, the suffixes *-er* and *-est*, when appended to the adjectives *young*, *strong* and *long*, lose their membership of Class II, since rebracketing affects them (as a result of lexical marking), for example

$$[[\text{long}]_{Ad} [+\text{est}]]_{Ad} \rightarrow [[\text{long}]_{Ad} +\text{est}]_{Ad}$$

Subsequently, the morphology–phonology mapping takes place

$$[[\text{long}]_{Ad} +\text{est}]_{Ad} \rightarrow ([[\text{long}]_{Ad} +\text{est}]_{Ad})_\omega$$

Clearly, the rule of G-deletion cannot affect this string as the voiced velar plosive is not followed by the edge of the phonological word.

Consider now the compounds such as *fireman*, which from the phonological point of view are simple words. Again, prephonological rebracketing can be claimed to take place

$$[[\text{fire}]_N [\text{man}]_N]_N \rightarrow [[[\text{fire}]_N \text{ man}]_N]_N$$

After the assignment of parenthesis

$$([[[\text{fire}]_N \text{ man}]_N]_N)_\omega$$

the item undergoes various p-word processes, such as vowel reduction.

Thus, for dual class (i.e. not uniform) affixes we suggest the mechanism of rebracketing: bracketless affixes can, under certain conditions, become bracketed affixes and vice versa: bracketed affixes may change into bracketless formatives. Such modifications are carried out by adjustment rules. In this way we are capable of handling both the morphological and phonological properties of dual class affixes, and accounting for the cases in which there is no isomorphy between the morphological and phonological structure of words.

A few words have to be said about the interpretation of inflectional affixes within the framework constructed here. SPE (p. 85) notes that they belong to word boundary affixes since, among other things, their attachment does not bring about any changes in stress. This means that they will be treated here as bracketed affixes, on a par with other Class II formatives. The implication thus is that there are no phonological differences between Class II affixation and inflection – a claim that Halle and Mohanan (1985) put into question. They argue that this distinction should be maintained since some phonological rules refer to it. However, the evidence Halle and Mohanan provide is very tenuous: according to them in some dialects of English the rule of vowel tensing needs to distinguish between Class II affixation and inflection. The facts provided by these authors are nevertheless rather questionable as seen in totally different accounts proposed by other researchers. Strauss (1982:172) claims, for example, that tensing (which in some dialects is manifested as stem-final lengthening) applies in the context of Class II affixes, but only when they begin with a vowel. Of the affixes which start with a consonant, some induce tensing, while others do not. Strauss concludes that the rule should be viewed as derivationally constrained with a list of suffixes that trigger it.[2] Yet a different interpretation of vowel tensing and stem-final lengthening (whose details are not relevant at the moment) has been put forward by Booij and Rubach (1987), where the alleged distinction between these two types of morphological processes is done away with as well.

An example which supports the non-existence of phonological differences between Class II affixation and inflection is supplied by the suffix -*ing*, which has a double morphological function: it is a derivational suffix that forms deverbal nouns (for example *cooking, letter-writing, baby-sitting*) and it functions as an inflectional ending used for forming the progressive form of verbs (for example *I am cooking dinner. I was baby-sitting all day yesterday*). Halle and Mohanan (1985:63) note this distinction and maintain that the derivational, nominalizing *-ing* is added in stratum 2 (together with other Class II affixes), while the inflectional, participial *-ing* is suffixed in stratum 4 (together with other inflectional affixes). Since rules such as vowel tensing and stem-final lengthening are assigned to stratum 3 (p. 84), they are supposed to affect the words with derivational, but not inflectional *-ing*. Consequently, we should expect differences in tenseness (or length) of the italicized vowels in the following pairs of sentences:

Stud*y*ing history is time-consuming.
I was stud*y*ing English history from 10 to 6.

I am very fond of cross-country sk*i*ing.
He is sk*i*ing down the hill.

To our knowledge, the words with the italicized vowels are pronounced in the same manner regardless of whether *-ing* is derivational or inflectional. We conclude that there is no convincing evidence which would necessitate separating Class II derivation from inflection in terms of their phonological interpretation. Consequently, both Class II affixes and inflectional formatives receive a pair of brackets, which ensures that they will be treated as separate p-words.

The latter statement, however, is in need of revision in view of the facts assembled in section 5.1.1, where we have stated that inflectional affixes are frequently syllabified with the stems. This situation is, in fact, predictable. In prosodic phonology the syllable, of which all larger units are composed, is the basic unit of the phonological hierarchy. Since every phonological word must consist of at least one syllable, it logically follows that if a nonsyllabic affix is appended, it must be prosodically incorporated into the adjacent p-word regardless of its morphological status.

Consider now the English plural morpheme (as well as the third person singular present tense ending and the genitive case exponent) and the regular past tense ending. If we assume that their underlying representations are /z/ and /d/ respectively, i.e. the suffixes in question are phonologically non-syllabic, then the well-formedness requirement that has just been mentioned will cause their prosodic assignment directly to the stems. Schematically,

$$[[beg]_V\ [+z]]_V \rightarrow (beg+z)_\omega$$
$$[[beg]_V\ [+d]]_V \rightarrow (beg+d)_\omega$$

which accounts for the facts of syllabification in a straightforward manner.

The problem arises, however, if we decide, the way Halle and Mohanan (1985) do, to handle the phonology not only of regular, but also irregular verbs. Examine past tense forms of the verbs *plead* and *bleed*. If in both cases the past tense suffix is /d/, as Halle and Mohanan (p. 107) suggest, then the following structures result

$$(pl\bar{e}d+d)_\omega \qquad (bl\bar{e}d+d)_\omega$$

Since segmentally these strings are identical, the same phonological rules should be applicable to them. Yet, to derive the correct output, in the first case the rules of vowel epenthesis and vowel shift are needed, whereas in the second instance the processes to apply are vowel shortening and degemination. Clearly, such derivations cannot be produced with the structures presented above. To be more exact, the issue concerns the approach proposed here, since in Halle and Mohanan's framework the correct forms are obtained due to suffixing the irregular -*d* in stratum 1, in which cluster shortening operates, and appending the regular -*d* at the level of inflection (stratum 3). Evidently, such a solution is not available to us.

We should like to suggest that the differences in the behaviour of past tense suffixes can be attributed to their phonological structures, which are not the same. The irregular endings are /d/ and /t/ (the latter suffix occurs in such forms as *lost, crept, bent*, etc.), in agreement with Halle and Mohanan's proposal, while the regular affix is underlyingly syllabic, i.e. it is /id/. Thus, the verbs under discussion have two different morphological structures [[blēd]$_V$ [+d]]$_V$ [[plēd]$_V$ [+id]]$_V$

which, after prosodic mapping become

(blēd+d)$_\omega$ (plēd)$_\omega$ (+id)$_\omega$

Since in the first case we are dealing with a single p-word, such word-level rules as cluster shortening and degemination apply, producing the desired form [bled]. In the second instance the past tense suffix remains a separate p-word (by virtue of its syllabic character) and does not affect the phonology of the root; the vowel is subject to vowel shift and the correct form ['pli:did] is yielded.

By analogy, the present tense suffix will also be represented as /iz/, i.e. syllabically, which, curiously, is also the result of Booij and Rubach's (1987) analysis carried out within the lexical framework. (Let us remind the reader that the phonological interpretation of English inflection has been the subject of controversy in the 1970s – see Anderson 1974.) Since the vowel of the suffix does not occur in many forms, for example

| wor[kt] | ro[bd] | mi[st] | analy[zd] |
| wor[ks] | ro[bz] | fi[ts] | go[z] |

a morphologically conditioned rule of vowel deletion is needed in such cases.

Contracted forms such as

Jack's (from *Jack is*)   What's (from *What is*)

also require the rule of vowel deletion. If inflectional endings are phonologically non-syllabic, we have to postulate vowel insertion for them and vowel deletion for contracted forms. Under the assumption that inflection is syllabic, the need for vowel insertion disappears altogether and vowel deletion can be extended to cover both cases.[3]

Naturally, the deletion of the vowel in the instances just discussed results in the emergence of non-syllabic p-words, which is inadmissible. To prevent such structures, resyllabification assigns such defective p-words to adjacent prosodic units, and nonsyllabic inflectional endings eventually merge with the verbs to which they are appended.

In brief, it appears that at the word-level a two-way distinction (between bracketed and bracketless affixes) is sufficient to handle the relevant phonological data of English.

5.1.3 Other prosodic categories

A significant issue, which has so far been avoided, is the status of a sequence of p-words. In other words, it is important to examine what larger units p-words are organized into.

Aronoff and Sridhar (1983) observe that those items in which Class II affixes are followed by Class I affixes, i.e. which consist of several p-words, have the properties of phrases in terms of stress placement. Thus, (p. 7) three p-words that form the noun *compartmentalization*

$(\text{compart})_\omega\ (\text{mental})_\omega\ (\text{ization})_\omega$

receive final phrase stress, in the same fashion as the syntactic phrase

combat mental elation

Similarly, it is impossible to distinguish the stress pattern of

$(\text{judge})_\omega\ (\text{mental})_\omega$

and the expression

Judge Mendel

We can therefore assume, along the lines suggested by Aronoff and Sridhar, that every p-word is stressed individually, and that the whole structure, having no head, receives final phrase stress.

Two types of words escape the above generalization. One of them is compounds, which require a different stress pattern from phrases. This can be illustrated with some well-known examples.

```
    1   2                    2   1
   hot dog         vs       hot dog
    1     2                  2     1
  White House              white house
    1    2                   2   1
   Red Coat                 red coat
```

Here compounds receive initial, while phrases final stress. Following Aronoff and Sridhar (p. 9), it can be suggested that, 'if the last p-word within a member of a major lexical category is itself a member of a major lexical category, then we have a compound, and we have compound stress'.

As observed by Fudge (1984:136), there exist compounds which nevertheless are stressed as phrases, for example

```
        2       1                    1      2
   Christmas pudding        (vs Christmas cake)
        2      1                    1     2
     London Road            (vs London Street)
```

In such cases an adjustment rule can, exceptionally, remove the specification of a compound from the problematic items so that they can function in phonology as phrases rather than compounds. Thus, the claim is that, apart from the differences in stress patterns, compounds and phrases are the same with regard to their remaining phonological properties.

This contention is questioned by Halle and Mohanan (1985), according to whom the rule of l-resyllabification must make a distinction between compounds and phrases. L-resyllabification makes the lateral in the rhyme the onset of the following syllable, provided the next vowel is found in the compound and not in the phrase. They (p. 65) support this claim with the following examples,

>   a wha[l]e edition   vs   the wha[ł]e and the shark
>   the sea[l] office   vs   the sea[ł] offered a doughnut

In the examples on the left, i.e. in compounds, the lateral is fronted, while in those on the right, i.e. in phrases, it is velarized.[4]

Halle and Mohanan's observations seem to be wrong, however. Gimson (1970:201), in his description of received pronunciation, gives many examples of phrases in which the lateral is clear, for example

fee[l] it   a[l] over   fa[l] out

Apparently l-resyllabification is not restricted to compounds, but operates within phrases as well. How, then, can the lack of resyllabification in Halle and Mohanan's examples be explained? It appears that much depends on the way in which the phonological phrase is defined. If we follow Nespor and Vogel's (1986:168) approach where there is no isomorphy between syntactic and phonological phrases, then it is clear that the troublesome cases are not phrases at all, but rather sequences of phrases (i.e. intonational phrases or even utterances). Thus, in Nespor and Vogel's framework the division of the offending structures into p-phrases would probably be the following

(a whale edition)$_\phi$ (the seal office)$_\phi$
(the whale)$_\phi$ (and the shark)$_\phi$
(the seal)$_\phi$ (offered)$_\phi$ (a doughnut)$_\phi$

(where ϕ means the phonological phrase). Under this approach the domain of l-resyllabification is the phonological phrase, and since compounds form p-phrases as well, the rule in question applies to them. In brief, there seem to be no compelling reasons for isolating a separate prosodic category of compounds as phonologically distinct from p-phrases.

The question that arises now is whether p-words are directly organized into p-phrases, or whether some prosodic units intermediate between these two should be isolated. According to Nespor and Vogel (1986), many languages require the clitic group as a domain of application of some phonological rules.

Consider a noun with three Class II affixes

$un_{II} + rest + less_{II} + ness_{II}$

prosodically interpreted as

$(un)_\omega (rest)_\omega (less)_\omega (ness)_\omega$

i.e. as consisting of four phonological words. If the whole string is regarded as a p-phrase, we should expect it to receive the final phrase stress, which evidently does not happen. Instead, stress falls on the root, as if the affixes were not there. This, in Aronoff and Sridhar's (1983:8) view, can be explained if Class II affixes are regarded as clitics, which always adjoin as weak sisters and, hence, never receive stress. Bisyllabic clitics, by virtue of their polysyllabicity, are stressed, for example

-'worthy   'super-   'counter-

Their clitical nature, however, can be seen in the fact that such affixes get only secondary stress, for example

```
   1      2          2      1
praise+worthy   counter+argument
```

Since Class II affixes are not, of course, true morphosyntactic clitics (they cannot change their host) and function as such only for the purposes of phonology, it follows that they must be specified as clitics by adjustment rules. The appropriate convention can be schematically presented as

$[+X] \rightarrow [+clitic]$

which means that Class II affixes are to be interpreted in phonology as clitics.[5] Consequently, items that contain such affixes will be treated as clitic groups.

According to Nespor and Vogel (1986:150), the need to distinguish between clitic groups and phrases is seen in the operation of palatalization, which is restricted to the former. Thus, it takes place in such cases as

```
[is Sheila   did you   don't you
    ↓           ↓          ↓
   [ž]         [j]        [č]
```

which can be viewed as clitic groups, but fails to apply in (examples taken from Kaisse 1985:37),

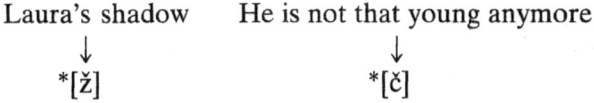

where we are dealing with phrases.

It should be noted that in clitic groups palatalization is optional. In our opinion this follows from the fact that expressions such as *is Sheila* do not have to be interpreted by all the speakers as clitic groups, but as p-phrases. If the former option is chosen, palatalization applies. If, however, a given sequence of p-words is regarded as a phrase, the rule in question is blocked.

A similar approach can be adopted to the optionality of vowel deletion in such expressions as

John is – John's   Who is – Who's
Where is – Where's What is – What's

Here the speaker has the choice of using either the full or the contracted form. The former amounts to interpreting a given sequence of p-words as a p-phrase, the latter as the clitic group. In other words, it can be assumed that the processes of contraction on the phonology part consists in cliticizing the auxiliary onto the preceding item. Once this decision is made, phonological consequences follow. Under the phrase approach the vowel is preserved since deletion is restricted to the domain of the clitic group (it affects the vowel of inflectional suffixes). If, however, a given structure is treated as a clitic group, the vowel is removed. This reasoning amounts to saying that in some instances a string of morphemes can be divided into prosodic units in more ways than one, which is reflected in the application or non-application of various phonological rules. The problem has to be examined in more detail to arrive at more than assumptions.

In the preceding pages we have been concerned with the phonology of English affixation. The apparatus proposed by prosodic phonology has been employed with the major conclusion that in English there is no identity between morphological and phonological words: Class I affixes form p-words with the bases to which they are affixed, whereas Class II formatives constitute independent p-words. Since the majority of phonological rules apply in the domain of the p-word, they do not affect Class II affixation. We have furthermore suggested that Class I affixes should be represented in the lexicon without any brackets, while Class II affixes should have brackets. Information expressed by bracketing is subsequently utilized by mapping conventions, which interpret morphological brackets for the purposes of phonology, or, to put it differently, translate morphological units into phonological units. This accounts for the phonological properties of Class I and Class II affixation. To handle dual class affixes, as well as other forms whose morphological and phonological features do not converge, we have suggested the adjustment mechanism of rebracketing: the change of bracketless affixes into bracketed ones, and of bracketed affixes into bracketless ones. In this way the phonological structure of words can be modified without any consequences for their morphology. Further examination of sequences of p-words has revealed that Class II affixes should be treated as clitics, and the items that contain them as prosodic clitic groups. The third unit which appears to play a significant role in English phonology is the phonological phrase. Thus, p-words are gathered into clitic groups which are further organized into p-phrases, and phonological rules have three different domains of application.[6] We have also noted that the morphology–phonology mapping does not always have to be identical for all the speakers, and that sometimes certain morphological structures might receive different prosodic interpretations, which has impact on the operation of phonological rules.

In order to evaluate the theoretical significance of these findings, it is necessary to examine a different language from a comparable perspective. In the next section we turn to the analysis of the phonology of Polish prefixes.

5.2 The phonology of Polish prefixation

In Chapter 2 it was stated that prefixes in Polish differ from suffixes in terms of their properties, i.e. they block the application of the majority of phonological rules. We have further demonstrated that the problem cannot be solved by claiming that prefixation constitutes a separate derivational stratum. The conclusion has been that level-ordering of lexical phonology is not capable of handling the phonology of Polish prefixes. As a matter of fact, although Polish prefixes have been analysed in a variety of frameworks, none of the suggested approaches appears fully satisfactory, and the problem of an adequate description of prefixation remains largely open.

In what follows, the major descriptive and theoretical issues pertaining to phonological properties of prefixes are taken up again and examined in some detail. First the basic facts are briefly presented. Then the previous generative analyses are critically discussed. Finally, we make an attempt at providing a solution to the problem which involves the use of prosodic categories and the phonological word in particular. The issue that will receive the most detailed treatment will be the operation of the lower rule in prefixed forms. Other processes, as less controversial and simpler, will be dealt with more cursorily.

We shall start with the presentation of the relevant data. First we list those phonological processes which fail to take place on prefixation (Group A).

Group A

1. Anterior palatalization, as was mentioned in Chapter 2, is blocked in the case of prefixes, for example *ro[z'+i]skrzyć* 'sparkle', not **ro[źi]skrzyć*, *prze[d'+i]mek* 'article, gram.', not **prze[dźi]mek*.
2. Vowel retraction, which retracts the high front vowel /i/ after nonpalatal coronal consonants, is not induced if the vowel in question is stem-initial, for example *ro[z'+i]skrzyć* 'sparkle', not **ro[zɨ]skrzyć*, *prze[d'+i]mek* 'article', not **prze[dɨ]mek*.
3. Vowel deletion, which deletes one vowel in the context of another, fails to apply when the vowels are separated by the prefix juncture, for example *p[o+u]czyć* 'teach', not **p[u]czyć*, *n[a+o]powiadać* 'tell', not **n[a]powiadać*.
4. Derived imperfective tensing, which can optionally affect a sequence of two back mid vowels, for example *osz[a]ł[a]miać* 'daze', never modifies the prefix vowel, for example *d[o]+s[o]lić* 'add salt' – *d[o]+s[a]lać* 'id. DI', not **d[a]s[a]lać*, *[o]+gł[o]sić*

'announce' – *[o]+gł[a]szać* 'id. DI', not **[a]gł[a]szać*.

On the other hand, however, some phonological processes do accompany prefixation (Group B).[7]

Group B

1. Surface palatalization, which softens hard consonants followed by the high front vowel /i/, affects also the prefix-final consonants, for example *ro[z'+i]skrzyć* 'sparkle', *prze[d'+i]mek* 'article'.
2. Voice assimilation, according to which an obstruent agrees in voicing with the following obstruent, operates in prefixed forms as well, for example *[s+p]aść* 'fall' vs *[z+b]udzić* 'wake', *po[t+s]koczyć* 'jump up' vs *po[d+v]ozić* 'give a lift'.
3. Vowel epenthesis, which breaks heavy consonantal clusters containing spirants, inserts the mid front vowel between the prefix spirant and the identical stem-initial fricative followed by another obstruent, for example *[ze+sk]oczyć* 'jump down' (vs *[z+gń]eść* 'crush'), *[ze+zv]olić* 'allow' (vs *[s+tr]ącić* 'knock off').
4. The stress rule, which usually assigns stress to penultimate syllables, treats prefixed forms in the same way as other words, for example *'przy+siad* 'knee bending', *'wy+lać* 'pour out'.

Finally, there is a third type of phonological processes, which display no uniform behaviour with respect to prefixed words (Group C).

Group C

1. Lower, which, as has been explained in the preceding chapters, is responsible for the e~ɸ alternation, in some cases affects the prefix-final lax vowels and brings out their emergence on the surface, for example *[ze+r]wać* 'tear off', *o[dem]knąć* 'open', whereas in others it is blocked, i.e. the yer is deleted rather than blocked, for example *be[s+k]rwawy* 'bloodless' not **be[zek]rwawy*, *o[t+p]chlić* 'de-flea' not **o[dep]chlić* – in all these instances the roots contain the lax vowel.
2. Palatal assimilation, which makes clusters of consonants uniformly palatal, with prefix consonants is sometimes obligatory, for example *[ś+ć]inać* 'cut off', *[ś+ć]erać* 'wipe off', sometimes optional, for example *ro[ś+ć]ąć* or *ro[s+ć]ąć* 'cut', *[ź+dź]erać* 'tear off' or *[z+dź]erać*, and in some cases it is blocked altogether,

for example *[z+ń]iszczyć* 'ruin' not **[źń]iszczyć*, *[z+l']iczyć* 'count' not **[zl']iczyć*.

3. Syllabification – in some instances the prefix is obligatorily syllabified with the stem, for example *z+no-sić* 'bear', *s+pa-dać* 'fall down', while in others it is syllabified separately, for example *od-dłubać* 'groove', *nad-druk* 'overprint', and with some items two possibilities are available: syllabification with the stem, for example *na-d+użyć* 'abuse', *po-d+oficer* 'non-commissioned officer' or separately, for example *nad-użyć*, *pod-oficer*.

5.2.1 Previous analyses

All major accounts of Polish phonology couched within the traditional generative framework note the exceptional behaviour of prefixes with regard to phonological rules. To deal with the issue they employ two types of devices, which are complementary in character. One of them is resorting to rule ordering, the other to the use of morphological boundaries.

First of all, it appears that there is morpheme structure condition on the phonological shape of Polish prefixes, according to which they all end in a vowel at the underlying level. Those prefixes which display the e~ɸ alternation, for example *z-/ze-*, *w-/we-*, *pod-/pode-*, *od-/ode-*, *nad-/nade-*, *roz-/roze-*, are represented phonologically with the final high lax vowel, which, in the course of phonological derivation, is either lowered to [e], or deleted.

It is obvious that under this approach many phonological rules are blocked in prefixed forms owing to the presence of prefix-final yers. To be more exact, such processes as anterior palatalization and vowel retraction, which precede lower are not applicable simply because their context is not met. Thus, in the standard generative model the blocking character of prefixation largely results from the assumed system of rules and representations.

Nevertheless these mechanisms are insufficient in the case of such rules as vowel deletion and DI tensing. These processes fail to affect prefix vowels even when no yers are involved. To put it differently, their non-application in prefixed words cannot be attributed to rule ordering as these processes do not interact with lower in the relevant cases. In such situations use can be made of morphological boundaries. The prefix boundary, which in the hierarchy of strength is situated between the morpheme and the word boundary, might be posited in prefixed items with the purpose of blocking the application of numerous phonological rules. This follows from a general convention, quoted in Chapter 1, according to which phonological processes can apply across the prefix boundary only when it is explicitly mentioned in their structural description.

Postulating the prefix boundary in Polish has many advantages. First of all, it allows for handling all the rules grouped under A, i.e. those instances in which prefixation blocks the operation of phonological processes. The application of the rules in B is not problematic either; as will later be demonstrated, they are all phrase-level rules, which take place across word boundaries. Consequently, the prefix boundary has no inhibiting effect on them. The most troublesome rules are those found in C, since in some cases they apply in prefixed items and in others they do not. Clearly, positing the prefix boundary in all such instances leads to incorrect results and cannot be considered fully adequate. In this situation employing lexical marking and exception features seems inevitable. These difficulties coupled with the problems of theoretical nature point to the inadequacy of the boundary approach, which in recent studies has generally been abandoned.

Within the cyclic description of Polish (Rubach 1981) distinct phonological properties of prefixes derive from their being processed on the last phonological cycle as well as from the division of rules into cyclic and postcyclic. This procedure has been introduced with the main purpose of accounting both for the application and the non-application of lower in prefixed forms, and can best be illustrated with some examples which involve the rule in question. The adjective *bezdenny* 'bottomless' has the following phonological structure:

/bezĭ+dĭn+ĭn+i/

i.e. it contains three lax vowels: in the prefix-final position, since *bez-* alternates with *beze-*, in the nominal root (cf. *[dn]o* 'bottom' – *[den]* 'id. gen. pl.') and in the adjectival suffix /-ĭn/. If this adjective is processed linearly, then the first two yers are lowered and the last one is deleted. This produces an incorrect result:

	/bezĭ+dĭn+ĭn+ɨ/
Lower	e e ɸ
	*[bezedennɨ]

Clearly, the first lax vowel must be deleted and not lowered. Within the cyclic analysis the unprefixed form *denny* is derived first. Then the prefix is processed with the rest of the base, but as the prefix yer is no longer followed by another yer (the root vowel having already been lowered to [e]), it undergoes deletion. In this way the correct form *bezdenny* is yielded. In large simplification the cyclic derivation of *bezdenny* can be presented as follows:

	/bezĭ+dĭn+ĭn+ɨ/
Cycle 2	/dĭn+ĭn/
Lower	e
Cycle 3	/den+ĭn+ɨ/
Lower	–
Cycle 4	/bezĭ+den+ĭn+ɨ/
Lower	– – –
Postcyclic rules	/bezĭdenĭnɨ/
Yer deletion	ɸ ɸ
	[bezdennɨ]

Take now the verb *zesłać* 'send down', of the following phonological structure:

/zĭ+sɨł+a+ć/

Here the root yer is preserved throughout all the cycles since it is not followed by another lax vowel. On Cycle 4 the prefix yer and the root yer occur in the neighbouring syllables, as a result of which the former is lowered, while the latter is deleted postcyclically:

Morphological versus phonological hierarchy

Cycle 4	/zĭ+sĭł+a+ć/
Lower	e

Postcyclic rules	/zesĭłać/
Yer deletion	ϕ
	[zeswać]

Thus, within the cyclic framework both the application (the *zesłać* type) and the non-application (the *bezdenny* type) of lower in prefixed forms can be accounted for. The operation of the rules in B causes no major difficulties either; they can be treated as postcyclic processes, which disregard word-internal structures, and, as such, affect prefixed items as well.

Unfortunately, there are problems with the cyclic description of prefixation. A theoretical difficulty is noted by Rubach (1984a) himself; in this model phonological rules are supposed to mirror the application of word formation rules and, since prefixes must often be appended prior to suffixes (see Chapter 2), their processing on the last cycle violates this requirement and necessitates a special stipulation. Several descriptive problems must be noted as well. As Nykiel-Herbert (1985) observes, the model under scrutiny is unable to produce the correct derivations of such prefixed forms as *bezkrwawy* 'bloodless' and *odpchlić* 'deflea'. Items of this type contain lax vowels in the neighbouring syllables: in the prefixes /bezĭ-/ and /odĭ-/ as well as in the roots (cf. *kr[e]w* 'blood' – *k[rf]i* 'id. gen sg.', *pch[e]ł* 'flea, gen. pl.' – *p[xw]a* 'id. nom. sg.'). Consequently, on the final cycle the prefix yers should be lowered. This, however, yields the incorrect forms **bezekrwawy* and **odepchlić*.

Cycle 4	/bezĭ+krĭv+av+ĭ/	/odĭ+pxĭl+i+ć/
Lower	e	e

Postcyclic rules	/bezekrĭvavĭ/	/odepxĭlić/
Yer deletion	ϕ	ϕ
	*[bezekrfavĭ]	*[odepxlić]

Moreover, processing prefixes on the last cycle cannot prevent the application of rules such as vowel deletion and DI tensing. These processes, as has already been mentioned, do not interact with lower in prefixed forms and are applicable on every cycle which involves prefixes. To block them, an appeal to the prefix boundary must be made, which is problematic for the reasons that have already been given.

In sum, the cyclic description of Polish has failed to come up with a satisfactory account of the phonological properties of prefixes.

In the lexical framework it is crucial that there should be no discrepancy between the order of application of WFRs and phonological rules, since both types of processes are intermingled. Therefore, processing prefixes on the last cycle, as incompatible with morphological facts, has to be abandoned in this approach. To handle the phonology of prefixation Rubach (1984a) suggests that, in addition to lexical mechanisms, use should also be made of the concept of the phonological word. He argues that in Polish morphological words are not always identical with phonological words; prefixes constitute separate phonological units, i.e. phonological words, while prefixed forms can be viewed as phonological compounds. Furthermore, phonological rules of Polish have at least two domains of application: the p-word and the p-compound. Those rules which are blocked by the prefix juncture have the p-word as their domain, whereas the remaining ones have the p-compound. The rule of lower is exceptional as it is supposed to apply in the domain of both the p-word and the p-compound.

The lexical approach, together with prosodic categories, is evidently superior to the previous descriptions, since it covers more cases. Thus, the non-application of rules in A can be attributed to their restriction to p-words. The processes in B might be viewed as postlexical and, hence, applicable to prefixed items as well. Only the processes in C appear more challenging for the framework under consideration. As a matter of fact, the lexical analysis does not handle all the relevant data.

Let us examine these rules briefly. As to syllabification, the problem is regarded as non-existent since, according to Rubach (1984a), the process obeys the p-word domain, which means that prefixes must always be syllabified separately.[8] This, however, disagrees with the intuition of the present author as well as several other native-speakers of Polish who have been consulted on the issue.

Morphological versus phonological hierarchy

The lexical description also fails to account for the peculiar operation of palatal assimilation in prefixed forms. Note that under the assumption that all prefixes are independent p-words we should expect either a general application of the rule to prefix consonants or its blocking. Yet, no generalization of this sort can be made: in some cases palatal assimilation affects prefixed words while in others it does not.

The major problem of the proposal in question lies in its inability to handle all the facts pertaining to the presence and absence of prefix vowels, i.e. to the operation of lower. It can easily be noticed that the problematic cases are exactly the same as in the cyclic framework. They concern those instances in which the prefix yer fails to emerge on the surface in spite of the presence of the required lax vowel in the following syllable. In such situations the lexical analysis incorrectly predicts the lowering of the prefix yer. This can be illustrated with a simplified lexical derivation of the words *bezpłciowy* 'sexless' (cf. *pł[e]ć* 'sex') and *odwszyć* 'de-louse' (cf. *w[e]sz* 'louse').[9]

	$(bezĭ)_\omega$ $(płĭć+ov̌+ĭ)_\omega$	$(odĭ)_\omega$ $(vĭš+ĭ+ć)_\omega$
WFR	$(płĭć+ov)_\omega$	$(vĭš+ĭ)_\omega$
Cycle 2		
Lower	–	–
WFR	$(bezĭ)_\omega$ $(płĭć+ov)_\omega$	$(odĭ)_\omega$ $(vĭš+ĭ)_\omega$
Cycle 3		
Lower	– –	– –
WFR	$(bezĭ)_\omega$ $(płĭć+ov+ĭ)_\omega$	$(odĭ)_\omega$ $(vĭš+ĭ+ć)_\omega$
Cycle 4		
Lower	– –	– –
p-compound erection	$(bezĭ+płĭć+ov+ĭ)_{\omega'}$	$(odĭ+vĭš+ĭ+ć)_{\omega'}$
Lower	e	e
Postcyclic rules	/bezepłĭćovĭ/	/odevĭšĭć/
Yer deletion	ϕ	ϕ
Other rules	w	f
	*[bezepwćovĭ]	*[odefšĭć]

In these derivations nothing important happens till Cycle 4 – the prefixes and the bases form separate p-words and the rule of lower is inapplicable. On Cycle 4 the p-words are gathered into phonological compounds and the context for lower is created. As now the prefix yers are followed by the root yers, the former undergo lowering, which leads to the wrong outputs. On the theoretical side it is not clear why, of all cyclic rules, only lower should have a special status and apply both within p-words and p-compounds. It is, moreover, questionable that one rule, i.e. lower, is allowed to apply twice on the same cycle.

To summarize, the lexical description appears to be capable of handling the set of phenomena presented in A, i.e. those cases in which prefixation blocks phonological rules, as well as those in B, where phonological processes apply across the prefix juncture. It cannot, however – at least in the shape subject to our scrutiny – account for the operation of those rules which display no coherent behaviour with prefixes, i.e. processes listed in C.

5.2.2 Lower

In the preceding section we have attempted to demonstrate that none of the existing descriptions of Polish phonology can handle the totality of phonological phenomena that concern prefixation. However, before we suggest a solution which is more adequate, we should like to examine the relevant facts once again, this time in greater detail. The focus of our analysis will be the rule of lower, which seems to be the source of greatest difficulty.

As has several times been mentioned, lower is peculiar in that sometimes it applies in prefixed forms, and in other cases it is blocked. Thus, two aspects of the process should be investigated: the application and the non-application of lower across the prefixal juncture. We shall start with the latter as it is more complex.

Lower appears to be blocked in several types of prefixed words.

Prefixed denominal adjectives

Pref[[ ]$_N$]$_{Ad}$

for example
bezsenny sleepless (*s[e]n* dream – *[sn]u* id. gen. sg.)
bezkrwawy bloodless (*kr[e]w* blood – *k[rf]i* id. gen. sg.)
bezpłciowy sexless (*płt[e]ć* sex – *p[wć]i* id. gen. sg.)
bezcłowy duty-free (*c[e]ł* duty, gen. pl. – *[cw]o* duty)

Laskowski (1975:36) observes that in prefixed denominal adjectives the prefix yer is deleted despite the fact that the root contains a high lax vowel in its phonological structure. This causes problems for both the linear and the cyclic/lexical descriptions alike. Yet the non-application of lower is absolutely regular in such instances. Moreover, all forms created from such adjectives, for instance, adverbs

bezsennie sleeplessly   *bezpłciowo* sexlessly

and abstract nouns

bezsenność insomnia   *bezpłciowość* sexlessness

behave exactly like their derivational bases, i.e. the prefix yer is deleted rather than lowered. The only exception to this generalization is the adjective *bezecny* 'infamous' and the noun formed from it, i.e. *bezeceństwo* 'infamy', whose synchronic morphological divisibility can be questioned.

Prefixed denominal nouns
$$\text{Pref}[[\quad]_N]_N$$
for example
odsetek percentage (*s[e]tka* hundred – *[st]o* hundred)
podpieniek honey fungus (*pi[e]ń* trunk – *[pń]a* id. gen. sg.)
naddniówka extra day's work (*dzi[e]ń* day – *[dń]a* id. gen.)
podszewka lining (*sz[e]w* stitch – *[šf]u* id. gen. sg.)

This group is not numerous, but its behaviour with regard to lower is consistent: in all cases both the roots and the prefixes contain lax vowels, yet the prefix yers fail to emerge on the surface. We have found only one exception to this generalization, i.e. the word *podeszwa* 'sole', which can be claimed to be derived from the noun *szew* 'stitch'. Synchronically, however, this relatedness is not very obvious and *podeszwa* can be regarded as a lexicalized morphologically simple word.

Prefixed denominal and deadjectival verbs

Pref[[ ]$_N$]$_V$ Pref[[[ ]$_N$]$_{Ad}$]$_V$

for example
 odpchlić de-flea (*pch[e]ł* flea, gen. pl. – *p[xw]a* id. nom. sg.)
 odwszyć de-louse (*w[e]sz* louse – *(fš]y* id. nom. pl.)
 wśnić się start dreaming (*s[e]n* dream – *[sn]u* id. gen. sg.)
 rozkrwawić cause to bleed (*kr[e]w* blood – *k[rf]i* id. gen. sg.)
 roztzawić draw tears (*t[e]z* tears, gen. – *[wz]y* id. nom.)

The items above confront us with a situation analogous to the two previous types: the prefix yer is deleted even though the roots contain a high lax vowel. As noted by Laskowski (1975:36), two denominal verbs appear with the prefix yer lowered

 rozednieć grow light (*dzi[e]ń* day – *[dń]a* id. gen. sg.)
 odemglać de-vaporate (*mgi[e]ł* fog gen. pl. – *m[gw]a* id. nom. sg.)

and are thus exceptions to the non-application of lower in this class of items.

The failure of lower in prefixed denominal nouns, verbs and adjectives, originally noted by Laskowski (1975), has been subject to Nykiel-Herbert's (1985) analysis. She has noted that in all problematic cases the prefix is not attached immediately to the base noun, but is separated from it by means of at least two brackets:

Pref[[ ]$_N$]$_N$ Pref[[ ]$_N$]$_{Ad}$ Pref[[ ]$_N$]$_V$
Pref[[[ ]$_N$]$_{Ad}$]$_V$

Consequently, Nykiel-Herbert proposes that in the context

Pref[[

lower should be blocked. Nevertheless, it appears that there are words in which the rule under consideration does not apply even though the prefix is directly attached to the stem.

Prefixed nouns

　　Pref[ ]$_N$

for example
　　bezsen insomnia (*s[e]n* dream – *[sn]u* id. gen. sg.)
　　bezdeń or *bezdno* abyss (*d[e]n* bottom, gen. pl. – *[dn]o* id. nom. sg.)
　　przeddzień the day before[10] (*dzi[e]ń* day – *[dń]a* id. gen. sg.)

As in the case of the items discussed earlier, in these instances the prefix yer fails to occur on the surface and, consequently, forms such as **bezesen* or **przededzień* do not appear. Since the bases are simple underived nouns, the peculiar behaviour of prefix yers cannot be explained by the presence of double brackets after the prefix. In brief, Nykiel-Herbert's approach is not helpful here.

Obviously, it is possible to claim that such formations are exceptional since there are only a few of them (which is true also of the types presented previously). Nevertheless, a different line of reasoning can also be adopted. The fact that the forms in question are not numerous might be viewed as resulting from at least two factors. First, only in a few cases can evidence be found that the first root vowel is a yer. Secondly, and more importantly, there are considerable restrictions on attaching prefixes to nouns and adjectives. Simply, prefixation is typical of verbs, and with other categories occurs relatively infrequently. Recently, however, an increasing tendency to form prefixed verbs can be observed. Thus, it is possible to use new items which are yet unattested in dictionaries such as

　　bezmech absence of moss (*m[e]ch* moss – *[mx]u* id. gen. sg.) – as *bezmocz* anuria, *bezsens* nonsense and not **bezemech*
　　nadlwy superlions (*l[e]w* lions – *[lv]a* id. gen. sg.) as *nadczłowiek* superman, *nadinspektor* superinspector and not **nadelwy*
　　przedsen pre-sleep (*s[e]n* dream – *[sn]u* id. gen. sg.) as *przedśpiew* prelude, *przedmecz* pre-match and not **przedesen*

All these potential words are well-formed, can easily be defined and might enter Polish vocabulary without any difficulty. Yet, none of the existing descriptions is capable of handling such items.

There is yet another class of prefixed forms, which has so far escaped attention, where lower fails to apply.

Words with two prefixes
Pref [Pref [

for example
przedzjazdowy preceding a congress
przedzlotowy preceding a rally
bezzwrotny irreclaimable
podzbiór subclass

All of these items are deverbal derivatives with a sequence of two prefixes:

przed+z+jazdowy   *bez+z+wrotny*   *pod+z+biór*

These prefixes are phonologically represented with final years:

/pšedĭ+zĭ/   /bezĭ+zĭ/   /podĭ+zĭ/

Since two lax vowels are found in the neighbouring syllables, we should expect the lowering of the first one. This, however, results in incorrect forms such as

*przedezjazdowy   *bezezwrotny   *podezbiór

Clearly, in such cases the first yer does not lower, but deletes.

At this point, with a mass of examples in which lower fails to affect prefixed items, it is legitimate to ask whether such instances constitute exceptions or regular forms. Notice that not isolated cases, but whole classes of derivatives are involved here. This seems to indicate that there is nothing unusual in such situations. Therefore, a reverse possibility should be considered, i.e., that it is the application of lower in prefixed forms rather than its non-application which requires explanation. In order to

Morphological versus phonological hierarchy

check the validity of this supposition, let us, in turn, examine those cases in which lower does take place across the prefixal juncture.

The analysis of words in which the prefix yer is lowered and not deleted reveals that this happens in verbs, in which prefixes are appended to about thirty roots. They are the following (the first member of every pair is a perfective verb, the other the corresponding derived imperfective).[11]

/dĭx/ – *ode+tchnąć* breathe – *od+dychać*
/zĭv/ – *ode+zwać* speak – *od+zywać*
/sĭx/ – *obe+schnąć* dry – *ob+sychać*
/sĭs/ – *we+ssać* suck in – *w+sysać*
/pĭx/ – *ode+pchnąć* push away – *od+pychać*
/bĭr/ – *ode+brać* take away – *od+bierać*
/dĭr/ – *ode+drzeć* tear off – *od+dzierać*
/pĭr/ – *ode+przeć* beat off – *od+pierać*
/pĭr/ – *ode+prać* wash off – *od+pierać*
/mĭk/ – *ode+mknąć* open – *od+mykać*
/tĭk/ – *ode+tkać* uncork – *od+tykać*
/sĭł/ – *ode+słać* send away – *od+syłać*
/sĭp/ – *ode+spać* sleep off – *od+sypiać*
/rĭv/ – *ode+rwać* tear off – *od+rywać*
/žĭr/ – *pode+żreć* eat up – *pod+żerać*
/tĭr/ – *we+trzeć* rub in – *w+cierać*
/gĭn/ – *ode+gnać* drive off – *od+gonić*
/łĭg/ – *ze+łgać* lie
/jĭr/ – *obe+jrzeć* watch
/mĭr/ – *ze+mrzeć* die
/lĭž/ – *ze+lżyć* abuse
/gĭr/ – *ode+grać* play – *od+grywać*
/jĭm/ – *ode+jmować* subtract, DI – *od+jąć* id. perf.
/łĭk/ – *prze+łknąć* swallow – *prze+łykać*
/pĭn/ – *od+piąć* unbutton – *od+pinać*
/gĭn/ – *od+giąć* bend – *od+ginać*
/žĭn/ – *wy+żąć* cut out – *wy+żynać*
/žĭm/ – *wy+żąć* wring out – *wy+żymać*
/čĭn/ – *za+cząć* begin – *za+czynać*
/tĭn/ – *od+ciąć* cut off – *od+cinać*
/klĭn/ – *za+kląć* charm – *za+klinać*

It is very striking that the roots which have just been listed have the same segmental make-up: they consist of a consonant, a high lax vowel and another consonant (only in the case of /klĭn/ are there two consonants in the root-initial position). It may thus be assumed that verbs with such roots constitute a class of systematic exceptions to the non-application of lower in prefixed forms. In other words, the suggestion is that lower generally fails to operate across the prefix boundary unless the verbs contain the roots of the specified structure. What remains to be explained is how this conclusion can be incorporated into the general description of Polish phonology.

5.2.3 *A prosodic solution*

The solution which we should like to suggest makes use of the notion of the p-word. Thus, we agree with Rubach (1984a) that in Polish, as in English, there is no identity between morphological and phonological words. A set of mapping conventions relates the two types of units and is responsible for the lack of isomorphy between them. Moreover, word-level rules of Polish have the phonological word rather than the morphological word as their domain of application. Other processes operate on larger units such as the phonological phrase.

Let us apply these general remarks to prefixes. It should be clear by now that prefixes, as generally non-cohering affixes, should be treated as separate p-words, with the exception of those cases in which they are attached to yer root verbs. This can be reflected by means of the prephonological convention of the following form

$$[\text{Pref}+[\ ]] \rightarrow \begin{cases} ([\text{Pref}+[C_1^2 \begin{bmatrix} V \\ +\text{high} \\ -\text{tense} \end{bmatrix} C(+VS)]]_V)_\omega \\ ([\text{Pref}+)_\omega ([\ ])_\omega \end{cases}$$

The upper part of this convention says that prefixes form one phonological word with simple verbs of the specified segmental structure. The lower expansion states that prefixes are to be interpreted as separate p-words elsewhere. The prediction thus is that in the former case phonological rules will apply to such items, whereas in the latter instances they will usually be blocked.[12]

The suggested procedure allows us to account for the properties of prefixes with regard to lower, both its application and non-application. The rule in question can be regarded as a word-level process that properly belongs to group A. This means that it will normally be blocked in prefixed forms unless the prefix is attached to a yer root. The word-level status of lower is additionally supported by its failure in prepositional phrases, for example

z psami with the dogs – (zĭ pĭs+ami) not **ze psami*
w dzień during the day – (vĭ dĭn+i) not **we dzień*

In these cases the lax vowels of the prepositions are not lowered but deleted, which shows that lower applies only in the domain of the p-word.

One point requires further clarification. According to our proposal lower operates in those prefixed verbs which contain yer roots. It should be noted that verbs such as *odpchlić* 'de-flea', and *rozkrwawić* 'cause to bleed', also have lax vowels in their roots, yet the prefix yers do not emerge on the surface. This happens due to the fact that such verbs are not simple, but denominal:

$$[[\text{Pref}+ [[C_1^2 \begin{bmatrix} V \\ +\text{high} \\ -\text{tense} \end{bmatrix} C]_N +VS]_V]_V$$

and have a structure which departs from that specified in the formulated mapping convention. Consequently, prefixes will not be phonologically directly attached to such verbs.

The proposed analysis does not mean, however, that lower is made totally without exception in prefixed words. Exceptions to it do exist, but now they are more clearly defined. These are forms in which lower fails to affect the prefix yer, even though the prefix is attached to simple verbs with yer roots. Another case is those items in which the rule does apply in spite of the fact that the prefix is appended to a non-yer root. Examples of the second kind have already been given. They include such exceptions as *podeszwa* 'sole', *bezecny* 'infamous', *rozednieć* 'grow light'. Here the mapping convention seems to have been relaxed to include also some non-verbal yer roots in its first clause.

Let us now present some exceptions of the first kind. Past forms of the verbs *iść* 'walk' and *schnąć* 'dry' belong to this group. Consider the verbs below.

w+szed+ł [fšedw] he went in – *we+sz+ł+a* [vešwa] she went in

roz+sech+ł [rossexw] he dried up – *roze+sch+ł+a* [rozesxwa] she dried up

Here both the prefixes and the roots contain yer vowels and should, according to our approach, form one p-word within which the prefix vowel is lowered. Yet lowering takes place only in feminine, but not in masculine forms. The exceptionality of such verbs is noted by Laskowski (1975:34), who observes that in the first person singular masculine forms such as

szed+ł+em I walked   *sch+ł+em* I dried

in the identical phonological and grammatical context, in one verb the root vowel appears on the surface, while in the other it does not.

Words which contain the root /jĭm/ often show certain idiosyncracies as well, for example

roze+jm truce   *na+jem* hiring
obe+jm embrace   *pod+na+jem* underlease
wy+na+jm hire   *wy+na+jem* hire

Here in the left-hand forms the root yer is dropped and in the right-hand ones is lowered. Clearly such forms must be viewed as lexicalized, as we are dealing here with an irregularity which escapes any systematic treatment.[13]

The next process which requires further discussion is palatal assimilation. The rule in question is troublesome as it displays no uniformity with regard to the way it affects prefixed words; in some cases it is optional, in others it is obligatory, and in yet others it is completely blocked. All these facts, it seems, escape any generalization, and we have no convincing solution to offer either. Booij and Rubach (1984) appear to be right in claiming that two types of palatal assimilation should be distinguished: one which is a p-word process, and another, which applies at the level of the p-phrase. An argument for splitting the rule into two parts is that its clauses are not identical, but only similar, and differ in several significant aspects: their scope, conditioning and optionality. The major difference is that the p-word palatal assimilation takes place in the context of sonorants such as [ń] and [l], for example

[zw]y bad – *[źl]e* badly
[sn]y dreams – *[śń]ić* to dream

which is completely impossible across words, for example

wó[s ń]ezły not a bad car, not **wó[ś ń]ezły*
la[s l]iściasty leaved forest, not **la[ś l]iściasty*

Interestingly, this type of assimilation is blocked in the case of prefixes, for example

[z+ń]iszczyć ruin, not **[źń]iszczyć*
[z+l]iczyć count, not **[źl]iczyć*

which supports treating it as a p-word rule and prefixes as separate p-words. This approach, however, does not work in the case of optional assimilation in (Karaś and Madejowa 1977),

ro[ś+ć]erać or *ro[s+ć]erać* grind
ro[ź+dź]erać or *ro[z+dź]erać* tear

which is independent of whether the prefix is a separate p-word or forms one phonological unit with the base.

With non-syllabic spirant prefixes palatal assimilation appears to be affected by spelling. In those cases where both consonants are spelt as palatals, assimilation is obligatory *ś+cinać* cut off [ść]   *ś+ciemniać* get dark [ść]

If the operation of the process in question is not marked in spelling, the rule is only optional

z+sinieć turn grey [śś]~[sś]
z+ziębnąć get cold [źź]~[zź]

The latter observations indicate that palatal assimilation is subject to non-phonetic restrictions. It seems that the rule is morphologized at the word level, i.e. it is blocked by the prefix bracket

[

In other words, the claim is that word-level palatal assimilation fails to affect the prefix consonants altogether, which is one of its idiosyncratic properties.[14] What, naturally, needs explaining is the fact that prefixed forms do display the effects of palatal assimilation. This we shall attribute to the phrase-level process sensitive to various factors, even spelling. Palatal assimilation which operates across words has the property of optionality, observed in the case of prefixes.

The third process of relevance to prefixed items is syllabification. At the beginning of section 5.2 it was stated that in some cases the prefix is obligatorily syllabified with the stem, in others it is syllabified separately, and with some words two possibilities are available. This statement requires some refinement. Of course with (phonetically) asyllabic prefixes there is no option – they must be obligatorily syllabified with the stem, for example

z+budować build: *zbu–do–wać*
w+ręczać hand in: *wrę–czać*

This follows from a well-known condition that every syllable must have a rhyme, which function cannot be performed by Polish consonants. Consequently, the deletion of prefix vowels brings about obligatory resyllabification. In other cases such as

od+dłubać groove   *nad+druk* overprint

there is only one possibility, namely that of syllabifying prefixes separately from the rest of the word. The reason is again phonetic and has to do with permissible syllable structure, in these particular instances, the impossibility of onsets that consist of a geminate followed by another consonant.

In many instances, however, there exist two ways of syllabifying prefixes: with the stem and separately, for example

nad+użyć abuse: *nad–u–żyć* or *na–du–żyć*
roz+ognić inflame: *roz–og–nić* or *ro–zo–gnić*

The first type of syllabification obeys the boundaries of the p-word, while the second follows the open syllable principle and is typical of single words. To put it differently, prefixed items behave as if they were sequences of p-words on the one hand, and single p-words on the other.

In order to explain this state of affairs, it is necessary to consider the prosodic status of prefixed words in some detail. In sections 5.1.2 and 5.1.3 we have argued that Class II affixes should be viewed as phonological clitics and Class II formations as clitic groups. A question arises whether prefixed forms in Polish should be treated in the same manner. Ample evidence reveals that they ought not to. One of the major properties of Polish clitics is their generally unstressed character, for example

zróbili+śmy we did   *zróbili+ście* you (pl.) did

In these words stress falls on the antepenultimate vowel instead of the usual penultimate one, which is due to the presence of the clitics *-śmy* and *-ście*, which do not affect stress placement. The same, however, cannot be said about prefixes, since words which contain them are stressed in the regular fashion, i.e. penultimately, for example

'od+ciąć cut off   *'pod+nieść* lift

The conclusion is that a combination word + clitic must be phonologically distinct from the sequence prefix + stem and that, consequently, prefixed forms cannot be regarded as clitic groups.

Another possibility is to treat such structures as phonological phrases. As a matter of fact, those processes that affect prefixed words and that we have listed under B, are phrase-level rules. Surface palatalization, for instance, operates across words, for example

pie[s' i]reny Irene's dog   *spo[d' i]gły* brand new

Voice assimilation is not restricted to single words either, for example

cho[ć t]utaj come here   *cho[dź d]o mnie* come to me

Vowel epenthesis is also known to operate in phrases, for example

w[e] wtorek on Tuesday (cf. *[v] niedzielę* on Sunday)
z[e] strachu out of fear (cf. *[z] głodu* from hunger)

We can conclude that such rules have the phonological phrase as their domain of application, i.e. they do not apply until p-words are gathered into p-phrases.

In this respect the processes just mentioned are opposed to the rules in A, which are restricted to p-words. This can be seen in their failure at word boundaries. Vowel deletion, for instance, is not applicable if vowel sequences occur in different words, for example

[o i]renie about Irene   *[u o]kna* at the window

Similarly, anterior palatalization and vowel retraction are blocked by word boundaries, for example

prze[d' i]nnymi before the others not **prze[dź i]nnymi* or
**prze[d i]nnymi*
prze[z' i]nnych because of the others not **prze[ź i]nnych* or
**prze[z i]nnych*

Clearly, these rules have the p-word as the domain of their application.

There is one process, however, which does not allow us to

regard prefixed words as p-phrases. The rule in question is stress; as has already been pointed out, it treats prefixed items as if they were single words, and falls on the penultimate syllable. This is not the case with phrase stress, which usually affects the last element, for example[15]

    2 1   2 1
mój dom my house   *zły pies* vicious dog

Evidently, for the purposes of stress assignment, forms with prefixes must be single p-words, rather than p-phrases. Nevertheless, this conclusion is in disagreement with our earlier observations, which point to the prosodic discreteness of prefixes.

The issue can be handled in a straightforward manner once we assume that prosodic structures can be reanalysed in the course of phonological derivation. Examples from Polish and English which involve syllable structure have already been given. The claim now is that similar changes might refer to larger prosodic units, such as p-words. In Polish the regularity seems to be that stress does not operate on monosyllables, and requires that they be attached prosodically to adjacent items. Thus, within words, prior to the application of word stress, the following convention is at work:

$$[(X)_\omega (Y)_\omega]_{N, Ad, V} \rightarrow (XY)_\omega$$
$$\text{when } X \vee Y = \sigma, \text{ and } Y \neq \text{Clitic}$$

This convention states that a sequence of two p-words within one morphological word is gathered into one prosodic word if one of the constituents is monosyllabic and no clitic is involved. It can be referred to as the monosyllable rule.

Polish prefixes are either monosyllabic (for example *od-*, *na-*, *przy-*) or bisyllabic (for example *roze-*, *nade-*, *ode-*). The latter end in the front mid vowel whose phonological source is a yer, subsequently lowered by the lower rule. As has earlier been demonstrated, such prefixes form one p-word with their bases, and undergo all p-word rules, including word stress. The remaining prefixes become prosodically united with the stems as a result of the monosyllable rule. This means that at the stage when word stress applies, there are no prosodic differences between prefixed forms: they are all single p-words and, consequently, receive penultimate stress, for example

'pod+skok jump up, noun   *o'de+zwać* speak
'wy+lać pour out   *ro'ze+rwać* tear apart

It must be made explicit that the monosyllable rule is not an *ad hoc* device, which is posited for prefixes exclusively. It has much broader applications, evident in the case of compounds. In compounds their individual elements constitute separate p-words, the fact reflected by means of the following convention:[16]

$$[[\ ] [\ ]]_{N\ V,\ Ad} \rightarrow (([\ ])_\omega ([\ ]))_\omega$$

After the elements of a compound are individually stressed, compound stress rule applies giving prominence to the head (Rubach and Booij 1985), for example

   2   1
cudzo+ziemiec foreigner
   1   2
kula ziemska globe

Compound stress rule fails to take place, however, if one of the elements is monosyllabic; in such cases penultimate stress is assigned, in the same fashion as in single p-words, for example

'troj+nóg tripod   *dusz+'pasterz* priest
ze'gar+mistrz clock-maker   *dw+u+'szereg* line
dalek+'o+pis teletype   *włócz+'y+kij* gadabout

What is clearly needed here is the monosyllable rule, which would gather both elements of a compound into a single p-word. It has to be added that these are all regular forms and not exceptions. In other words, compounds of the type presented above are not lexically marked as subject to the rule under discussion. This can be seen when plural forms are created; here the addition of an inflectional ending removes the context for the monosyllable rule and, consequently, the compound stress rule applies, for example

$$\overset{2}{dusz}+\overset{1}{pasterz}+e \text{ priests} \quad \overset{2}{zegar}+\overset{1}{mistrz}+e \text{ clock-makers}$$

It is also significant to note that the monosyllable rule cannot be viewed as a prephonological mapping convention. Thus, the verb *wśnić* start dreaming must be interpreted as two p-words

$$(vĭ)_\omega \ (sĭn+i+ć)_\omega$$

to ensure the blocking of lower. Only after the prefix vowel has been removed can the remaining consonant be incorporated prosodically into the adjoining item. Similarly, the compound *dusigrosz* scrape penny of the initial structure

$$(dus+i)_\omega \ (groš+ĭ)_\omega$$

where the final lax vowel is the marker of the nominative singular of masculine nouns, cannot be subject to the monosyllable rule, since it consists of two bisyllabic p-words. Once lower deletes the yer, the context for the rule in question is created and, after it has applied, word stress assigns prominence to the penultimate syllable

$$dus+'i+grosz$$

Clearly, the monosyllable rule must be placed among phonological processes, i.e. after lower and before word stress.[17]

Let us return to the problem of syllabifying prefixed forms. As has been argued, their prephonological prosodic status is different; some of them are single p-words (when they contain yer roots), others are sequences of p-words (when they contain non-yer roots). Nevertheless, at the end of phonological derivation they are all single p-words due to the monosyllable rule. This fact explains two possible syllabifications of prefixed words: the first one applies when the prefix and the stem are separate prosodic items, the second one operates after new p-words have been created. This is contingent with the assumption that whenever a p-word is formed, it must acquire syllabic structure.

Let us briefly restate the major results of this section. The issue at stake has been how to account for the phonology of Polish prefixes. The analysis of several earlier generative treatments of the problem (the boundary solution, the cyclic and the lexical approaches) has demonstrated that none of them is fully adequate. This conclusion has led us to seek an alternative solution. The concept of the prosodic word has been employed, enabling us to account for the majority of facts which pertain to the phonology of prefixation. We have assumed that prefixes are of two types: those that are cohering and form one p-word with the stem, and those that are non-cohering and constitute separate p-words. The first kind comprises prefixes attached to roots with yer vowels, the other kind all the remaining cases. This distinction is introduced by a prephonological mapping convention, which interprets the morphological structure of items in terms of prosodic words, and which refers to the segmental makeup of morphological strings. This approach enables us to account for the fact that lower applies in some prefixed forms (the first type), but is blocked in the others (the second type). We have also noted that there are certain properties that all prefixed words share: they are stressed as single items and can often be syllabified in two ways. It has been possible to account for these phenomena by positing the monosyllable rule, which performs prosodic reanalysis in the course of the phonological derivation. The remaining phonological rules that affect forms with prefixes belong to phrase-level phonology, and operate both within and across words. In brief, the present analysis appears to cover phonological properties of Polish prefixes.

5.3 Conclusion

It should be useful to compare now the results of our analysis of English affixation and Polish prefixation. First of all, it has been demonstrated that important gains are obtained if units of the phonological hierarchy are employed in phonological description. A mass of evidence from both Polish and English suggests the significance of the notion of the phonological word, called into question by some linguists (for example Selkirk 1984). Our analysis supports the need for isolating prosodic words in both languages. A striking analogy is that neither in English nor in Polish are morphological words identical with phonological words. Thus, in English, Class II affixes, but in Polish, prefixes appear to function as separate p-words, within which the majority of phonological rules operate. An important difference between English and Polish non-cohering affixes is, however, that English Class II affixes appear to be distinct from Class I affixes both in terms of their phonology and morphology, while prefixes in Polish are differentiated from the remaining formatives at the phonological, but not at the morphological level. In other words, in English, phonology reflects morphological structures to a greater degree than it does in Polish.[18]

The latter statement holds true of regular Class I and Class II formations, but not of dual class affixes, in which case numerous instances of morpho–phonological discrepancies have been observed. Our proposal has been to enrich the adjustment apparatus with rebracketing rules whose function is to prepare morphological structures for phonological interpretation whenever the relationship between the two escapes systematic treatment.

The lack of identity between morphological words and phonological words necessitates the introduction of the mapping mechanism that relates the former with the latter. In English mapping employs the information concerning the bracketing of two types of affixes, which is supplied by the morphological component as well as rebracketing rules. In Polish, in addition to morphological factors, phonological, or, more exactly, segmental structure of items plays an important role in morphology–phonology mapping.

Moreover, we have noted that the prosodic status of a given unit may undergo changes in the course of phonological derivation. This might happen due to the operation of phonological rules which modify the segmental (and, hence, the syllabic) structure of items. In English, for instance, inflectional suffixes (different from *-ing*) enter the derivation as separate p-words, but, after the vowel of the suffix has been deleted, they merge prosodically with the stem, due to the constraint that disallows non-syllabic p-words. In Polish prefixes have been claimed to lose their prosodic independence as a result of the monosyllable rule.

We should like to emphasize that there is evidence from other languages which points to the necessity for rules of phonological reanalysis in the course of phonological processing. Hungarian, for example, appears to parallel Polish in this respect. Nespor and Vogel (1986:123), following Booij (1984), observe that vowel harmony, according to which vowels must agree in backness, has the phonological word as its domain. Its operation is illustrated with the examples below,

ház+unk+nak for our house   *szék+ünk+nek* for our chair

In the first case all vowels are back, in the second they are front. Elements of compounds may have vowels differing in backness, for example

gyógy+szer medicine   *jár+mü* vehicle

which shows that they are separate p-words. The same is true of verbal prefixes whose vowels do not have to harmonize with those in the stems, for example

le+dolgoz+ni work off   *oda+men+ni* go there

(*-ni* is the infinitival suffix). Thus, prefixes are separate p-words as well. Yet, the stress rule, which gives prominence to the first syllable, treats all these items as single words. Consequently, their initial syllables receive stress, for example

'Buda+pest Budapest   *'ki+zar+ni* lock out

This means that before the application of the stress rule both compounds and prefixed forms are reanalysed as one prosodic unit. We conclude that the rules of prosodic interpretation are not always placed before phonological processes, but must often be interspersed with them.

Another significant aspect of mapping has to be mentioned. We have assumed that it does not consist in the replacement of morphological units by the phonological ones, but rather in the enriching of morphological structure with prosodic categories.

This view contrasts with Nespor and Vogel's (1986) approach, according to which mapping wipes off morphological units. This is possible owing to the fact that in their framework all morphologically conditioned rules apply in the lexicon in the fashion suggested by lexical phonology. Mapping takes place after lexical rules and before postlexical processes. This, in consequence, means that rules dependent on morphological structure cannot refer to prosodic categories. We find this view difficult to uphold, particularly in the case of Polish. As has been shown, many 'lexical' rules (such as vowel deletion, DI tensing, palatalization) must be prevented from affecting prefixes. This cannot be done by postulating different derivational levels, and appeal must be made to phonological words. To put it differently, at the stage where 'lexical' rules apply, prefixes must already be marked as p-words, and the processes in question must be restricted to the p-word domain. Thus, the morphology–phonology mapping must take place before the application of such rules.

Moreover, it is clear that word-level rules frequently refer not only to prosodic, but to morphological categories as well (for instance, DI tensing to the presence of the suffix -*aj*). It logically follows that morphological structure must be available for the proper application of such processes. The conclusion thus is that phonological units do not replace morphological entities, but complement them.

Another issue which we have encountered in our analysis is the prosodic status of sequences of p-words. We have argued that in English Class II affixes should be viewed as clitics, and words that contain them as clitic groups. The same approach cannot be extended to prefixed forms in Polish; at the end of phonological derivation they all acquire the status of single p-words. The term 'clitic group' is therefore restricted in Polish to the items with true syntactic clitics (such as -*śmy* and -*ście*).

As to compounds, in both languages their individual elements appear to function as separate p-words, and a sequence of such p-words usually has the properties of the phonological phrase. An exception to this generalization is English compounds such as *fireman*, which are reinterpreted by adjustment rules (and subsequent mapping) as single p-words, and Polish compounds with at least one monosyllabic element, which are also subject to prosodic reanalysis as p-words.

It has also been interesting to note that the mapping of the morpho-syntactic units onto the prosodic hierarchy admits a certain amount of variation. Thus, some structures (for example *John is*) can be viewed either as clitic groups or as p-phrases, which decision has phonological consequences in the form of optionality of some phonological rules.

In brief, the introduction of prosodic units, and the p-word in particular, results in increasing the adequacy of phonological description.

Final remarks

The main objective of the present book has been to investigate various ways in which phonological rules of Polish and English interact with the morphologies of both languages, as well as to explore the best model for describing these interactions. In other words, our primary concern has been the role of 'grammatical prerequisites' to phonological analysis of the abstract generative type. Similarly to Pike (1947:155) we believe that, 'when phonological and grammatical facts are mutually dependent, the treatment of phonology without reference to grammar is a concealment of part of a most important set of structural facts pertinent to phonology'.

The issue of paramount importance has been to decide what is the mutual relationship of the morphological and phonological components. Two approaches, which have been termed 'integrational' and 'separational', have been put side by side and applied to the description of selected problems of Polish and English phonology as well as, to a lesser extent, morphology. The question thus has been posed whether phonological rules should be integrated with WFRs in the lexicon, as suggested by lexical phonology, or whether the morphological component ought to precede phonology, as assumed in the traditional generative model.

First we have demonstrated that the integrational approach with lexical levels finds no support in Polish, where it is incapable of handling the phonology of prefixes without resorting to various non-lexical means. Nevertheless the bulk of our argument against the integration of the two components has been based on the discussion of English data. We have focused our attention on numerous cases of discrepancy between the morphological and phonological properties of English words, and concluded that they make a meaningful integration of phonology and morphology impossible. The so-called dual class affixes are a particularly strong evidence against lexical phonology, since they show that morphological and phonological levels or classes cannot be viewed as identical. We have concluded that the integrational lexical approach should be abandoned in favour of a separational framework.

We have then passed to examining the ways in which morphology determines the application of phonological rules. The issue of morphological bracketing and its role in phonology was taken up first. In abstract varieties of generative phonology it is largely uncontroversial that some phonological rules are grammatically conditioned and must be provided with the information concerning the lexical and/or grammatical categories of words. Therefore, morpho-syntactic brackets are needed for the proper operation of such rules. However, in cyclic phonology brackets have yet another function: they determine the mode of application of phonological rules. Those rules that refer to them are cyclic and those which do not are postcyclic. This assumption has been subject to our critical analysis. We have examined two most typical examples of allegedly cyclic rules: trisyllabic laxing in English and palatalization in Polish, and shown that regarding them as cyclic does not bring the desired results. In the first case it appears that TSL does not apply in every derived environment, but requires a specific placement of the morpheme boundary. In the second case it has been argued that there is no connection between the application of palatalization and the derived environment condition: the rule in question operates both inside morphemes and across morpheme boundaries, and frequently fails to apply in these two contexts. The concept of strict cyclicity has thus been rejected.

Nevertheless, the idea of phonological rules applying more than once in the derivation of one lexical item has been reconsidered in Chapter 3. Our analysis of verbs and deverbal derivatives in Polish has demonstrated that neither the traditional nor the cyclic/lexical framework are tenable since they are incapable of handling the forms in question in an adequate way. The problem is that some rules (such as verb suffix truncation and DI tensing) appear to operate in two different manners depending on the morphological structure of items: on phonological strings with simple verbs, and on surface forms of complex verbs. To account for such cases, we have introduced the mechanism of the multiple application of phonological rules. This means that the structures created by WFRs and specified as cyclic are processed by phonological rules, then return to the word formation component and undergo another operation of the phonology. Such procedure is possible due to the loop from the phonological component to the morphological component.

More evidence for the loop and the return from the output of phonological rules to the input of WFRs has been brought forward in Chapter 4, in which we have dealt with the nature of forms that are subject to morphological processes. It has been shown that WFRs such as comparative degree formation, imperative formation and augmentative back-formation in Polish require inputs that are neither phonological nor intermediate, but phonetic, i.e. resulting from the application of word-level phonological rules – a possibility inadmissible in both the traditional separational and the lexical integrational approaches. We have argued that some morphological processes must be marked as operating on structures already processed by the phonology, which procedure is applicable not only to the three WFRs of Polish, but also to *-al*, *-ful* and *-(e)teria* suffixations in English and *-rice* formation in Dutch. To put it differently, the phonology–morphology loop appears to have broader applicability and is not restricted to one language only. We have furthermore suggested that in certain cases (for example nominalizations of prepositional phrases in Polish) going back from (phrase-level) syntax to the morphological component is also necessary.

The approach to the phonology–morphology interaction pursued here has numerous advantages. First of all, it allows us to retain simple, general formulations of both phonological and morphological rules discussed in this book. Moreover, due to it we can produce the correct derivations of many classes of items (for example simple and complex verbs, deverbal formations, comparative degree adjectives, imperative forms of verbs, augmentative back-formed nouns), which are problematic in different frameworks. The phonology–morphology loop also enables some WFRs to have access to the information provided by phonological rules. This is done without integrating morphology and phonology in one common component, which correctly predicts that only some, and not all WFRs require such information. Finally, our approach makes it possible for morphological and phonological properties of items to be different – a situation frequently encountered not only in Polish and English. With the separation of the two components it comes as no surprise that morphological and phonological processes are often governed by different principles and are sensitive to various factors.

We should like to point out that the procedure suggested here is not arbitrary in the sense that it is subject to empirical (dis)confirmation. Thus, the assumption that WFRs operate on phonetic structures can be falsified if such processes are shown to refer to some intermediate level of representation, i.e. to the information that is present neither underlyingly nor phonetically, but at some stage between the two, and is subsequently removed by the application of phonological rules.

The analysis of English affixation and Polish prefixation embarked on in Chapter 2 has been further developed in Chapter 5. It has demonstrated that purely morphological distinctions are insufficient to account for the phonological properties of English and Polish words. Phonological rules of both languages have appeared to be sensitive to the units of the prosodic hierarchy frequently different from morphological entities. For instance, we have shown that in English and Polish there is no one-to-one correspondence between morphological and phonological words. In English Class II affixes, but in Polish prefixes, are separate p-words, since their attachment blocks the application of word-level phonological rules. The conclusion has been that it is the phonological rather than the morphological word which acts as the domain of such rules.

In view of the lack of identity between morphological and phonological words, a set of rules that map the former onto the latter has to be postulated. Mapping rules are language specific and complement morphological strings with prosodic structure. They make use of the information concerning the types of affixes as well as the segmental make-up of words. We have observed that the morphology–phonology mapping does not wipe off

Final remarks

morphological bracketing, since phonological rules frequently need to refer to the units of both hierarchies. Moreover, it has been argued that the prosodic structure of lexical items is not only established prephonologically, but must often undergo significant modifications in the course of phonological derivation.

Apart from mapping rules, which have the character of mechanical conventions, additional statements are required in those instances in which morphological and phonological structures cannot be related in any regular fashion. In such situations we have posited rebracketing rules which adjust morphological bracketing for the purposes of phonology in lexically marked cases. Such adjustment rules are particularly important in English, where dual class affixes often display divergent morphological and phonological properties. In short, rebracketing rules are responsible for all non-systematic cases of morphophonological discrepancy.

The incorporation of prosodic units, particularly the phonological word, into the phonological description of Polish and English allows us to handle phonological properties of Class I, Class II and dual class affixes in English, as well as prefixes in Polish in a more adequate way than the boundary approach of the traditional generative model and the level approach of lexical phonology.

Apart from morphological bracketing, in the traditional generative framework phonological brackets frequently refer to morphological boundaries, which count as the second major type of non-phonetic information in phonology. As noted in Chapter 1, recent years can be characterized as a period in which a campaign against boundary distinctions in both phonology and morphology has been launched. First, different boundaries have been attacked for their morphological arbitrariness. Then lexical phonology has demonstrated that the theory of level ordering eliminates the need for different boundary symbols altogether. Boundaries have also been criticized from the quarters of prosodic phonology, in which they are regarded as totally redundant. It is therefore significant to ask whether boundary distinctions are needed in the model of the phonology–morphology interaction proposed in this study.

Two morphological boundaries, the morpheme and the word boundary, have always been assumed necessary in phonology, and have largely been uncontroversial since they are morpho-syntactically motivated. However, other boundaries, intermediate between the two just mentioned, have also been postulated (i.e. the word-internal and the prefix boundary). It is significant to see what purpose they were meant to serve. Kenstowicz and Kisseberth (1977:104) correctly note that, 'the basic concept underlying the notion of boundaries is the degree of cohesion that linguistic forms exhibit. . . . Morphemes cohere to form larger units – words, but in some cases it is possible to distinguish different degrees of cohesion within the word.' To put it differently, within one morphological word there are frequently smaller units, distinct from syllables and feet, which function as the domain of application of phonological rules. Our examination has shown that in English, phonologically speaking, words are divided into stems and Class II affixes, while in Polish prefixes stand out from the remaining part of lexical items. The proposal has been to regard such non-cohering units as p-words. As has been demonstrated, the division of a given form into p-words is sometimes morphologically motivated (as with English regular Class I and Class II affixes), and in some cases somewhat arbitrary, i.e. not determined by morphology (English dual class affixes and Polish prefixes). In other words, the degree of morphological cohesion is not always identical with the degree of phonological cohesion.

These observations explain why the traditional boundaries of the SPE model have been so objectionable: they have been supposed to be morphologically motivated (they counted as non-phonetic information in phonology), but have been postulated for the sake of phonological rules only. To put it differently, boundaries have been meant to be morphological, but were, in fact, phonological in character. Moreover, the lack of iso-morphy between morphological and phonological structures explains why morphological bracketing has not been sufficient as a mechanism of rule conditioning and blocking, and why resorting to such half-morphological and half-phonological devices has been necessary.

Nevertheless, the conviction that it is possible to find morphological correlates of phonological differences is still present, although in a modified form, in more recent approaches as well. The theory of lexical levels and phonological rules assigned to them advocated by lexical phonology is clearly one of these. The source of its failure lies precisely in its attempt to justify all phonological properties of words in terms of their morphological structure. Consequently, the lexical model works when such correlation exists, but fails when it does not. As demonstrated, cases of the latter kind are very frequent in both Polish and English.

Within the approach advocated here, the majority of these problems are non-existent. Since morphology precedes phonology, the two types of structures do not always have to be identical. Thus, the division of morphological words into phonological words does not have to be morphologically motivated in all instances. A few more detailed remarks on the SPE boundaries in the framework assumed here seem in order.

It is, no doubt, evident that the inclusion of the p-word in the phonological description eliminates the need for a separate prefix boundary. If prefixes are systematically distinct from the remaining affixes in terms of their phonological properties (as is the case with Polish prefixes as well as English Class II prefixes), then they should be treated as separate p-words. In other instances prefixes should be regarded as cohering affixes that behave in the same fashion as the remaining formatives. Nevertheless, it might happen that a given phonological rule which operates in the domain of the p-word is morphologized and needs to refer to the prefix boundary (for example the rule of palatal assimilation in Polish blocked in the case of prefixes). In such situations, it seems, no reference to the traditional prefix juncture is needed. Rather use ought to be made, along the lines suggested by Strauss (1982), of morphological bracketing. Thus, prefixes are attached with the left bracket

[

and phonological rules can simply refer to it by including [in their structural description. If brackets are preserved throughout phonological derivation, they might as well serve in the formulation of phonological rules.

The concept of the p-word also makes it possible to dispense with the word internal boundary. Now the p-word can act as the domain of the application of word-level rules, and if they need to refer to some junctures, these should be the edges of the p-word. In short, the need for the # symbol in the formulation and application of phonological rules can be eliminated.

A significant issue is whether the remaining junctures, i.e. the morphological word boundary and the morpheme boundary, are needed in phonology. The answer clearly depends on whether these two morphological units, i.e. the word and the morpheme, play a role in the operation of phonological rules. To put it differently, the question is whether the concept of the p-word renders superfluous the use of these two units in phonology.

As to the role of the morphological word, it seems that its domain function is frequently fulfilled by the p-word. Thus, phonological rules discussed so far operate within p-words, rather than within morphological words. Moreover, many processes traditionally formulated as referring to the beginning or the end of a word (for example g-deletion, cluster simplification and sonorant syllabification in English) can be reformulated in such a way as to make use of the edges of the p-word. Finally, since in many cases word boundaries coincide with syllable boundaries, the former can be replaced with the latter in the formulation of some phonological rules. Note that this replacement is not motivated by the willingness to get rid of the word boundary at all costs, but by a considerably greater adequacy of formulations which employ syllable structure. Nevertheless, if some phonological rule needs to differentiate between the p-word and the morphological word boundary, it can do so by referring to morphological bracketing. Thus, the traditional word-final position is the right labelled bracket

]

followed by the null string, i.e. not followed by another right labelled bracket. In sum, the traditional word boundary is not necessary in the cases which have been subject to our scrutiny.

If three boundaries can be eliminated from phonology, the issue is whether the same can be done with the remaining one, i.e. the morpheme boundary. In other words, the question is whether morphemes play a role in the application of phonological rules. In order to answer this question, recall the discussion of trisyllabic laxing in Chapter 2. We have argued that it is

Final remarks

insufficient and inadequate to claim that the vowel subject to TSL must be the third from the end of the p-word, with the morpheme juncture located somewhere in the input string. For the rule to operate properly, the morpheme boundary must be placed exactly after the vowel to be shortened (optionally followed by one or two consonants). We have expressed this requirement in our formulation of TSL (see section 2.3.1), which comprises the plus symbol after the antepenultimate vowel.

It is now legitimate to ask whether '+' can be replaced by some morphological bracket. This, in turn, depends on the adopted system of bracketing. In a model in which suffixes are bracketed in a different way than prefixes, the morpheme boundary appears indispensable. Consider the formulation of TSL once again. If, instead of the plus symbol, we introduced

]

into the rule, this would incorrectly exclude laxing in prefixes, for example in such examples as

trĭ+meter   trĭ+colour

A different bracket, i.e.

[

would deal with laxing in prefixed, but in suffixed forms. The problem here is that while there exist right and left brackets, we have not one symbol which would mean 'bracket in general'. Clearly, the formulation of TSL with the morpheme boundary is the simplest possibility.

No problems of this sort arise with autosegmental notation: as shown in Chapter 1, it is possible for a string of segments to belong simultaneously to both the prosodic and the morphological hierarchies, which is expressed by appropriate association lines. Clearly, the morpheme boundary symbol is unnecessary in this approach.

Nevertheless, for practical reasons it seems useful to preserve '+' in morphology and phonology. First of all, it allows us to simplify rules and representations in those cases in which the

Final remarks

multidimensional character of the latter is unimportant. Secondly, if the morpheme boundary symbol is present in the lexical representation of affixes, we can distinguish them easily from free morphemes, as argued in Chapter 5. Moreover, the placement of the plus indicates in a straightforward manner on which side of an item an affix is appended. Finally, the plus symbol can be used to express other significant phonological and morphological distinctions.

Kenstowicz and Kisseberth (1977:87–8) claim that phonological rules in various languages sometimes need to distinguish between roots and affixes, as well as between derivation and inflection. If such distinctions are indeed significant, an adequate description must be able to reflect them.

The first case, i.e. distinguishing between roots and affixes, is non-problematic if pluses are allowed to appear as part of the morphological specification of affixes. Then roots can be treated as [ ], with no internal occurrences of brackets or pluses.

The second case refers to the difference between derivation and inflection. Recall the rule of verb suffix truncation in Polish, which was discussed in Chapter 3. It truncates verbalizing suffixes before derivational, but not before inflectional suffixes. This rule is very troublesome to express formally; if all morphemes are associated with brackets, then there is no formal difference between derivation and inflection. Compare, for example, the verb *kopać* 'dig' and the noun derived from it, i.e. *koparka* 'digging machine'

$$[[[\text{kop}]\ a]_V\ \acute{c}]_V \quad [[[[\text{kop}]a]_V\ a\check{r}k]_N\ a]_N$$

in which bracketing does not reflect the fact that some of the affixes in these words are inflectional and some are derivational. If we, however, assume, as Strauss (1982:6–13) does, that inflection is attached inside derivational brackets (it never changes the lexical category of words), i.e. it has no brackets of its own, the formulation of VST becomes trivial:

$$\text{VS} \rightarrow \phi\ /\ \underline{\quad}\ ]$$

Its application can be shown in the examples below.

Final remarks

$$[kop+a+ć]_V \quad [[kop+a]_V +arik+a]_N$$
$$ \downarrow$$
$$\text{no VST} \phi$$

In the first case the verb suffix does not delete, since no right bracket follows it directly, *-ć* being the infinitival inflectional ending bracketed together with the rest of the verb. In the second case VST takes place, since the nominalizing suffix *-arka* is appended outside the verbal bracket. In this way the distinction between derivation and inflection can be expressed for the sake of adjustment and phonological rules.[1]

To conclude, it appears that in a framework which employs phonological units such as p-words and syllables, as well as morphological bracketing, there is no need for the traditional boundary distinctions of the SPE type. The morpheme boundary symbol has been preserved, however, mainly in its concatenative function.

It is fitting to close this book with a presentation of the model of the phonology–morphology interaction that has emerged from our analysis. In a largely simplified form, it can be claimed to have the following shape:[2]

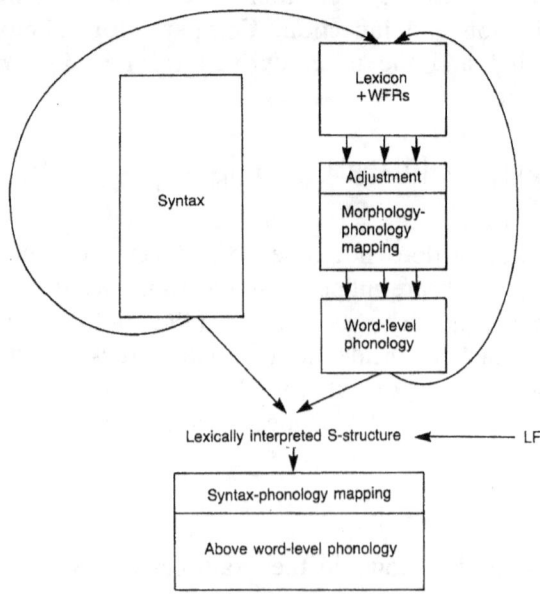

Final remarks

In this model the lexicon and WFRs provide fully bracketed structures which are subject first to adjustment and then to morphology–phonology mapping. Then word-level phonological rules apply, where by word we mean the p-word. Those structures which are marked in the lexicon as cyclic (by virtue of being subject to WFRs which take phonetic inputs, or by having morphological structure which is a cyclicity trigger) return to the morphological component via the phonology–morphology loop and then, together with the remaining affixes, pass through adjustment rules and phonological processes once again. After the final operation of word-level rules brackets are removed, and the items thus obtained are subject to lexical insertion. Lexically interpreted surface structure is then subject to another set of mapping rules, which divide syntactic strings into larger prosodic units such as the phonological phrase, the intonational phrase and the utterance. Then the remaining, above word-level phonological rules apply. The loop from syntax to morphology indicates that syntactic structures may act as inputs to WFRs.

The model of the phonology–morphology interaction presented here can be viewed as a compromise between the traditional SPE model and the lexical framework. On the one hand, the morphological and the phonological components are separate, but, on the other, the loop from the latter to the former allows for the multiple application of phonological rules, as well as access of WFRs to the information supplied by the phonology.

The division of the phonological component into word-level phonology and above word-level phonology has been based on studies by Selkirk (1984), Kaisse (1985) and Nespor and Vogel (1986). These authors have demonstrated convincingly that it is necessary to isolate phonological rules which apply in connected speech and are frequently sensitive to such factors as speech rate and syntatic environment. This does not mean, however, that a single word cannot be subject to such rules. After it has been assigned syntactic structure, it can be interpreted as a one-word phonological phrase and an utterance, and undergo appropriate rules. In this way the unnecessary repetition of rules can be avoided.

It should be observed that mapping rules are found in two places: between morphology and word-phonology, and between syntax and sentence-phonology. These rules are evidently not the same. The former refer to the units within the p-word, the latter to the items larger than the p-word.

Thus, the crucial role in our model of the phonology–morphology interaction is assigned to morphological bracketing, which may be referred to in the formulation of phonological rules. Moreover, certain bracket configurations, together with input conditions on WFRs, act as cyclicity triggers, i.e. they induce the multiple application of phonological rules. Furthermore, morphological brackets frequently determine the assignment of phonological parentheses, i.e. the mapping of morphological words onto the prosodic words. Since the erection of prosodic structure does not wipe off morphological brackets, phonological rules can make use of both types of units. Another consequence of this approach is that boundary distinctions are no longer necessary.

An important element of the proposal pursued here is adjustment rules. Apart from their usual function of modifying some morphemes in the context of some other formatives, they perform the operation of rebracketing in those cases in which no regular correspondence between morphological and phonological properties of words can be found.

Finally, our analysis would not be possible without prosodic units and the phonological word in particular. Let us merely mention here that due to it numerous facts of both languages can be accounted for in a more adequate fashion than in any other approach which has been scrutinized in this study.

A word of caution is also necessary. The material gathered here concerns two languages only, and the theoretical proposals that have been advocated by us must, of course, be tested against the background of other languages before any conclusions as to their universality can be drawn. We do hope, however, that some concepts presented in this book will prove of greater applicability than to Polish and English only.

In these final remarks we have so far concentrated on the major theoretical aspects of our analysis and its contribution to establishing the model of the phonology–morphology interface. To complete this overview, it has to be added that the present work has dealt with various detailed problems of Polish and English phonology and morphology. With respect to English, we have offered an analysis of two classes of affixes, and proposed a mechanism accounting for rule conditioning and rule blocking. Moreover, we have suggested a method of handling dual class affixes, whose adequate description is very troublesome for other approaches. We have also discussed in some detail the rule of trisyllabic laxing, and modified its formulation.

For Polish, a new way of approaching the phonology of prefixes has been suggested, which solves many problems other models are incapable of dealing with. Much attention has been devoted to the correct derivation of complex verbs and deverbal derivatives. Moreover, some rules of Polish phonology, such as DI tensing, lower and VST, have been examined with their proper formulation and application in focus. We have also analysed three morphological processes of Polish, i.e. comparative degree formation, imperative formation and augmentative back-formation, with respect to the nature of their input forms.

Finally, we have discussed and evaluated critically many theoretical as well as descriptive proposals put forward in recent years.

Although much of what has been proposed here will no doubt be supplemented, modified and revised by further research, we hope that a significant step has been taken towards describing the phonology–morphology interaction in Polish and English in a coherent and satisfactory fashion.

Notes

Notes to Chapter 1: Separation versus integration

1. The root-final consonant in *permissive*, after having undergone spirantization, is subject to devoicing before *-ive*.
2. In this chapter we concentrate on the relation between the phonological and the morphological components and, for the sake of clarity, disregard the interaction of phonological rules with syntax. We return to this issue in Final Remarks.
3. In this book we employ the SPE term 'trisyllabic laxing', although there are reasons to believe that the process consists in shortening the antepenultimate vowel rather than its laxing.
4. As a matter of fact, stress is the only phonological rule which applies on the first cycle, due to its structure-building character (Kiparsky 1982a).
5. Booij and Rubach (1987) argue, however, for a distinction between postcyclic lexical and postlexical (non-cyclic) phonological rules.

Notes to Chapter 2: Levels and cycles

1. As a matter of fact, according to Gussmann (1980a) and Rubach (1984a), palatalization in such cases is triggered by the lax vowel /ĭ/, which is later deleted by the rule of lower (see Chapter 3).
2. This does not exhaust all the alleged phonological advantages of adopting the lexical framework (see, for example, Kaisse and Shaw 1985; Mohanan 1982). Many of them, however, do not follow from integrating phonological rules with morphology, but from other principles. For instance, the limitation on the abstractness of phonological representations results from adopting the strict cyclicity condition.
3. In some models of lexical phonology the cyclicity of phonological rules must be suppressed rather than stipulated. For example, in Halle and Mohanan's (1985) framework some lexical strata are non-cyclic. At such levels phonological rules must be prevented

from applying cyclically, although they also take part in the
formation of lexical items.
4. Rubach's (1984a) lexical description of Polish is largely a
restatement of his (1981) cyclic account; one chapter on the lexical
framework is added, in which we learn that the only significant
modification with respect to the cyclic approach concerns the
treatment of prefixes (discussed in Chapter 5).
5. For the criticism of Rubach's (1984a) lexical approach to Polish see
Gussmann (1985b). See also Gladney (1986) for other pertinent
remarks.
6. Sometimes this significant and non-trivial issue is, amazingly,
ignored. For instance, Selkirk (1982:79), who is not a lexicalist, but
who accepts the AOG and the division of English affixes into two
classes, states that, 'I leave it to the readers to assure themselves
that all of the suffixes and prefixes tabulated here do indeed display
the distributional and phonological properties implied by their
classification.'
7. The majority of English data are taken from Lehnert (1971), *The
Shorter Oxford English Dictionary* (1973), Jones (1982) and
Kenyon and Knott (1953).
8. In what follows we shall not be concerned with the semantic factor.
As has been mentioned, cases of the disparity between the
morphological and semantic structure of words constitute a serious
problem for the lexical model.
9. For the reasons of the failure of TSL in some examples, see
section 2.3.1.
10. The denominal character of these verbs is proved by their
semantics. For example, *parenthesize* means to 'state in
parenthesis', *emphasize* 'to impart emphasis to' (*The Shorter
Oxford English Dictionary*).
11. Following Marchand (1969:251), we assume that *-ant* and *-ent* are
mere spelling variants.
12. Some *-ive* words function also as nouns, for example, *explosive,
captive, sedative*.
13. It should be added that morphological evidence for the Class II
status of *-ive* is quite scarce. Nevertheless, even if we regard *-ive* as
a member of Class I from the morphological point of view, it
remains a dual class affix in terms of its phonology.
14. Like Aronoff (1976:121), we treat *-able* and *-ible* as mere spelling
variants.
15. We do not mean here that fluctuating forms are found in the speech
of one person; a given speaker will probably use only one form.
Nevertheless, within the same idiolect some of the suffixes under
discussion will cause the shift in stress, while others will be stress-
neutral.
16. According to Hayes (1980), suffixes such as *-ant*, *-ive* and *-able* are
all extrametrical, i.e. they do not take part in stress rules. In his
framework this means that these suffixes cause stress to fall on

Notes

heavy syllables immediately to their left, otherwise two syllables to the left. This procedure accounts for the placement of stress in

    'illustrate – i'llustrative   con'serve – con'servative

(here -*ative* behaves, according to Hayes, as a single suffix), but not in

    'legislate – 'legislative (*le'gislative)

17. Aronoff (1976:125) is wrong in his claim that the occurrence of *un*- with Class I -*able* forms is infrequent. Numerous examples of this sort can be given, for example

uncommunicable	uncultivable	uninvestigable
unsatiable	unnavigable	uneducable
unfrustrable	unexpugnable	unimpugnable

18. In this section we have discussed selected dual class suffixes leaving aside the problem of prefixes. Nevertheless, it seems that the majority of our objections raised with regard to suffixes are directly applicable also to prefixes. The prefix *un*-, for example, frequently assigned to both classes, in all cases fails to undergo nasal assimilation.
19. Halle and Mohanan (1985:65) seem to be aware of the danger that such cases create for their framework and introduce the device of the loop. They argue that it 'allows a stratum distinction for the purposes of phonology without imposing a corresponding distinction in morphological distribution'. However, the loop is postulated from stratum 3 to stratum 2, i.e. from compounding to Class II derivation. Consequently, it does not account for Class I and Class II forms subject to our analysis. Positing the additional loop from level 2 to level 1 would further weaken the advantages of the lexical model.
20. Yet another way of handling the phonology and morphology of English affixes has been put forward by Selkirk (1982). However, her approach is based on the validity of the AOG and suffers from all the shortcomings discussed here.
21. Kiparsky (1982a) claims that it is possible to view strict cyclicity as derived from the elsewhere condition and the concept of lexical entries as identity rules. This is of no importance to our considerations since in the cases under discussion the results of applying strict cyclicity and Kiparsky's proposal are the same.
22. The formulation of TSL given here does not account for the failure of the rule with Class II affixes, i.e. it disregards the domain of rule application. The issue is taken up again in Chapter 5, in which TSL is treated as a rule which operates within the domain of the phonological word, to which Class II affixes do not belong.

23. Some linguists (most explicitly Selkirk 1984) are of the opinion that TSL is not a productive phonological rule, but a morphologized process which applies only in the context of certain diacritically marked suffixes. Kiparsky (1982:151) argues against this approach since 'it misses the generalization embodied in the *phonological* environment of the rule and therefore enormously adds to the *lexical* arbitrariness of the rule'.
24. The discussion of TSL presented in this section should not be viewed as a comprehensive analysis of the process. Many facts require further investigation, for instance, the relation between stress and TSL.
25. Following earlier generative accounts, Rubach accepts also absolute neutralization between high tense and lax vowels. Thus, the failure of palatalization in

    do[m+e]k house, dim.   *la[s+e]k* forest, dim.

    is attributed to the presence of the back lax vowels of the diminutive suffix /ɨk/. Curiously enough, in both cases in which palatalization does not take place resort is made to abstract, phonetically non-occurring segments.
26. The underlying /ž/ is exempted from depalatalization by virtue of the fact that the process in question does not affect continuants. The phonological /r/ is palatalized to /r'/, which is turned to phonetic [ž] or undergoes depalatalization before coronal consonants (Gussmann 1980a:20–2).

Notes to Chapter 3: The cycle revisited

1. Below we present some phonological facts which refer to verb suffixes,
    - the suffix -*i* emerges as the retracted vowel [ɨ] after hard consonants, for example *sko[č+ɨ]ć* jump.
    - the vowels of the VSs -*e* and -*ej* are phonologically tense and change to [a] before the past tense suffix -*ł*, for example *wisi+e+ć* hang – *wisi+a+ł* it hung.
    - the VSs -*i*, -*e* and -*a* are deleted before other vowels, for example *pis+a+ć* write – *pisz+e+sz* you write.
    - verbs with the suffixes -*aj* and -*ej* are given in the third person plural present tense forms as the palatal glide is deleted before the following consonant, as well as word-finally in the third person singular present tense forms, for example *czyt+aj+ą* they read vs *czyt+a+m* I read, and *czyt+a* he reads.
    - the suffix -*owa* is replaced by -*uj* in present tense forms, for example *ład+owa+ć* load – *ład+uj+e* he loads.
    - the suffix -*ną* /nɨn/ is realized as -*n* before vowels, for example *puch+ną+ć* swell – *puch+n+ę* I swell. The suffix vowel

247

Notes

alternates with [o], for example *płon+[o]+ł* it burnt and [e], for example *płon+[e]+ł+a* she burnt.

2. One may wonder whether indeed the nominalizing suffix is *-iciel* and not *-ciel*, since the stem vowel is the same as the initial vowel of the suffix, which seems to be a needless repetition. There are reasons to believe, however, that in Polish all derivational suffixes begin with a vowel. Furthermore, the exceptions to the *-iciel* suffixation, i.e. those cases in which the suffix is appended to verbs with different VSs than *-i*, indicate that the front vowel must indeed be a part of the suffix. Otherwise its presence in the forms below could not be accounted for, for example

   myśl+iciel thinker from *myśl+e+ć* think
   okaz+iciel bearer from *okaz+a+ć* show

3. In order to avoid postulating VST, it can be claimed that the formation of verbs consists not in suffixation, but in conversion, for example

   $[rown]_{Ad} \rightarrow [rown]_V$

   This is not convincing, however, since, in addition to conversion, another rule would also be needed, i.e. the process which would attach VSs to converted nouns and adjectives. Such an approach complicates the description considerably and serves no other purpose than getting rid of VST.

4. VST can be shown to take place before such early rules as palatalization, for example

   wykła[d]+a+ć cover – *wykła[dź]+in+a* cover, noun
   wypłu[k]+a+ć rinse – *wypłu[č]+yna* rinsing
   zeskro[b]+a+ć scrape – *zeskro[b']+in+a* scraping

5. To aid the reader, all derivations in this as well as in the following chapters are simplified with respect to those details which have no direct bearing on the issues under discussion and which, if presented, might obscure the argumentation. For instance, in the derivation of *tokarz* turner, we disregard the problem of the inflectional ending (see note 12 for explanation). A technical difficulty must also be mentioned here. Square brackets have two functions in this book: they either mean morphological bracketing or mark phonetic representations. We hope that no confusion will be caused by this ambiguity.

6. In some cases it can be argued that verbalization and prefixation are not ordered, but simultaneous. For example, the adjective *nowy* new serves as a base for the formation of such prefixed verbs as *od+now+i+ć* renew and *wz+now+i+ć* resume, while the unprefixed verb **now+i+ć* does not exist at all.

7. The fact that prefixes in Polish never change the grammatical category of words to which they are attached is expressed by a convention (adopted from Lieber 1980), according to which the category of the base is automatically percolated onto the prefixed form, for example

tracić lose – *utracić* id. perf.
$[\text{trat}+i]_V \rightarrow [u+[\text{trat}+i]_V]_V \rightarrow [u+[\text{trat}+i]]_V$

Another convention, employed also by Strauss (1982:6–13), is that inflection is attached inside derivational brackets, for example (-*ć* is the infinitival ending)

utracić lose $[u+[\text{trat}+i+ć]]_V$

8. The suffix -*ywa* has an allomorph -*wa* after the majority of stems ending in the palatal glide (which itself is deleted before the following consonant – see note 1)

$u+my+j+ą$ they will wash – $u+my+wa+ć$ id. DI
$za+truj+ą$ they will poison – $za+tru+wa+ć$ id. DI

9. A different interpretation of the suffix -*ywa* is provided by Gussmann (in press), who suggests that the distinction between [i] and [ɨ] is only phonetic and has no parallel at the underlying level. Thus, in all instances the quality of the high unround vowel is determined by the preceding consonant: [i] occurs after palatalized consonants, [ɨ] elsewhere. This interpretation, however, is possible within the autosegmental approach to palatalization (see Chapter 2).

10. It should be added that according to Gussmann (1980a:50) gliding is a phonological rule which operates before all non-high vowels. It seems, however, that it is more proper to treat it as an allomorphy rule since it has several idiosyncratic properties. For instance, it fails to affect the VS -*i* before -*aj* in

zale[ś]ić afforest – *zale[ś]ać* id. DI (*zaleszać)
rozgałę[ź]ić branch – *rozgałę[ź]ać* id. DI (*rozgałęzać)
zażela[ź]ić iron – *zażela[ź]ać* id. DI (*zażelażać)

Moreover, in some cases gliding must be extended to other contexts as well. It takes place (together with the subsequent palatalization) before the suffix -*arnia* in

wę[dź]ić smoke – *wę[dz]arnia* smoke house
kwa[ś]ić pickle – *kwa[š]arnia* pickling plant

Notes

but not in

to[č]yć turn – *to[k]arnia* turnery
pa[l]ić smoke – *pa[l]arnia* smoking room

which requires lexical marking as to which forms are subject to gliding and which are not.

11. The list of verbs presented here does not include those nasal vowel stems which do not display any changes in the imperfective forms. For example

    wyw[ē]szyć nose out – *wyw[ē]szać* id. DI
    przeci[ō]żyć overload – *przeci[ō]żać* id. DI
    zniech[ē]cić discourage – *zniech[ē]cać* id. DI

    These verbs are problematic since there is no agreement as to the phonological interpretation of nasal vowels – an issue whose discussion goes beyond the scope of this book. We shall assume that the rule of vowel nasalization precedes DI tensing, which does not affect [o] and [e]. It is interesting to note that in colloquial speech occasionally this restriction is lifted and forms such as

    wył[an]czać switch off (from *wył[ō]czyć*)

    although banned by normative dictionaries, can frequently be heard.

12. The high lax vowel is the marker of several inflectional endings, for example of the nominative case of singular masculine nouns – for justification see Gussmann (1980a).

13. Nykiel-Herbert (1984) suggests the following formulation of DI tensing, 'tensing is assigned to the rightmost non-yer vowel of the stem. If there is no other vowel, the yer is tensed.' Clearly, such a rule is not easily formalizable. Moreover, it does not explain the failure of DI tensing in those verbs which contain a sequence of two high lax vowels.

14. It should be noted that when *-ywa* verbs are subject to nominalization, only *-a* is deleted, for example

    w+łam+ywa+ć break in → *w+łam+yw+acz* burglar
    prze+kaz+ywa+ć transmit → *prze+kaz+yw+acz* transmitter

    We propose to account for this fact by assuming that *-ywa* is bimorphemic, i.e. has the structure /-ɨv+a/, and that VST deletes only the morpheme which is immediately followed by a derivational suffix. The same is true of another VS, i.e. *-owa*; on nominalization *-ow* is usually preserved and only *-a* is truncated, for example

        hod+owa+ć breed – *hod+ow+c+a* breeder
        prac+owa+ć work – *prac+ow+nik* worker

    It can therefore be claimed that *-owa*, just like *-ywa*, consists of two morphemes, *-ow* and *-a*, and only the last one is subject to VST.

15. Double imperfectives can be claimed to be derived from iterative verbs such as

        skakać jump   *latać* fly

    Iterative verbs are unprefixed, but resemble DIs in that they comprise the suffix *-aj*, which evinces the tensing of the root vowel.

16. A similar view is presented by Gussmann (1985a) in his analysis of vowel length in Icelandic.

17. What should be considered is whether the multiple processing of complex verbs always brings the correct results. We have found some examples in which this procedure fails to produce the desired output, for example

        $ręk+a_N$ hand → $po+ręcz+y+ć_V$ guarantee → $po+ręk+a_N$ guarantee, noun (**poręcza*)
        $cen+a_N$ price → $prze+cen+i+ć_V$ put on sale → $prze+cen+a$ sale (**przecenia*)

    If the verbs *poręczyć* and *przecenić* are regarded as denominal, the wrong forms are produced. It might be claimed that such verbs have lost their connection with the nouns *ręka* and *cena*, and are synchronically underived.

Notes to Chapter 4: Phonetic inputs to WFRs

1. The superlative degree of adjectives is formed by adding the prefix *naj-* to the comparative, for example

        głup+sz+y more silly – *naj+głup+sz+y* most silly

    or by means of the adverb *najbardziej* most, for example

        interesujący interesting – *najbardziej interesujący* most interesting

    Thus, no special phonological or morphological problems are created by such forms.

2. It should be observed that the attachment of *-ejsz* and *-sz* brings about the application of palatalization. Therefore, the latter suffix can be phonologically represented as /-ĭš/, i.e. with the high lax

Notes

vowel, which, after triggering palatalizaton, is deleted by lower. In some cases no palatalization can be noted, for example

now+sz+y newer   *tward+sz+y* harder

This happens due to the rule of depalatalization, which affects palatalized dentals and labials before the following consonant. This means, in practice, that the effects of palatalization are preserved only in the case of phonological velars, although some exceptions such as

dzi[k']+i wild – *dzi[k]+sz+y* wilder

occur as well.

3. According to the normative Polish dictionary by Doroszewski and Kurkowska (1980), in many cases only one comparative form of *st* adjectives is possible, and they warn against using the other one (which, of course, means that some people employ it), for example

prost+y simple – *prost+sz+y* simpler (**prości+ejsz+y*)
pust+y empty – *puści+ejsz+y* more empty (**pust+sz+y*)

4. We assume that these adjectives contain the suffix -*k* (phonologically /ɨk/). Some evidence for it is provided by forms such as

lek+k+i light – *lż+ejsz+y* lighter

which are discussed later in this section.

5. Throughout this section we present only the second person singular forms of the imperative. The first person plural and the second person plural are formed by the addition of the suffixes -*my* and -*cie* to the verbal stems, for example

myj wash, 2nd person sg. *myj+my* let's wash *myj+cie* wash, 2nd person, pl.

The suffixes -*my* and -*cie*, which are clitics, do not reveal any new aspects of the imperative and will be disregarded here.

6. The imperatives of verbs with the VSs -*owa* and -*ywa* display the presence of -*uj*, which, as noted in the preceding chapter, occurs also with all present tense forms, for example

prac+owa+ć work – *prac+uj* id. imper.
z+gad+ywa+ć guess – *z+gad+uj* id. imper.

7. In Gussmann's (1980a) analysis the deletion of -*i* and -*e* is effected by the phonological rule of vowel deletion.

Notes

8. The high lax vowel in the imperative suffix /-ijĭ/ is motivated solely by the need to prevent the deletion of [j] in the word-final position. This is not necessary in our analysis, since we assume that the palatal glide is removed only in a specific grammatical context, i.e. word-finally in the third person singular present tense forms.
9. There is only one verb in which the root yer is lowered before -ną, i.e. *zdechnąć* 'die' (of an animal) derived from

    /zĭ+dĭx+nĭn+ć/

    This form is clearly an exception with regard to lower since the prefix yer fails to emerge as [e] in spite of the presence of another lax vowel in the following syllable.
10. As Bethin correctly observes, in those verbs which admit both the longer and the shorter imperative, there are frequently additional factors that determine the choice of the suffix. For instance, some speakers prefer the longer form with monosyllabic verbs such as

    wielb+ij adore   *wątp+ij* doubt

    but use the shorter form when the prefix or the negative particle *nie-* is added, for example

    u+wielb adore, perf.   *nie wątp* don't doubt

11. Two imperatives, *bierz* 'take', and *pierz* 'wash', cannot be derived in the fashion proposed here. It seems, however, that these forms are exceptions since their stems /bĭr+a/ and /pĭr+a/ are exactly like those in *spać* 'sleep' and *zwać* 'name', yet they take the suffix /ĭ/ and not /ij/. Moreover, the root vowel is unusual in that it alternates with [o] in *bi[o]re* 'I take' and *pi[o]rę* 'I wash', instead of the expected zero (cf. *we[tr]ę* 'I will rub in', *obe[žr]ę* 'I will eat up'). Thus, lexical marking is unavoidable in these cases.

    Other irregularities of the verb system are also reflected in the imperative. Thus,

    jedz eat   *powiedz* say

    show the reflexes of j-palatalization and not i-palatalization. The verb *zrozumieć* 'understand' with the VS *-ej* forms the short imperative *zrozum*. Other irregularities are

    być be – *bądź* id. imper.
    znaleźć find – *znajdź* imper.

12. It should be added that the suffix subject to truncation cannot be the diminutive suffix /ĭk/. This is understandable since the removal of the diminutive formative would result not in an augmentative,

Notes

but in a semantically neutral form. In some cases it can be questioned whether -*k* is a suffix at all.

13. The rule of augmentative back-formation is not complete as it mentions no semantic or morphological constraints on the input strings, which are of no relevance here. The symbol C_0^2 means that sometimes more consonants than one can be replaced by the velar spirant, for example

    towarzy[stf]o company – *towarzy[x]o* id. augm.
    kapu[st]a cabbage – *kapu[x]a* id. augm.

14. Some nouns appear to form two augmentatives; one through k-truncation, another through both k-truncation and consonant modification, for example

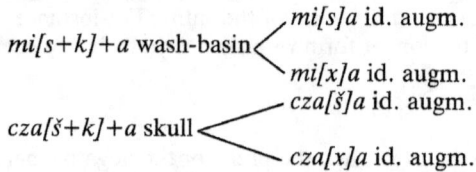

15. The point of interest is whether we are dealing here with two separate, but mutually ordered processes of k-truncation and consonant modification, or with one rule with two simultaneously applying clauses. Following Szymanek (1986) we accept the latter possibility.

16. The derivation of *wiącha* is simplified. According to Gussmann (1980a:105–6), nasal vowels are first tensed and then the rule of nasal vowel distribution assigns the feature of backness in agreement with the specification for tenseness. These two rules are conflated here.

17. A group of exceptions has to be mentioned. These are words which contain the voiceless velar plosive, for example

    be[č+k]+a barrel – *be[k]+a* id. augm. (*becza)
    ty[č+k]+a pole – *ty[k]+a* id. augm. (*tycza)
    pa[č+k]+a package – *pa[k]+a* id. augm. (*pacza)

    Here the suffix /ĭk/ appears to be truncated before its vowel palatalizes the preceding plosive

    /bek+ĭk/ → /bek/

    If such items are processed prior to the truncation, incorrect starred forms are produced.

Notes to Chapter 5: Words

1. Class II prefixes appear to share more features with elements of compounds than with Class II suffixes (for example the possibility of being 'factored out', attaching iteratively, etc. – see Strauss 1982). This has led Selkirk (1982) to claim that the majority of Marchand's (1969) prefixes are not really prefixes but bound roots which act as compounding elements. The problem is largely morphological and has no direct bearing on the analysis suggested here. Phonologically speaking, Class II prefixes have the properties of p-words.
2. It should be added that according to Strauss we are dealing here with laxing rather than with tensing – a fact of minor importance for our reasoning.
3. According to Kaisse (1985:42), [z] of *is* cannot be productively derived from /iz/. We see no reason why this should be the case.
4. Facts concerning the distribution of dark and clear /l/ are much more complex. First of all, not all laterals in the rhyme can be resyllabified; syllabic laterals do not undergo this process in Received Pronunciation (Gimson 1970:204), for example

    special edition   little Ann

    Thus, the rule of resyllabification should refer to the lateral not in the rhyme, but rather in the coda. Furthermore, phonetically speaking, it is more proper to talk about 'darker' and 'clearer' types of the lateral. Gimson states, for instance, that syllabic [ł] may tend to become clearer when a vowel follows, for example in

    finally   middle of the road   little or nothing

5. Forms such as *judgemental* show that the sequence of a Class II affix followed by a Class I affix is no longer a clitic, but a p-word. This might stem from the polymorphemic character of such structures (clitics appear to be monomorphemic). It should be noted that no definition of a clitic is provided. This is because we believe that this notion should be defined on syntactic grounds. The term is used here in the phonological sense, i.e. as a unit which is phonologically dependent on the adjacent word, but which does not merge phonologically with its host to the extent regular affixes do.
6. This is not to say that we deny the existence of prosodic units larger than the phonological phrase. Simply, we have not investigated the issue to the extent which would allow us to formulate any definite claims in this respect.
7. We disregard here some phonostylistic processes which refer to the optional simplification of consonantal clusters.
8. Separate syllabification of prefixes is, in Rubach's (1984a:226) view,

Notes

general except for phonetically asyllabic prefixes. The problem is given some attention in section 5.2.3.

9. It is not clear whether after the erection of the phonological compound phonological rules are still allowed to refer to p-words or not, i.e. whether after the formation of bigger units rules can be restricted to smaller units. In Rubach (1984a) only one lexical derivation is presented, which makes it difficult to form definite judgements with regard to this issue.

10. The word *przeddzień* 'the day before' has, however, an inflected form *w przede+dniu*, in which the prefix yer is lowered. This may be attributed to the exceptional, lexicalized character of such phrases.

11. Several verbs with yer roots do not form derived imperfectives. Moreover, some of them do not combine with yer prefixes. No lowering of the prefix yer can be observed if the root vowel is found in the nasalizing context (before a nasal consonant followed by another consonant). This happens due to the rules which affect such vowels prior to the application of lower (Gussmann 1980a). In some cases we are dealing with additional allomorphy.

12. A question worth asking is whether all prefixes in Polish have the same morphological status. As we have not investigated the morphology of prefixation in much detail, we are not in a position to decide the issue. Let us merely point out that there is a considerable difference between prefixes attached to verbs on the one hand, and prefixes appended to nouns and adjectives on the other. In the former case prefixation is very frequent, but the semantics of prefixed forms is largely non-compositional. Nouns and adjectives are prefixed less often, but such forms are semantically transparent.

13. Other exceptional forms are some nouns derived from prefixed verbs, for example

    od+dech breath   *od+zew* response

where, despite the presence of yers in the prefixes and the roots, prefix yers are deleted and not lowered. The behaviour of the root yer is, in such cases, irregular as well: sometimes it is lowered and in other cases in the identical context it is deleted, for example

od+zew response – *od+zew+u* id. gen. sg.
po+zew summons – *po+zw+u* id. gen sg.

Lower applies irregularly also in such set phrases as

ze wsi from the country   *we krwi* in blood

since the yer of the preposition is vocalized in the context of

256

another yer in the following word. Clearly, such phrases must exceptionally be rebracketed as words.
14. As a matter of fact, palatal assimilation is far from regular within single words as well. For instance, there exist alternative pronunciations of the word initial clusters in

Zdzisław masc. name [źdź]~[zdź]
ssie it sucks [śś]~[sś]

The variation can probably be attributed to the operation of palatal assimilation on the one hand, and spelling (without the palatalized consonant) on the other.
15. Phrase stress depends on the grammatical category of items. Thus, in a prepositional phrase that consists of a preposition and a pronoun, the former is stressed, for example

'*od nas* from us   '*przez nich* because of them

Such phrases, for the purposes of stress assignment, should probably be reinterpreted as single p-words.
16. Many compounds in Polish contain the so-called connective vowel between their elements (the vowels are either -i- or -o-, and, in some rare cases, -u-). Rubach (1984a:224) observes that if a compound possesses a connective vowel, the vowel in question is attached prosodically to the first element. This is supported by the fact that the connective vowel is always syllabified with the first element and takes part in stressing it. For example, the compound adjective

zielon+o+czerwon+y green and red

consists of two p-words

$(zielon+o)_\omega \ (czerwon+y)_\omega$

If the second element of a compound is monosyllabic, however, stress falls on the connective, for example

piorun+'o+chron lightning conductor
włócz+'y+kij gadabout

17. Sometimes in colloquial speech the monosyllable rule is extended to clitics as well. Thus, often penultimate stress can be heard in such words as

robi'li+śmy we did   *robi'li+ście* you (pl.) did

Speakers who use such forms have apparently generalized the rule so that it applies to all monosyllables, including clitics.

18. In this chapter we employ traditional generative terminology, such as the p-word. It should be added that p-words can be treated as units placed on separate tiers which are later conflated, along with McCarthy's proposals.

Notes to Final Remarks

1. The proposal concerning the bracketing of inflection does not seem to be applicable to English inflectional endings, which, as argued in Chapter 5, are bracketed outside their bases and form separate p-words. To put it differently, English inflectional suffixes have, idiosyncratically, the properties of clitics, which information must be supplied by adjustment rules.
2. Several comments on this model are in order. First of all, the placement of the loop between syntax and morphology must be made more precise; we have to go back not from the output of the whole syntactic component, but rather from phrase-level syntax. Moreover, it is possible that lexical insertion takes place not into the surface structure, but into deep structure. These inexactitudes result from the fact that we have not made any detailed examination of the syntatic component.

References

Allen, M. R. (1978) *Morphological Investigations*, doctoral dissertation, University of Connecticut, Storrs.
(1980) 'Semantic and phonological consequences of boundaries: a morphological analysis of compounds', in M. Aronoff and M-L. Kean (eds) 9–27.
Anderson, S. R. (1974) *The Organization of Phonology*, New York: Academic Press.
(1985) *Phonology in the Twentieth Century. Theories of Rules and Theories of Representations*, Chicago and London: The University of Chicago Press.
Archangeli, D. (1984) 'An overview of the theory of Lexical Phonology and Morphology', in M. Speas and R. Sproat (eds) 1–14.
Aronoff, M. (1976) *Word Formation in Generative Grammar*, Cambridge, Mass.: MIT Press.
(1980) 'The treatment of juncture in American linguistics', in M. Aronoff and M-L. Kean (eds) 29–36.
Aronoff, M. and Kean, M-L. (eds) (1980) *Juncture*, Saratoga, Cal.: Anma Libri.
Aronoff, M. and Sridhar, S. N. (1983) 'Morphological levels in English and Kannada or Atarizing Reagan', in *Papers from the Parasession on the Interplay of Phonology, Morphology and Syntax*, Chicago: Chicago Linguistic Society, 3–16.
Bartmiński, J. (ed) (1981) *Pojęcie derywacji w lingwistyce*, Lublin: Wydawnictwo Uniwersytetu Marii Curie-Skłodowskiej.
Bethin, Ch. (1987) 'Syllable structure and the Polish imperative desinence', to appear in *Slavic and East European Journal* 31.
Bloomfield, L. (1933) *Language*, New York: Holt.
Bochner, H. (MS) 'Exceptions to palatalization in Polish'.
Booij, G. (1977) *Dutch Morphology. A Study of Word Formation in Generative Grammar*, Lisse: the Peter de Ridder Press.
(1981) 'Rule ordering, rule application and the organization of grammars', in W. U. Dressler (ed) 45–56.
(1983) 'Principles and parameters in prosodic phonology', *Linguistics* 21: 249–80.

References

(1984) 'Neutral vowels and the autosegmental analysis of Hungarian vowel harmony', *Linguistics* 22: 629–41.

(1985a) 'The interaction of phonology and morphology in prosodic phonology', in E. Gussmann (ed) (1985a): 23–34.

(1985b) 'Coordination reduction in complex words: a case for prosodic phonology', in H. van der Hulst and N. Smith (eds) (1985b): 143–60.

Booij, G. and Rubach J. (1984) 'Morphological and prosodic domains in Lexical Phonology', *Phonology Yearbook 1*: 1–27.

(1987) 'Postcyclic versus postlexical rules in Lexical Phonology', *Linguistic Inquiry* 18: 1–44.

Brame, M. (ed) (1972) *Contributions to Generative Phonology*, Austin: University of Texas Press.

Brogyányi, B. (ed) (1979) *Studies in Diachronic, Synchronic and Typological Linguistics: Festschrift for O. Szemerényi*, Amsterdam: J. Benjamins.

Chomsky, N. (1970) 'Remarks on nominalization', in R. A. Jacobs and P. S. Rosenbaum (eds): 184–221.

Chomsky, N. and Halle, M. (1968) *The Sound Pattern of English*, New York: Harper and Row.

Dingwall, W. O. (ed) (1971) *A Survey of Linguistic Science*, College Park: University of Maryland.

Dinnsen, D. A. (ed) (1979) *Current Approaches to Phonological Theory*, Bloomington: Indiana University Press.

Doroszewski, W. and Kurkowska, H. (1980) *Słownik Poprawnej Polszczyzny*, Warszawa: Państwowe Wydawnictwo Nankowe (PWN).

Dressler, W. U., Pfeiffer, D. E. and Rennison, J. R. (eds) (1981) *Phonologica 1980*, Innsbruck: Institut für Sprachwissenschaft.

Elert, C. C., Johanson, J., and Strangert, E. (eds) (1984) *Nordic Prosody III: Papers from a Symposium*, University of Umeå.

Fischer-Jørgensen, E. (1975) *Trends in Phonological Theory. A Historical Introduction*, Copenhagen: Akademisk Forlag.

Fisiak, J. (ed) (in press) *Further Insights into Contrastive Linguistics*, Amsterdam: J. Benjamins.

Fisiak, J. and Puppel, S. (eds) (in press) *Polish Phonology in the 1980s*, Amsterdam: J. Benjamins.

Fokker, A. A. (1965) 'Derivation of nouns from verbs in contemporary literary Polish', *Lingua* 13: 240–73 and 385–450.

Fudge, E. C. (1984) *English Word Stress*, London: George Allen and Unwin.

Fujimura, O. (ed) (1973) *Three Dimensions of Linguistic Theory*, Tokyo: TEC.

Gimson, A. C. (1970) *An Introduction to the Pronunciation of English*, London: Arnold Publishing Company.

Gladney, F. (1986) Review of J. Rubach (1984a) *Lingua* 67: 337–52.

Goldsmith, J. (1976) 'An overview of Autosegmental Phonology', *Linguistic Analysis* 2: 23–68.

(1979) 'The aims of Autosegmental Phonology', in D. A. Dinnsen (ed): 202–22.

References

Goyvaerts, G. K. and Pullum, G. K. (eds) (1974) *Essays on 'The Sound Pattern of English'*, Ghent: E. Story-Scientia P.V.B.A. Scientific Publishers.

Grzegorczykowa, R. (1979) *Zarys Słowotwórstwa Polskiego. Słowotwórstwo Opisowe*, Warszawa: PWN.

Grzegorczykowa, R., Laskowski, R., and Wróbel, H. (eds) (1984) *Morfologia. Gramatyka Współczesnego Języka Polskiego*. Warszawa: PWN.

Grzegorczykowa, R. and Puzynina, J. (1979) *Słowotwórstwo Współczesnego Języka Polskiego. Rzeczowniki Sufiksalne Rodzime*, Warszawa: PWN.

Gussmann, E. (1978) *Contrastive Polish-English Consonantal Phonology*, Warszawa: PWN.

—— (1980a) Studies in Abstract Phonology, *Linguistic Inquiry Monograph* 4, Cambridge, Mass.: MIT Press.

—— (1980b) 'The phonological structure of the Polish imperative', *Studia Gramatyczne* III: 34–46.

—— (ed) (1985a) *Phono-Morphology. Studies in the Interaction of Phonology and Morphology*, Lublin: Katolicki Uniwersytet Lubelski.

—— (1985b) 'The morphology of a phonological rule: Icelandic vowel length', in E. Gussmann (ed) (1985a): 75–94.

—— (1985c) Review of J. Rubach (1984a), *Linguistics* 23: 609–23.

—— (1986) Review of S. L. Strauss (1982), *Studia Anglica Posnaniensia* 18: 241–4.

—— (ed) (1987) *Rules and the Lexicon. Studies in Word Formation*, Lublin: Katolicki Uniwersytet Lubelski.

—— (in press) 'Back to front. Non-linear palatalization and vowels in Polish', in J. Fisiak and S. Puppel (eds).

Halle, M. (1959) *The Sound Pattern of Russian*, The Hague: Mouton.

—— (1973) 'Prolegomena to a theory of word formation', *Linguistic Inquiry* 4: 3–16.

—— (1979) 'Formal vs functional considerations in phonology', in B. Brogyányi (ed): 325–41.

—— (1986) 'On the phonology-morphology interface', MS.

Halle, M. and Clements, G. N. (1983) *Problem Book in Phonology*, Cambridge, Mass.: MIT Press.

Halle, M. and Mohanan, K. P. (1985) 'Segmental phonology of Modern English', *Linguistic Inquiry* 16: 57–116.

Halle, M. and Vergnaud, J-R. (1980) 'Three-dimensional phonology', *Journal of Linguistic Research* 1: 83–105.

—— (1987) 'Stress and the cycle', *Linguistic Inquiry* 18: 45–84.

Hayes, B. (1980) *A Metrical Theory of Stress Rules*, Bloomington: Indiana University Linguistics Club.

Hooper, J. B. (1976) *An Introduction to Natural Generative Phonology*, New York: Academic Press.

Hulst, H. van der and Smith, N. (eds) (1982) *The Structure of Phonological Representations*, vol. 1, Dordrecht: Foris Publications.

References

(1985a) 'The framework of nonlinear Generative Phonology', in H. van der Hulst and N. Smith (eds) (1985b): 3–55.

(1985b) *Advances in Nonlinear Phonology*, Dordrecht: Foris Publications.

Ingeman, F. A. (ed) (1983) *Proceedings of the 1982 Mid-America Linguistics Conference*, Lawrence: University of Kansas.

Jacobs, R. A. and Rosenbaum, P. S. (eds) (1970) *Readings in English Transformational Grammar*, Waltham, Mass.: Ginn and Company.

Jones, D. (1982) *English Pronouncing Dictionary*, revised by A. C. Gimson, London: J. M. Dent and Sons Ltd.

Kahn, D. (1976) *Syllable-based Generalizations in English Phonology*, Bloomington: Indiana University Linguistics Club.

Kaisse, E. M. (1985) *Connected Speech. The Interaction of Syntax and Phonology*, Orlando: Academic Press.

Kaisse, E. M. and Shaw, P. A. (1985) 'On the theory of Lexical Phonology', *Phonology Yearbook* 2: 1–30.

Karaś, M. and Madejowa, M. (1977) *Słownik Wymowy Polskiej*, Warszawa: PWN.

Kastovsky, D. (1987) 'Boundaries in English and German morphology', paper presented at 23rd International Conference on Contrastive Linguistics in Błażejewko, Poland.

(forthcoming) 'Word formation, boundaries and the concept of motivation'. in J. Roggenhofer and B. Asbach-Schnittker (eds).

Kean, M-L. (1974) 'The strict cycle in phonology', *Linguistic Inquiry* 5: 179–203.

Kenstowicz, M. J. and Kisseberth, Ch. W. (1977) *Topics in Phonological Theory*, New York: Academic Press.

Kenyon, J. S. and Knott, T. A. (1953) *A Pronouncing Dictionary of American English*, Springfield, Mass.: G. G. Merriam.

Kiparsky, P. (1968) 'How abstract is phonology?' Mimeographed by Indiana University Linguistics Club, a revised version published as P. Kiparsky (1973).

(1971) 'Historical linguistics', in W. O. Dingwall (ed): 576–649.

(1973) 'Phonological representations', in O. Fujimura (ed): 1–137.

(1982a) 'From Cyclic Phonology to Lexical Phonology', in H. van der Hulst and N. Smith (eds) (1985b): 131–75.

(1982b) 'Lexical Morphology and Phonology', in *Linguistics in the Morning Calm*, Seoul: Hansin.

(1983) 'Word-formation and the lexicon', in F. A. Ingeman (ed): 3–29.

(1984) 'On the Lexical Phonology of Icelandic', in C. C. Elert, I. Johansson, and E. Strangert (eds): 135–64.

(1985) 'Some consequences of Lexical Phonology', *Phonology Yearbook* 2: 83–138.

Laskowski, R. (1975) *Studia nad Morfonologia Współczesnego Języka Polskiego*, Wrockław: Ossolineum.

(1977) 'Morfologia w gramatyce transformacyjno-generatywnej (w poszukiwaniu modelu opisu)', *Studia Gramatyczne* 1: 103–33.

(1981) 'Derywacja słowotwórcza', in J. Bartmiński (ed): 107–25.

References

Lehnert, M. (1971) *Reverse Dictionary of Present-day English*, Leipzig: VEB Verlag Enzyklopädie.
Liberman, M. Y. and Prince, A. (1977) 'On stress and linguistic rhythm', *Linguistic Inquiry* 8: 249–336.
Lieber, R. (1980) *On the Organization of the Lexicon*, Bloomington: Indiana University Linguistics Club.
—— (1982) 'Allomorphy', *Linguistic Analysis* 10: 27–52.
Lubaszewski, W. (1982) *Struktura Morfemowa Polskiego Czasownika* (próba opisu generatywnego), Wrocław: Ossolineum.
McCarthy, J. (1979) *Formal Problems in Semitic Phonology*, doctoral dissertation, MIT, Cambridge, Massachusetts.
Malicka-Kleparska, A. (1985) *The Conditional Lexicon in Derivational Morphology. A Study of Double Motivation in Polish and English*, Lublin: Katolicki Uniwersytet Lubelski.
Marantz, A. (1982) 'Re Reduplication', *Linguistic Inquiry* 13: 435–82.
Marchand, H. (1969) *The Categories and Types of Present-day English Word-Formation*, München: C. H. Beck Verlagsbuchhandlung.
Mascaró, J. (1976) *Catalan Phonology and the Phonological Cycle*, Bloomington: Indiana University Linguistics Club.
Mohanan, K. P. (1982) *Lexical Phonology*, Bloomington: Indiana University Linguistics Club.
Nespor, M. (1985) 'The phonological word in Italian', in H. van der Hulst and N. Smith (eds) (1985b): 193–204.
Nespor, M. and Vogel, I. (1986) *Prosodic Phonology*, Dordrecht: Foris Publications.
Nykiel-Herbert, B. (1984) *Phonological and Morphological Analysis of Prefixation in Polish and English*, doctoral dissertation, Adam Mickiewicz University, Poznań.
—— (1985) 'The vowel-zero alternation in Polish prefixes', in E. Gussmann (ed) (1985a): 113–30.
Paulsson, O. (1974) *Aspects of Polish Verb Morphology and Phonology*, Göteborg: Göteborg University.
Pesetsky, D. (1979) 'Russian morphology and lexical theory', MS.
Pesetsky, D. (1985) 'Morphology and logical form', *Linguistic Inquiry* 16: 193–246.
Piernikarski, C. (1970) 'O tożsamości leksykalnej czasowników typu: pisać, napisać', *Poradnik Językowy 1970*: 297–308.
Pike, K. L. (1947) 'Grammatical prerequisites to phonemic analysis', *Word* 3: 155–72.
Pulleyblank, D. (1986) *Tone in Lexical Phonology*, Dordrecht: D. Reidel Publishing Company.
Roggenhofer, J. and Asbach-Schnittker, B. (eds) (forthcoming) *Festschrift for Herbert E. Brekle*.
Ross, J. R. (1972) 'Reanalysis of English word stress', in M. Brame (ed): 229–323.
Rubach, J. (1981) *Cyclic Phonology and Palatalization in Polish and English*, Warszawa: Wydawnictwa Uniwersytetu Warszawskiego.

References

(1984a) *Cyclic and Lexical Phonology. The Structure of Polish*, Dordrecht: Foris Publications.
(1984b) 'Segmental rules of English and Cyclic Phonology', *Language* 60: 21–54.
(1985) 'On the interaction of word formation and phonological rules', in E. Gussmann (ed) (1985c): 131–55.
Rubach, J. and Booij, G. (1985) 'A grid theory of stress in Polish', *Lingua* 66: 281–319.
Saloni, Z. (1976) *Cechy Składniowe Czasownika Polskiego*, Wrocław: Ossolineum.
Satkiewicz, H. (1969) *Produktywne Typy Sło votwórcze Współczesnego Języka Polskiego*, Warszawa: Wydawnictwa Uniwersytetu Warszawskiego.
Scalise, S. (1986) *Generative Morphology*, Dordrecht: Foris Publications (2nd edition).
Schenker, A. M. (1954) 'Polish conjugation', *Word* 10: 469–81.
Selkirk, E. (1980) 'Prosodic domains in phonology: Sanskrit revisited', in M. Aronoff and M-L. Kean (eds): 107–29.
(1982) *The Syntax of Words*, Cambridge, Mass.: MIT Press.
(1984) *Phonology and Syntax. The Relation between Sound and Structure*, Cambridge, Mass.: MIT Press.
Siegel, D. (1974) *Topics in English Morphology*, published in 1979, New York and London: Garland Publishing, Inc.
Speas, M. and Sproat, R. (eds) (1984) *MIT Working Papers in Linguistics 7*.
Spencer, A. (1985) 'A non-linear analysis of vowel-zero alternations in Polish', *Journal of Linguistics* 22: 249–80.
Sproat, R. (1984) 'On bracketing paradoxes', in M. Speas and R. Sproat (eds): 110–30.
(1985) *On Deriving the Lexicon*, doctoral dissertation, MIT, Cambridge, Massachusetts.
Strauss, S. L. (1979) 'Against boundary distinctions in English morphology', *Linguistic Analysis* 5: 387–419.
(1982) *Lexicalist Phonology of English and German*, Dordrecht: Foris Publications.
Szober, S. (1962) *Gramatyka Języka Polskiego* (12th edition) Warszawa: PWN.
Szpyra, J. (1985) 'Cyclic Phonology – a counterproposal to the SPE model?' *Studia Gramatyczne* 6: 97–131.
(1987) 'Inputs to WFRs – phonological, intermediate or phonetic?' in E. Gussmann (ed) (1987): 169–203.
(in press a) 'Morphological and phonological levels in Polish and English', in J. Fisiak (ed).
(in press b) 'The phonology of Polish prefixation', in J. Fisiak and S. Puppel (eds).
Szymanek, B. (1985) *English and Polish Adjectives. A Study in Lexicalist Word Formation*, Lublin: Katolicki Uniwersytet Lubelski.
(1986) 'Extended exponence and rule-ordering in morphology', MS.

The Shorter Oxford English Dictionary on Historical Principles (1973) Oxford: Clarendon Press.
Tokarski, J. (1951) *Czasowniki Polskie*, Warszawa: PWN.
Zaron, Z. (1976) *Cechy Składniowe Czasownika Polskiego*, Wrocław: Ossolineum.

Index of subjects

absolute neutralization 15, 79, 82
adjustment of rules 12–14, 191, 196, 198, 200, 226, 234, 240–2; *see also* allomorphy rules, readjustment rules, rebracketing, truncation rules
affix ordering generalization 23, 41, 45, 68; violations of 38, 49–50, 60
allomorphy rules 12–13, 14; in English 41, 53, 55, 56, 58, 60–1; in Polish 101, 145–7
alternation condition 15–16
autosegmental phonology 20, 82, 238

boundaries, morphological 2, 14, 15, 24, 27, 181–3, 234–40; criticism of 11, 182–3, 234–7; full word boundary 4, 183, 234–5, 237; internal word boundary 4, 6, 7, 11, 12, 23, 182–3, 204, 235–7; morpheme boundary 4–5, 7, 12, 16, 18, 23, 73–82, 181–5, 186, 231, 234–40; prefix boundary 4, 6, 11, 24, 204, 235–6
bracket adjustment *see* rebracketing
bracket erasure 17, 25, 67, 172
bracketing, morphological 2, 10, 19, 27, 69, 172, 184–90, 193–4, 200, 226, 231, 234–40, 242
bracketing paradoxes 38–9, 45, 68

classes of affix in English 7–8, 22–4, 26, 30, 38, 40–68, 72, 226; properties of, morphological 41, phonological 41, semantic 42; prosodic interpretation of 179–200, 234; *see also* dual class affixes, prefixes in English
clitic group 197; in English 197–200, 228–9; in Polish 220, 228
clitics in Polish 220, 228, 252, 257–8
compounds 20; in English 39, 65, 190, 196, 228; in Polish 223–4, 228; *see also* phonological compound
cyclic phonology, assumptions of 17–19, 70, 204–5, 231; criticism of 69–82, 93–7, 206–7, 210, 231; *see also* strict cyclicity principle
cyclic rules *see* transformational phonological rules, strictly cyclic rules
cyclic strata 70

derived environment 16–17, 72–3, 78–82, 93, 231; *see also* strict cyclicity principle, strictly cyclic rules
dual class affixes 42, 45–62, 180, 187, 231, 243; phonological properties of 47–9, 51–2, 54, 57–8, 60–1; morphological properties of 49–50, 52–3, 55–6,

266

Index

58–61, 181, 187; prosodic treatment of 186–91, 226, 235
Dutch 170–1, 179

Finnish 16
foot 19–21

Hungarian 227

inflectional affixes in English 191–4, 258
intonational phrase 20, 197, 241
Italian 179

level-ordered morphology 22–3, 26, 37, 43
lexical features 8–9
lexical levels 25–7, 35–6, 39, 235–6; in English 23–6, 37, 39–40, 43, 45, 50–1, 63, 66–8, 178; in Polish 29–36, 68, 178, 228, 230
lexical phonological rules 25, 27, 228
lexical phonology, assumptions of 24–8, 70, 114, 207; advantages of 35–7, 207; criticism of 235–6, in English 38–68, in Polish 30–6, 93–7, 99–100, 114–15, 119–20, 136–7, 153–4, 173, 207–9, 210, 231–2
loop *see* phonology-morphology loop
loop in lexical phonology 39, 246

mapping *see* morphology-phonology mapping, syntax-phonology mapping
metrical phonology 20
morpheme 20–2, 237–9
morpholexical rules 13, 82, 90
morphological boundaries *see* boundaries
morphological word 20–2, 168–9, 170, 171–4, 178–9, 183–5, 226, 233, 237, 242
morphology-phonology mapping 179, 226–9, 233–4, 240–2; in English 186–90, 193–4, 200; in Polish 215–16, 224–5
multiple application of phonological rules *see* morphology-phonology loop

natural generative phonology 15

phonological clitics 198; *see also* clitic group
phonological compound 197, 207–9, 256
phonological phrase 8, 20, 241; in English 197–200, 228–9; in Polish 215, 220, 228
phonological utterance 20, 197, 241
phonological word 20–2, 178–9, 225–7, 229, 233–4, 236–7, 241–2, 255, 258; in English 183–200; in Polish 207, 215–16, 218–25, 228–9
phonology-morphology loop 115–16, 121–3, 125, 130, 132, 139, 154–8, 165–6, 167, 232–3, 240–1
postcyclic rules 17–19, 25, 45, 70, 115, 153, 204–6, 231
postlexical rules 25, 228
prefixes, in English 38–9, 42, 45, 53, 55, 59, 61, 64, 198, 238; in Polish 30–4, 96–7, 98, 123, 178, 200–26, 235
prosodic phonology 19–21, 178–9
prosodic reanalysis 194, 222–5, 226–7

readjustment rules 2, 7, 8, 11–14, 19, 27, 28
rebracketing 188–91, 200, 226, 234
Russian 19

SPE, assumptions of 1–9, 14, 181–2; criticism of 9–12, 14–15, 182–3; treatment of exceptions in 9

Index

strict cylicity principle 17–18, 25, 29, 36, 69–82, 231
strictly cyclic rules 16–18, 25, 70, 153, 231; in English 16–17, 72–7, 82, 204–6; in Polish 78–82, 93–7
syllable 15, 19–22
syntax-morphology loop 174–7, 232, 240
syntax-phonology mapping 2, 240–2

transformational phonological rules 2–4, 10, 18
truncation rules 12–14; in English 41, 44, 50, 58–9, 60–1; in Polish *see* verb suffix truncation

Index of rules

English

cluster shortening 193–4
cluster simplification 42, 48, 52, 58, 65, 180, 184, 237
compound stress 3, 195–6

degemination 41, 64, 180–1, 184, 193, 194

g-delegation 41, 49, 58, 66–7, 180, 184, 237

laxing 49, 52, 193
l-resyllabification 196–7, 255

nasal assimilation 26, 38, 41, 61, 66–7, 180, 184

palatalization: inside words 4, 45, 52; across words 198–9
phrase stress 195–6

sonorant syllabification 6–7, 41, 48, 57–8, 180–1, 184, 189–90
spirantization 5–6, 41, 45, 52, 244
stem-final lengthening 191–2, 255
stress 19–20; *see also* compound stress, phrase stress, word stress
s-voicing 6
syllabification 183, 192–3

tensing *see* stem-final lengthening
trisyllabic laxing 16–18, 41, 48, 63–4, 71–7, 82, 180–1, 184, 186, 187, 231, 237–8, 244, 246–7

velar softening 5–6, 9
vowel deletion 194, 199
vowel epenthesis (insertion) 193–4
vowel reduction 3, 65, 190
vowel shift 18, 193
vowel shortening *see* cluster shortening, laxing, trisyllabic laxing

word stress 2–3, 6, 7–9, 10, 23–4, 26, 41, 46, 47–8, 51–2, 54, 57, 60, 62–3, 170, 180–1, 183, 184, 188, 244–6

Polish

a-deletion 156

backing 104, 120, 121, 125, 129–30, 162–3, 164, 166, 174

compound stress 223–4

degemination 144
depalatalization 80–1
derived imperfective tensing 30, 102–16, 118, 119, 120, 121, 124–6, 174, 201, 203, 206, 228, 232, 243

Index

final devoicing 94, 144
fronting 100
front vowel truncation 143–4, 155, 156

gliding 101–2, 114

j-delegation 102, 104, 105, 106, 112, 113, 114, 146–7, 157
j-insertion 144, 157

k-truncation 135, 140–1

lower 105, 122, 129, 143, 168–9, 174, 243; exceptions to 210, 211, 216–7, 253, 256; in augmentative nouns 161–2, 164, 165, 166, 168; in comparatives 136–7, 139, 141; in derived imperfectives 106–14, 119, 125; in imperatives 143, 144, 146–7, 151, 155–8; in prefixed forms 202–15, 224

monosyllable rule 222–5, 257–8

nasal tensing 163, 164, 166, 168, 169, 174
ną-allomorphy 145–7, 157

palatal assimilation 144, 157, 202–3. 208, 217–19, 236
palatalization 77–82, 93–7, 99–100, 104, 105, 106, 108, 113, 114, 115, 117, 118, 120, 129–30, 136–7, 139, 140, 141, 142–4, 146, 147, 151, 155, 156, 157, 163, 228, 231; anterior 30, 33–4, 201, 203, 221; j-palatalization 101–2, 142, 144; second velar 9; surface 30, 202, 221; surface velar 100
phrase stress 222

raising 105, 151, 160–1, 164, 165, 168, 169, 174
r-lowering 106

stress *see* compound stress, phrase stress, word stress
syllabification 151, 155, 156, 157, 203, 207, 219–20, 224–5

verb suffix truncation 89–95, 98–9, 113, 114, 115, 118–26, 174, 231, 239, 243, 248, 250–1
voice assimilation 172, 202
vowel adjustment 113; *see also* fronting, vowel retraction
vowel deletion 30, 144, 157, 201, 203, 206, 221, 228
vowel epenthesis 202, 221
vowel nasalization 166
vowel retraction 30, 201, 203, 221

word stress 202, 220, 223–4

yer deletion 115, 136, 143, 205–6, 208; *see also* lower

For Product Safety Concerns and Information please contact our EU
representative GPSR@taylorandfrancis.com
Taylor & Francis Verlag GmbH, Kaufingerstraße 24, 80331 München, Germany

www.ingramcontent.com/pod-product-compliance
Lightning Source LLC
Chambersburg PA
CBHW071810300426
44116CB00009B/1264